Managing Transition

T0384595

Examining the factors that shaped the first interim governments of Tunisia and Libya, which were formed in the immediate aftermath of the 2011 uprisings that brought down the governments, *Managing Transition* analyzes each interim government to enhance our understanding of how political transition occurred within the two North African countries. Tracing the importance of the key decisions made during these transition periods, Sabina Henneberg demonstrates the importance of these decisions taken during the short period between authoritarian collapse and the first post-uprising elections, including decisions around leadership, institutional reform, transitional justice, and electoral processes. By documenting, in close detail, the important events of the 2011 Arab uprisings, and the months that followed, this study shows that while pre-existing structures strongly influence the design and behavior of the first interim governments, actors' choices are equally important in shaping both immediate and longer-term phases of transition.

SABINA HENNEBERG is a visiting scholar for the African Studies Program at Johns Hopkins University School of Advanced International Studies, where her research has focused on political transition in North Africa. She is the author of articles in journals including the *Journal of North African Studies, British Journal of Middle Eastern Studies, Journal of International Affairs, Foreign Affairs* and *Foreign Policy*. She is currently the Tunisia Country Specialist with Amnesty International USA.

Managing Transition

The First Post-Uprising Phase in Tunisia and Libya

SABINA HENNEBERG
Johns Hopkins University

CAMBRIDGE
UNIVERSITY PRESS

Shaftesbury Road, Cambridge CB2 8EA, United Kingdom

One Liberty Plaza, 20th Floor, New York, NY 10006, USA

477 Williamstown Road, Port Melbourne, VIC 3207, Australia

314–321, 3rd Floor, Plot 3, Splendor Forum, Jasola District Centre, New Delhi – 110025, India

103 Penang Road, #05–06/07, Visioncrest Commercial, Singapore 238467

Cambridge University Press is part of Cambridge University Press & Assessment, a department of the University of Cambridge.

We share the University's mission to contribute to society through the pursuit of education, learning and research at the highest international levels of excellence.

www.cambridge.org
Information on this title: www.cambridge.org/9781108816069

DOI: 10.1017/9781108895729

© Sabina Henneberg 2020

First published 2020
First paperback edition 2022

A catalogue record for this publication is available from the British Library

ISBN   978-1-108-84200-6   Hardback
ISBN   978-1-108-81606-9   Paperback

For mom and dad

Contents

Acknowledgments   *page* ix
Note about Terms and Definitions   xii
List of Abbreviations   xiv

1   Introduction   1
    An Interim Government Forms   1
    First Interim Governments: A Unique Moment   3
    The Study of Interim Governments during Transition from
      Authoritarian Rule   5
    Questions, Design, and Argument   11
    Plan of the Book   14

2   The Tunisian Provisional Administration   17
    Historical Backdrop   18
    Immediate Attempts to Appoint New Leadership   20
    Establishing a Way Forward   24
    Balancing Continuity and Change   28
    Setting Up Interim Institutions   33
    Securing Legitimacy   39
    Building Consensus for a New Political System   51
    Organizing Elections   57
    Conclusion   59

3   Impacts of the Tunisian Provisional Administration   60
    Constraints   61
    Formation of the National Constituent Assembly and Troika   65
    Drafting a New Constitution, Polarization, and National Dialogue   67
    Reforming Institutions   74
    Dealing with Questions of Transitional Justice   88
    Conclusion   97

4   The Libyan National Transition Council   99
    Historical Backdrop   100
    Formation of the National Transition Council   102

Garnering Legitimacy through Recruitment 106
Establishing New Governing Institutions 118
Prioritizing International Assistance 130
Developing a Roadmap 139
Organizing Elections 142
Conclusion 145

5 Impacts of the National Transition Council 147
Forming a New Government 148
Restoring (In)stability 149
Establishing Authority 154
Impacts of International Assistance 158
Drafting a Constitution 160
Addressing Human Rights and Transitional Justice 162
Conclusion 169

6 Impacts of the Tunisian Provisional Administration
and National Transition Council in Later Years 170
Tunisia 170
Libya 188
Conclusion 204

7 Conclusions 206
Review of the Questions and Arguments 207
Tunisia and Libya's Different "Starting Conditions" 208
Summary of Findings 210
What Have We Learned? 215
Contributions 219
Toward a Theory of Interim Governments 221

Appendix A Tunisia Chronology 228
Appendix B Libya Chronology 232
Bibliography 236
Index 256

Acknowledgments

I am grateful to everyone who supported this project. I received research support as a doctoral student from the Cosmos Scholars Foundation and the National Security Education Program, and a critical year of funding as a Provost's Postdoctoral Fellow from Johns Hopkins University. Several organizations and individuals were also crucial aids to the work during my time in Tunisia. These include my Arabic teachers, Najla Abbes and Mohammed Laabidi; the kind sisters at the Maison Diocésaine; the staff at the Centre d'Études Maghrébines à Tunis (CEMAT) and the National Library of Tunisia; and the fellow researchers and journalists (both Tunisian and foreign) I met who supported me and offered suggestions. I also owe thanks to the inspiring women working at the regional office of Amnesty International in Tunis for hosting me several times in recent years.

The most important people during my fieldwork were of course the interview subjects themselves. I have kept them anonymous in order to avoid putting them at risk, but I will forever be indebted to them for sharing their time and experiences and humbled by their extraordinary courage. Several people met with me more than once, shared resources, and spoke to me over the phone; this book would not have been possible without their efforts. I am equally grateful to the individuals who met with me in Washington, in London, and on Skype throughout the research process.

At the John Hopkins School of Advanced International Studies (SAIS), I have been fortunate to work with excellent advisors, especially Peter Lewis, Bill Zartman, and Karim Mezran. I am also grateful to Jennifer Seely and Eva Bellin for serving as external committee members during my dissertation defense. The reference librarians and entire library staff have been consistently friendly and supportive since I arrived as a master's student in 2006. I would particularly like to thank Linda Carson, Kate Pickard, Steve Sears, Jenny Gelman, Jenny

Kusmik, and Sheila Thalhimer, as well as Susan High and Josh MacDonald.

Dan Brown, Atifa Jiwa, Thomas Haynes, and Maria Marsh from Cambridge University Press all played a role in realizing this book, and I am thankful to them for making the publishing process such a pleasant experience. Feedback from two anonymous reviewers also helped improve the work. I also consulted many others in the process of publishing the manuscript, including the senior acquisitions editor from Michigan University Press, Elizabeth Demers, and the series editor from Columbia University Press, Marc Lynch. I am grateful for their time and advice, and to the three anonymous reviewers from Michigan University Press whose feedback on the proposal I also incorporated when revising the manuscript.

Several peers and mentors were kind enough to share their advice on book publishing, including Taylor Boas, Narges Bajoghli, Lisel Hintz, Dan Honig, Teddy Khan, Liz Nugent, Patrick Quirk, Jennifer Seely, Jonathan Stevenson, Betsy Super, and Fred Wehrey. Mietek Boduszynski, Tom Carothers, Elizabeth Phelps, and Susan Waltz all took the time to provide feedback on draft pieces of the manuscript; the book also would not have been the same without Ben Gedan and Jason Pack's comments on the proposal and Bill Zartman, Peter Lewis, and Karim Mezran's help when it was still a dissertation project. Jacob Mundy facilitated work on the ground in Tunis, and his invitation to contribute to a special issue of *Middle East Law and Governance* led to valuable anonymous reviews that helped me deepen my understanding of the Libya case.

I also benefited from the opportunity to present pieces of the research at various venues, including the annual conferences of the Middle East Studies Association, the African Studies Association, the Center for the Study of Islam and Democracy, the Bureau of Conflict and Stabilization Operations at the Department of State, and the publication *Realités*. An invitation from my mentor and friend, Bob Lee, to co-teach with him at Colorado College provided yet another opportunity to present the work before fresh eyes. Anonymous feedback from reviewers at the *Journal of North African Studies* and the *British Journal of Middle Eastern Studies* also contributed to my thinking about the larger project. Charafa al-Achalhi and Kaoutar el-Mernisi both worked with me extensively on Arabic.

Several individuals at SAIS offered support as administrative staff, mentoring faculty, and friends. These include Stephanie Cancienne Hedge, Eamonn Gearon, Allison Janos, David Kanin, Seth Kaplan, Starr Lee, Chichi Nwankwor, Gabby Roberts Hendy, Bruce Parrott, Guadalupe Paz, Camille Pecastaing, Isabelle Talpain-Long, Bridget Welsh, Mark White, Jon Youngs, and the ever-friendly and kind engineers and facilities staff. Jeanne Choi, Lili Diaz, and Amanda Kerrigan have been my champions and inspiration.

Finally, the project would not have been possible without the support of my family and friends, especially Chrissy, Mo, Bina, Sid, and my dear partner, Mike. My mother, Jeanne, not only read and commented on every draft of every page but frequently listened as I tried to sort through complicated ideas. There are no words to express how grateful I am to her and to my late father, Matthias, whose love also made this work possible.

Note about Terms and Definitions

This book is about interim governments. It borrows the operational definition of interim governments offered by Allison Stanger, in her contribution to Yossi Shain and Juan J. Linz's 1995 volume *Between States*, which itself is built on their paper delivered at the American Political Science Association's annual conference in 1991. Stanger defines an interim government as "the administration that rules 'in the hiatus between the breakdown of the authoritarian regime and the selection of a new government as a result of free and contested elections.'"[1] This book also draws inspiration from Jennifer Seely's work on interim governments (which she calls transition governments) in Benin and Togo. Seely specifies that "A transition government is defined as a temporary leadership body that is appointed by an existing government or occupying authority (rather than popularly elected) to serve for a limited term with the intention of creating conditions for new leadership to be chosen."[2] The key elements of an interim (or transition) government are thus that it (1) is temporary (2) is unelected (3) presides over the period immediately following the collapse of an authoritarian regime, and (4) presides over democratic elections.[3]

When I first conceived this study, I struggled to differentiate "transition" government from "interim" or "provisional." My work on this project began as dissertation research in 2013, when the uprisings in Tunisia and Libya were relatively fresh and the question of whether or not either country was transitioning to anything – in other words,

---

[1] Shain and Linz, eds., *Between States*, 256.
[2] Seely, *The Legacies of Transition Governments*, 11.
[3] Although in Libya during the first several months of the National Transition Council's existence, the authoritarian regime it sought to replace had not actually collapsed, it nonetheless meets these criteria, and permits me to study it alongside the transition government in Tunisia. The term "government-in-waiting" deployed by Rangwala is thus also useful for making this distinction between the Libyan and Tunisian cases.

whether either was experiencing a regime change, defined by Ronald Francisco as "major shifts in two or more categories of political structure" – was unresolved.[4] Indeed, scholars of regime transition or regime change generally agree that identifying the point when this transition has occurred is difficult.[5] Thus, while I initially avoided calling the processes under study here "transition" and the actors "transition governments," my decision to apply these terms also acknowledges that both countries examined in this book – as is the case with Benin, Togo, and many other places – have been experiencing *attempted* transition, and have even used the term themselves.[6]

I also struggled to figure out whether I was studying "governments" or "administrations." Although "administrations" appeared to be the safer choice, if for no other reason than that we tend to think of governments as being elected or formally instated in some way,[7] I ultimately consider both terms relevant to the tasks and roles of the two interim bodies studied here. Although, as this book will show, both these bodies tried hard to avoid the appearance of having seized power undemocratically, and often did not consider themselves mandated to take many decisions, they indeed both took decisions as a government and executed them as an administration. I term the Tunisian case a "provisional administration" because it was made up of several bodies that collectively – even if not intentionally[8] – took charge of public affairs. I use this term to refer to all the interim Tunisian institutions and actors discussed here.[9]

---

[4] Francisco, *The Politics of Regime Transition*, 3.
[5] E.g. Linz and Stepan, *Problems of Democratic Transition and Consolidation*, 3–5.
[6] Tunisia's Ben Achour Commission, a central institution within the Tunisian Provisional Administration (TPA), used in its name the Arabic word "*intiqali*" (transitional), as did the NTC.
[7] According to *Webster's Dictionary*, the definition of "government" includes more emphasis on recognized authority, while "to administer"/"an administration" emphasizes execution of decisions, rather than decision-making.
[8] This is why they did not give themselves, as a collective, a name.
[9] This includes the members of the first iterations of the TPA's interim cabinet. In the Libyan case, the disparate groups that formed tended to call themselves "councils" (*majlis*), but because they did not divide the management of public affairs according to sector or task, as was roughly the case in Tunisia, I do not term them an "administration."

Abbreviations

AMT   Tunisian Magistrates' Association
ARP   People's Representative Assembly
ATCE   Tunisian External Communications Agency
AU   African Union
CDA   Constitution Drafting Assembly
CNPR   National Council for the Protection of the Revolution
DL   Decree Law
EMB   Electoral Management Body
FDTL   Democratic Forum for Work and Liberties
FIT   Tunisian Islamic Front
GNC   General National Congress
HAICA   High Independent Authority for Audio-Visual Communication
HNEC   High National Elections Committee
HOR   House of Representatives
ILE   Independent Local Electoral Authority
INRIC   National Commission for Information and Communication Reform
IRIE   Independent Regional Electoral Authority
ISIE   Independent High Electoral Authority
ISIS   Islamic State in Iraq and Syria
LCG   Libya Contact Group
LIFG   Libyan Islamic Fighting Group
LTDH   Tunisian Human Rights League
MENA   Middle East and North Africa
MMC   Misrata Military Council
NCA   National Constituent Assembly
NCLO   National Conference of Libyan Opposition
NTC   National Transition Council

PDP	Democratic Progressive Party
PSC	Peace and Security Council
RCD	Constitutional Democratic Rally
SMT	Tunisian Magistrates' Syndicate
TDC	Truth and Dignity Commission
TPA	Tunisian Provisional Administration
UGTT	General Tunisian Workers' Union
UNSC	United Nations Security Council
UNSMIL	United Nations Support Mission in Libya
UTICA	Tunisian Union of Industry, Commerce, and Handicrafts
WMC	Western Military Council

1 | *Introduction*

An Interim Government Forms

On January 13, 2011, Tunisian President Zine al-Abidine Ben Ali appeared on national television in an attempt to quiet a powerful anti-government uprising that had begun four weeks earlier. He announced a series of sweeping democratic reforms and price cuts and promised that he would not seek reelection. At the end of the speech, delivered in the local dialect, Ben Ali alluded to Charles de Gaulle's famous 1958 remarks in Algiers, in which he told the French settlers of the colony that was fighting bitterly for its independence "I have understood you" (*"fahimtikum"*). The Tunisian people's response to Ben Ali was "Get out" (*"dégage"*).

The next day, the government declared a state of emergency. Ben Ali fired nearly his entire cabinet and announced that legislative elections would take place within six months. Yet thousands of Tunisians took to the streets demanding Ben Ali's immediate resignation. They gathered first in front of the headquarters of the national trade union, l'Union Générale des Travailleurs Tunisiens (UGTT), at Mohammed Ali Square, and then moved to the front of the Ministry of Interior. Around five o'clock that evening, President Ben Ali and his wife, Leila Trabelsi, boarded a plane for Saudi Arabia in exile.

In the chaotic weeks following Ben Ali's flight, protest leaders entered into negotiations with remaining elites from the *ancien régime*. These negotiations resulted in a succession of interim governments (prime minsters and their ministerial cabinets), with gradual elimination of the outgoing regime. Meanwhile, a wide group of political and civil society actors organized themselves into various interim committees and governing structures to help prepare for elections of a National Constituent Assembly, which would draft a constitution and organize elections for a new permanent government. I call this ensemble of structures the Tunisian Provisional Administration (TPA);

1

2 Introduction

it became the first interim government in Tunisia's attempted political transition and was in place until October 23, 2011, when it began transferring authority to the Assembly.[1]

Meanwhile, in neighboring Libya, the first rumblings of an anti-authoritarian movement began – not by coincidence – in January 2011. Encouraged by what had happened to Ben Ali in Tunisia that month, Libyan protestors gathered in the cities of Bani Walid and Benghazi to denounce the government's failure to provide adequate housing. These protests quickly spread to towns such as al-Baida and Derna in the east and Sebha in the south. The government, led by Colonel Moammar Qadhafi, responded swiftly, ordering the police to avoid violent clashes and not to fire live ammunition, and instructing clerics to call for calm during their sermons.

Soon, an opposition group of exiled activists, the National Conference for Libyan Opposition (NCLO), called for a Libyan "Day of Rage" on February 17 in all cities, intended as massive protests against the government.[2] The government responded to the NCLO's message by reaching out to associated individuals and sending Colonel Qadhafi's son Saadi, a Special Forces commander, and Abdullah al-Sanusi, head of internal security, to Benghazi.[3]

On February 15, security forces arrested human rights lawyer Fathi Terbil – one of several political activists detained[4] – who was known for defending the families of victims of a massacre at Abu Salim prison in 2006. His arrest sparked protests in Benghazi (ahead of the planned Day of Rage), which quickly became violent. Protests also broke out in the eastern cities of al-Baida and Tobruk. Qadhafi let it be known that live bullets would be fired on people who joined the protests, and that anyone associated with organizing demonstrations would be arrested.

[1] TPA is not an official term; it is a term I created. At the time, what was thought of as the interim government in Tunisia was more limited than what I describe here, so I have chosen to use the term TPA to distinguish it.

[2] This date was chosen purposefully, as significant anti-regime protests had occurred in Benghazi on February 17, 2006, led by families of the victims of the Abu Salim massacre.

[3] Several sources (e.g. *Middle East Journal*, "Chronology," 482; Bell and Witter, *Roots of Rebellion*) report the release of political prisoners over the month of February. Some of these meetings and warnings also reportedly involved regime figures like Saif al-Islam giving warnings "not to further inflame the situation" (Bell and Witter, *Roots of Rebellion*).

[4] Another important arrest was that of Terbil's colleague Faraj al-Sharani (Mundy, *Libya*, 55).

The conflict between government forces and protestors continued over the next few days, and the violence escalated.[5] Unlike Tunisia's TPA, which did not form until President Ben Ali had fled, Libya's first interim government was led by an organization that formed before the Qadhafi regime fell, which called itself the National Transition Council (NTC). The NTC was based in Benghazi and originally comprised primarily lawyers and former dissidents, many of whom had been living abroad. It operated through an executive branch, with individuals assigned to discrete portfolios (such as foreign affairs, interior affairs, and finance), a legislative branch with representatives from around the country, and a military branch, which attempted to coordinate military operations in the fight against the Qadhafi regime and control various local militias.

During the five months after it formed, the NTC drafted a constitutional declaration and a roadmap to elections. Its first major step after Qadhafi was removed[6] was naming a postliberation government. This first "official" interim government was tasked with adopting electoral legislation and overseeing the transition to a constitution and elections for a General National Congress (GNC). Elections for the GNC were held on July 7, 2012, seventeen months after the NTC had formed.

First Interim Governments: A Unique Moment

These extraordinary and virtually simultaneous events in Libya and Tunisia constitute a poorly understood but critical phase of attempted transition to democratic rule – the short period between authoritarian collapse and the first post-authoritarian elections. During this phase, a struggle unfolds between forces calling for continuity with the past and those pushing for change, with the result captured in a phenomenon I call a "first interim government." This book examines the forces that

---

[5] On February 18 and 19 it would get much worse, with regime forces firing on a funeral procession in Benghazi and a retaliation by protestors in which they attack national army barracks – including that of the dreaded Khamis (32nd) Brigade in a siege that lasted three days (see Chorin, *Exit the Colonel*, 195; Bell and Witter, *Roots of Rebellion*). Human Rights Watch counted eighty-four dead by February 19 (*Middle East Journal*, "Chronology," 65, no. 3, 482).
[6] Several sources (e.g. Gaynor and Zargoun, "Gadhafi Caught Like 'Rat' in a Drain, Humiliated and Shot") document the violent manner in which he was killed near his hometown of Sirte.

shaped the first interim governments in Tunisia and Libya and seeks to understand how each one influenced the events that followed.

The TPA in Tunisia and the NTC in Libya emerged from two very different (though both brutally harsh) experiences of authoritarian rule. The two countries' different "starting conditions"[7] undeniably contributed to some of the differences between the TPA and the NTC. However, to make a direct connection between these historical experiences in Tunisia and Libya and their divergent trajectories in the years following the 2011 authoritarian collapse would be to ignore the critical decisions each interim government took immediately after the uprisings. A comparison of these two first interim governments, operating in the same timeframe and the same geographic region, offers a unique opportunity to examine how those who emerge as political leaders can take advantage of the authoritarian collapse, and how they are simultaneously constrained by the structures and legacies they inherit.

The dramatic differences between events in Tunisia and Libya during the first several years following the TPA and NTC, respectively, also reveal the critical importance of seminal decisions and actions taken during the initial phase of attempted transition. In Tunisia, the first round of elections (organized by the TPA) gave way to increasing instability and political polarization under its successor, the National Constituent Assembly (NCA), and the troika government it formed. Eventually, key actors from the TPA stepped in to overcome the governance stalemate and help the NCA complete the draft constitution. With a new constitution in place to define the principles, structure, and procedures of a new governance system, elections for the first democratically elected and non-interim president and unicameral legislature could be held. In Libya, by contrast, the elected congress, the GNC, that replaced the NTC was almost immediately overwhelmed by the demands of armed militia and other societal groups. The GNC struggled to organize elections for a constitutional committee as intended, in large part due to interference by a proliferating number of militia with independent funding and "revolutionary" prestige. Thus, while the first interim government in each country managed to hand over power to a second representative body,

---

[7] I am indebted to Seth Kaplan for creating this term.

subsequent events couldn't have been more different. These differences would become even more apparent in later years.

The Study of Interim Governments during Transition from Authoritarian Rule

First interim governments take on a unique responsibility and face daunting challenges. While interim governments across history have assumed a variety of forms and functions, their legitimacy has been accorded based, in part, on the historical time period in which they have appeared.[8] Today, most interim governments that follow an authoritarian overthrow – whether as the result of a popular uprising, a military coup, or violent conflict – must promise to hand over power to a government chosen by the people.

McGuire describes how interim governments are paradoxically in a position to both be extremely influential and work under conditions of limited capacity:

An interim government comes into being precisely when it announces the certainty of its own demise. Why should anyone take seriously the preferences of political actors who are just marking time until more enduring rulers are chosen? Moreover, interim governments are not themselves elected, and usually come into being when the crisis that led to the authoritarian regime has long passed. Their decisions may therefore lack the weight of those made either by authoritarian incumbents at their height, or by elected officials with democratic legitimacy.[9]

In other words, interim governments face the challenge of establishing legitimacy in the eyes of those they represent without having been elected, and knowing that they must soon leave office. Thus, they must purport to following certain rules while also trying to set new rules of governance and convince people of their authority. The ways they achieve (or don't achieve) this difficult task has important implications for understanding the larger processes of transitions.

Despite their importance, interim governments have remained an understudied aspect of attempted democratic transition since its

---

[8] Shain and Linz, *Between States*, 8.
[9] McGuire, "Interim Governments and Democratic Consolidation: Argentina in Comparative Perspective" (in Shain and Linz, eds., *Between States*), 180.

emergence as a subfield of comparative politics.[10] Samuel Huntington's "third wave" of transition from authoritarianism began with the
popular overthrow of the Portuguese, Greek, and Spanish regimes in
the mid-1970s.[11] These first cases helped scholars understand transition actors (such as militaries, elites, and mass protest movements) and
their decision-making contexts. Studies of the transitions that unfolded
in the subsequent years in Latin America gave more insight into the
roles of actors like labor movements as well as the influence of economic conditions on bargaining elites.[12]

The unique context of the Eastern European transitions in the early 1990s
highlighted the role of outside actors (the Soviet Union and the United States
and its allies) in shaping transition processes.[13] These events also gave rise
to studies of how the different Communist parties either adapted to new
forms of government or disappeared and how they negotiated with the
rising civil society movements that challenged them. This era, which was
characterized by a series of "roundtable" negotiations on the shape of
the new political order, led to a literature on constitutional design.[14]

Several sub-Saharan African countries in the early 1990s also experienced popular uprisings that destabilized the dictatorships that had
been ruling since independence. As the roundtable talks had in Eastern
Europe, the National Conferences organized in several of these African
countries provided important transition mechanisms for study.[15] The

[10] A few exceptions exist, and have offered a critical foundation for this study. See
especially Shain and Linz, *Between States*, and Seely, *The Legacies of Transition
Governments*. To my knowledge, the only other studies that directly examine
the challenge for interim governments of establishing legitimacy are Guttieri and
Piombo, *Interim Governments* and Rangwala, "The Creation of Governments-
in-Waiting." However, both these works focus on the involvement of the
international community in creating interim governments, which is not the
model of interim government experienced in Tunisia and Libya in 2011–2012.
[11] Huntington, *The Third Wave*.
[12] E.g. Collier and Collier, *Shaping the Political Arena*; Haggard and Kaufman,
"The Political Economy of Democratic Transitions." The latter set of authors
includes some Asian cases.
[13] Rose et al., *Democracy and Its Alternatives*.
[14] The broader literature on constitutional design generally includes works by Jon
Elster (e.g. *The Roundtable Talks and the Breakdown of Communism*) and the
scholars associated with the Comparative Constitutions Project (such as Tom
Ginsburg, Zachary Elkins, and James Melton).
[15] Such countries include Benin, Chad, Comoros, Congo, Gabon, Mali, Niger,
Togo, and former Zaire. See Heilbrunn, "The Social Origins of National
Conferences"; Bratton and van de Walle, *Democratic Experiments in Africa*.

role of civil society organizations such as the church also began to come to the fore.[16] Michael Bratton and Nicholas van de Walle brought together these and other factors (including the preexistence of democratic institutions) in a multivariate model that sought to explain variation in transition paths across the continent.[17] Scholars such as Richard Joseph contributed to the debate by highlighting the importance of changes in the international economy on these events.[18]

Before the uprisings of 2011, the literature on political transitions in the Middle East and North Africa (MENA) had not succeeded in explaining why waves of democratic transition had passed over the region.[19] Studies in MENA countries were limited to exploring patterns of opposition and participation and patterns of authoritarian rule.[20] The lack of transitions from authoritarian rule in the region gave social scientists much to explore in terms of factors permitting the "persistence of authoritarianism."[21] Their works provide a rich collection of resources on specific institutions such as political parties, civil society, and elections and electoral processes, as well as evaluations of state strength and governance.[22]

---

[16] Heilbrunn, "The Social Origins of National Conferences"; Widner, *Political Parties and Civil Societies in Sub-Saharan Africa* (cited in Seely, *The Legacies of Transition Governments*, 7–8). The church also played an important role in many Latin American cases.

[17] Bratton and Van de Walle, *Democratic Experiments in Africa.*

[18] Joseph, "Challenges of a 'Frontier' Region."

[19] One exception is Turkey, where, until relatively recently, the country was considered a case of secular democracy after 1945 (despite being punctuated by military coups).

[20] E.g. Anderson, "Lawless Government and Illegal Opposition"; Lust-Okar, *Divided They Rule.*

[21] E.g. Salamé, *Democracy without Democrats?*; Schlumberger, ed., *Debating Arab Authoritarianism*; Bellin, "The Robustness of Authoritarianism in the Middle East." It should be acknowledged that there were rounds of popular protest during these years in several MENA countries. Some of the most widely cited protests and riots in North Africa are Algeria in 1988, Tunisia in 1977, 1983, and 2008; and the "bread riots" of Egypt in 2007. Even Libya in 2006 experienced protests in Benghazi, which related more to human rights than economic demands.

[22] On political parties, see, for example, Lust and Zerhouni, eds., *Political Participation in the Middle East*; Storm, *Party Politics and Prospects for Democracy in North Africa.* On civil society, see, for example, Norton, ed., *Civil Society in the Middle East*; Cavatorta and Durac, *Civil Society and Democratization in the Arab World.* On elections, see, for example, Blaydes, *Elections and Distributive Politics in Mubarak's Egypt.* On state strength and governance, see, for example, Dawisha and Zartman, eds., *Beyond Coercion:*

The events of 2011 were unprecedented in postcolonial North Africa and the Middle East. Scholars have had few reference points as they have sought to identify causes of the regime downfalls in North Africa and Yemen, as well as the varying patterns of uprising and regime response across the region. Some have identified themes such as the role of social media and the changing public; others have focused on studying more closely the events themselves.[23] Several edited volumes with contributions on countries from across the MENA region bring together the range of factors and dynamics that made up the events and their aftermath.[24] In general, as Kao and Lust assert, this literature reflects the tendency within comparative politics to focus on macro-historical accounts and structural variables at the expense of decisions by local actors.[25]

Despite its valuable contributions to our understanding of attempted transitions from authoritarian rule, the existing literature fails to resolve whether structural variables or agency variables matter more during regime transition. On the one hand, this debate is easy to resolve, because scholars generally agree that in any transition, *both* types of variables shape outcomes. However, few studies take as their *problématique* the issue of how these types of variables interact. Our understanding of how political transitions unfold and why they unfold

---

The Durability of the Arab State; Ayubi, *Over-Stating the Arab State*; Salamé, ed., *The Foundations of the Arab State*.

[23] E.g. Lynch, *The Arab Uprising*; Tessler and Robbins, "Political System Preferences of Arab Publics" (in Lynch, ed., *The Arab Uprisings Explained*); Brynen et al., eds., *Beyond the Arab Spring*; Zartman, ed., *The Arab Spring*; Bayat, *Revolution without Revolutionaries*. A common theme throughout these studies is the role of the Islamist parties in the unfolding dynamics of regime destabilization. Several individual works have also been devoted to that topic, including works specifically on Tunisia. See, for example, Wolf, *Political Islam in Tunisia*; McCarthy, *Inside Tunisia's Al-Nahda*.

[24] To name only a few, Lynch, ed., *The Arab Uprisings Explained*; Diamond and Plattner, eds., *Democratization and Authoritarianism in the Arab World*; Kienle and Sika, eds., *The Arab Uprisings*; Diwan, ed., *Understanding the Political Economy of the Arab Uprisings*. A few studies focus specifically on North Africa, e.g. Frosini and Biagi, eds., *Political and Constitutional Transitions in North Africa*; Volpi, *Revolution and Authoritarianism in North Africa*.

[25] Kao and Lust, "Why Did the Arab Uprisings Turn Out As They Did? A Survey of the Literature." In their special issue of *Comparative Political Studies* published shortly before the uprisings, Capoccia and Ziblatt attempt to address this same tendency within the literature (Capoccia and Ziblatt, "The Historical Turn in Democratization Studies.")

as they do can be enhanced by closer examination of the array of variables that interact during attempted transition and the stages at which different variables matter.

Moreover, neither aggregated analyses nor individual case studies adequately take into account how decisions made in the *first phase* of an attempted transition take on a particular importance in directing what follows. While explanations of narrow aspects of transitions, such as negotiated pacts or electoral processes, are informative, these tend to occur relatively late in a rapidly unfolding and blurry sequence of events. Similarly, studies of class structure and other social or economic features of the attempted transition overlook the fact that actors during the *immediate* stages of authoritarian collapse may have been relatively free from these institutional constraints. Without examining the options and choices taken by actors in those moments, and *how* they worked within those constraints, we cannot know how much weight to give to the structures transition actors inherit.

Studying the phase of attempted democratic transition that is delineated by the appearance of an interim governing body on one end and by first democratic elections on the other requires the study of several key decisions. Is a foundational governing document, such as a constitution – even if temporary – needed for the transition to proceed? If so, by what procedures should it be written and adopted? What should be the role of existing state institutions during this period, including the military, especially if this is not clearly defined by an interim constitution or statement? What steps should be taken to ensure the closure of and to perhaps punish the former regime? How much assistance should be accepted or requested from foreign powers? Should the first elected authority be a constitution-drafting body or a new legislature and/or head of state, and when should elections take place?[26] Finally, who should be allowed to participate in those elections, and in what capacity?

Existing scholarship on regime transitions has dealt with many of these questions but not as a comprehensive set of decisions that can influence a country's trajectory during authoritarian collapse. Critical questions of constitution writing, for example, as noted above, have been treated extensively by Jon Elster and colleagues, including debates

---

[26] Presumably, elections should take place as soon as possible, but someone must be charged with determining exactly when that is.

over the institutional design best suited for emerging democracies, especially for countries emerging from violent conflict, as well as over issues of individual rights and the spatial separation of power.[27] Others have brought to the fore the importance of the "constitution-making environment"[28] as well as the actors involved in the writing process and the constraints they face.[29]

But how is the stage for that constitution-writing process set? The authorities who govern between authoritarian collapse and the launching of a constitution-writing phase (often through the establishment of a constituent assembly) play a key role in determining those actors, environments, and constraints. For example, in both Tunisia and Libya, as in other Arab-uprising countries, the authorities who took charge produced texts meant to acknowledge the role of a constitution in securing democratic governance. These texts, both by the content they contained (or omitted) and the processes by which they were adopted, played an important role in determining later events and structures.

Similarly, the scholarship considering the question of which leaders should succeed an outgoing authoritarian ruler takes into account both a country's "starting conditions" and the identity and actions of individuals involved in the transition. Linz and Stepan, for instance, highlighted the role of "initiators of transition."[30] More recently, and in regards to specific cases, Jennifer Seely has studied the actors involved in Sovereign National Conferences in Benin and Togo, and Glen Rangwala and Alice Alunni have highlighted the role of unique actors such as diaspora communities and other external actors in both creating and legitimating interim governing forces.[31] No less attention has been given to the question of "founding elections" following

---

[27] E.g. Cheibub, *Presidentialism, Parliamentarism, and Democracy*; Carey and Shugart, "Incentives to Cultivate a Personal Vote"; Horowitz, "Comparing Democratic Systems"; Lijphart, "The Political Consequences of Electoral Laws: 1945–85"; Sisk, *Democratization in South Africa*.

[28] Linz and Stepan, *Problems of Democratic Transition and Consolidation*, 66–83.

[29] See Zachary Elkins, "Constitutional Engineering," in Bertrand Badie, Dirk Berg-Schlosser, and Leonardo Morlino, eds., International Encyclopedia of Political Science (Thousand Oaks: SAGE Publications, 2011): 414–416.

[30] Linz and Stepan, *Problems of Democratic Transition and Consolidation*, 66–83. On this, also see Francisco, *The Politics of Regime Transition*, 48.

[31] Alunni, "Long-Distance Nationalism and Belonging in the Libyan Diaspora"; Rangwala, "The Creation of Governments-in-Waiting"; Seely, *The Legacies of Transition Governments*.

authoritarian breakdown, including their role as a signifier and tactic as actors vie to maintain or gain control.[32] Yet the underlying assumption in this literature is that the process of electoral contestation and the outcome of this process matter more than decisions around their timing or the conditions under which they take place.[33] Overlooking such important factors may result in a significant misreading of the transition process.

Finally, a rich literature exists on questions of transitional justice, or measures to address past human rights abuses, including through punishments directed at members of the former regime. These works have advanced our understanding of how these processes fit into the transition process.[34] Few, however, directly ask about the decisions taken (or not taken) to produce those measures in the first place. What choices did the designers of these measures face, what information did they have or not have at their disposal, and what challenges or threats did they face?[35] Studying such questions can help clarify both how a transition is or is not preordained by legacies and decisions of the past, *and* how it is shaped by the first struggle between those clinging to the past and those looking to the future.

Questions, Design, and Argument

This book focuses on the governing processes that emerge during the first phase of attempted transition from authoritarian rule. This phase begins the moment the ruling autocracy starts to crumble and ends when an elected government takes over. The book explores two central research questions. First, to what extent are first interim governments

---

[32] E.g. di Palma, *To Craft Democracies*, 82–86.

[33] As the case of Libya shows, neglecting to establish proper consensus over key issues about these electoral rules, or to reassure security and other surrounding conditions, can have grave consequences.

[34] E.g. Teitel, *Transitional Justice*; Elster, *Closing the Books*. For a good treatment of transitional justice questions following from the 2011 MENA uprisings, see Sriram, ed., *Transitional Justice in the Middle East and North Africa*.

[35] An important exception here is the volume by Shain and Linz, who argue that interim governments play an influential role in the process of "evening the scores" that occurs in transition from authoritarian rule, and that the impact of interim governments on this process can only be truly understood after much time has passed. Many of their case studies also illustrate how various interim governments have dealt with this issue (see Shain and Linz, eds., *Between States*, 97–98).

shaped by preexisting structures, and to what extent are actors able to shape them? Second, to what extent do first interim governments influence the phases of political change that follow them?

I argue that while preexisting structures, whether formal governance institutions or the institutionalized expressions of established social interactions (such as tribal relations),[36] strongly influence the design and behavior of first interim governments, too often overlooked are actors' (agents') choices, which affect not only immediate events but also later phases of governance. Studying first interim governments – what determines their structure and actions and the legacies they leave – shows how individuals can sometimes work within limiting structures and institutions to affect longer-term reforms.

In order to address the extent to which first interim governments are shaped by preexisting structures and the extent to which actors are able to shape them, I examine the formation and actions of the TPA in Tunisia and the NTC in Libya. As described briefly above, the TPA emerged as the first interim government in January, 2011, after the flight of Ben Ali, and lasted until late October of that year, when the National Constituent Assembly was elected to draft a constitution. The NTC formed in February 2011, before Qadhafi fell, and lasted until July 2012, when the General National Congress was elected. The two interim governments had some structural and behavioral similarities as well as many differences. Both the TPA and NTC assumed as their self-determined mandate the maintenance of day-to-day governance and the organization of democratic elections, but the ways they chose to carry out these tasks, as well as the issues they faced and their choice of action in dealing with these issues, were characterized by stark contrasts.

To address the second research question – the extent to which first interim governments influence the phases of political change that follow them – I trace the direct effects of the key decisions taken by the NTC and TPA onto the second "transition phase" in each country. I delimit this second phase to a roughly two-year time period following the first post-uprising election in each country. In Tunisia, this second phase ended with the adoption of a new constitution in January 2014; in Libya, it ended with the emergence of two rival governments in

---

[36] I credit Bill Zartman with this formulation.

summer of that same year.[37] Following this second phase, the increasingly violent and irreconcilable conflict in Libya diverged sharply from the trajectory followed in neighboring Tunisia, where a political compromise led to the peaceful election of a first post-authoritarian (non-interim) government, which then gave way to five years of halting political transition. Again, an examination of these interim governments' direct impacts helps clarify the extent to which structures channeled the actions of decision-makers, versus their ability to break free of what came before.

The study is based on a set of interviews conducted in Tunisia, in London, and in Washington, DC, with actors involved in these interim governments in some form and analysts with unique insight into the questions driving this study.[38] The majority of interviews were conducted during several brief or extended visits to Tunis between 2013 and 2019. I also reviewed an extensive set of additional sources covering facts about the period. I identified these sources using three chief methods: (1) being directed to them by interviewees; (2) through keyword searches and perusing of academic databases and journals; and (3) through reading other secondary sources. The sources I collected include primary documents, such as laws and other official texts written at the time; secondary analyses such as books, journal articles, and reports published by international organizations; and news articles taken from credible media outlets.

Political transitions are a complicated, messy process. Creating a government that is responsive to the people from the not-quite-cold corpse of an autocracy is not necessarily the rational plan of the actors involved. Rather, democratic arrangements often represent the most satisfactory compromise for all sides following protracted negotiations, usually among elites.[39] In other cases, negotiations following

[37] The cutoff point for this second transition phase is defined by the major events specific to each country. I also wanted the phases to be roughly equivalent in length, although this was not as important as the role of the cutoff events in changing the focus of the transition process.

[38] I was fortunate to meet with several Libyan actors residing in Tunis or Washington, DC, and to speak with others over Skype.

[39] E.g. O'Donnell and Schmitter, eds., *Transitions from Authoritarian Rule*; Higley and Burton, "The Elite Variable in Democratic Transitions and Breakdowns"; Higley and Gunther, *Elites and Democratic Consolidation in Latin America and Southern Europe*.

authoritarian ouster can break down before such an arrangement is reached, or the agreement itself collapses shortly thereafter. Transitions – whether or not they end in democratic consolidation – are difficult because they are characterized by a combined desire to reject the past with a fear of the unknown future.

This book applies the theories and analytical tools developed in studies in southern and eastern Europe, Latin America, and Africa of attempted transitions from authoritarian rule to two recent cases in North Africa.[40] Whereas to date most studies of the 2011 Arab uprisings and their aftermath have focused on social and other structural variables and the nature of the outgoing regime, this book aims to restore the importance of local agents' choices in critical moments during the transitions.[41] It also helps refocus attention within this scholarship on the dynamics of democratization, rather than the religious-secular divide that has consumed so many analysts.[42] Additionally, the book provides empirical material for the study of transitions by providing close descriptions of the events and of decisions taken – and the tension between structural conditions and human agency reflected in them – during a key transitional phase.

Plan of the Book

The book is organized as follows. In Chapter 2, I argue that the first interim government in Tunisia formed in order to prepare for elections of a constituent assembly but by nature of its position also took other highly consequential decisions along the way. Such decisions included the composition of the interim government itself, the declaration of an interim constitution and roadmap, the promulgation of other interim laws and formations of other interim committees, and the organizing of foundational elections. The account of each event covers the conditions under which inherited structures guided actors' decisions, and those under which actors were able

---

[40] And to a limited extent, Asia.

[41] E.g. Hinnebusch, "Historical Sociology and the Arab Uprising"; Brownlee et al., *The Arab Spring*.

[42] E.g. Lust et al., "After the Arab Spring"; Hamid, *Temptations of Power*.

to shape the trajectory of the new political regime. Chapter 3 describes the events in the phase immediately following the work of the first interim government, showing how consequential that government was both in the decisions it took and the ways it had been constrained.

Chapters 4 and 5 analyze the Libyan case. Chapter 4 discusses how the first interim government, the National Transition Council, formed to determine a transitional roadmap and hold elections for a body to draft a constitution. In order to do this, the NTC also made consequential decisions about security and other pressing matters. In Chapter 5, I demonstrate how the next phase of Libya's attempted transition reflected the NTC's actions (and inactions).

Chapter 6 offers a high-level overview of the events in Tunisia and Libya following the phase of the first interim government in each country and the work of the second interim government each one helped elect.[43] In Tunisia, the TPA had given way to a constituent assembly that – with great difficulty, and thanks to help from members of the TPA – overcame conflict and produced a new constitution. The context in which this constitution was written – which had been shaped by the TPA – led it to contain several features that continued to shape Tunisia's attempted transition. In Libya, meanwhile, the NTC had created a General National Congress, which was meant to organize elections for a constituent committee (or constitutional drafting assembly, the CDA). However, the GNC had been so plagued by the features and decisions of the NTC – among others, its inability to control armed groups or assert a shared Libyan vision – that the next several years were defined by spiraling conflict among groups with varying goals and identities.

The final chapter summarizes how and why the TPA in Tunisia and the NTC in Libya took different approaches to their common mandate of maintaining stability in government during authoritarian breakdown and holding democratic elections. Bringing these findings into broader context, the chapter concludes that the actions of first interim governments are critical for understanding how and why attempted transitions to democratic governments unfold the way they do. It offers a tentative research agenda for future scholars to more precisely

---

[43] I trace events during the roughly five-year period, until the end of 2019, in each country.

measure the impact first interim governments have on attempted transition from authoritarian rule. The extremely short period of time that immediately follows an authoritarian overthrow and precedes elections encapsulates the struggle that actors who forge a new political path face in striking a balance between continuity and change.

2 | *The Tunisian Provisional Administration*

This chapter analyzes Tunisia's first post-uprising transition government, the Tunisian Provisional Administration (TPA). The TPA formed in order to fill the void left in the wake of Ben Ali's departure – a void defined not simply by the absence of a leader but by the collapse of an entire political system. This entailed filling the positions of interim prime minister, president, and cabinet ministers in such a way that would satisfy protestors; developing a transition roadmap that would respond to protestors' demands, particularly in regards to a new constitutional framework; organizing itself into a functioning set of institutional structures; and organizing and overseeing elections for a new government. Accomplishing these tasks also entailed balancing continuity and change by relying both on individuals considered independent from the outgoing regime and on individuals with governing experience, and using various strategies such as building consensus and drawing on historical traditions to convince the Tunisian people of its legitimacy.

At the time it was in place, the Tunisian Provisional Administration was hardly considered a government. Indeed, this book considers as part of the TPA the entire ensemble of individuals and organizations who worked to step in and manage the attempted transition that began when Ben Ali fled. The TPA brought together an array of actors in an ad hoc fashion, worked through institutions that were a mix of existing and improvised or new, and deployed a variety of strategies for managing its daunting tasks. Nonetheless, the distinct features characterizing TPA actors facilitated their working relationship and the TPA's relatively cohesive institutional framework. Its strategies helped prevent it from succumbing to challengers or external forces.

The chapter first presents a historical backdrop in order to set the stage for the work of the TPA. It then describes the various features, decisions, and actions taken by the various bodies and individuals who are termed here the TPA. Although the TPA sought to adhere to its defined mandate of managing day-to-day affairs and organizing elections, in seeking to organize itself and establish its own legitimacy, as well as draft a plan for transition, it dealt with several other issues relevant to any transitional process. This chapter describes how the TPA dealt with these myriad issues all during its short tenure.

Historical Backdrop

Tunisia's history as a geographical entity is somewhat longer than its Maghreb neighbors, dating back to the fifteenth and sixteen centuries.[1] It also distinguishes itself from the others in the development of its national identity following independence, which emphasized unity, development, and modernity blended with its traditional roots. When Habib Bourguiba, the country's first president following independence from France, sought to foster this national identity, he emphasized the country's historical sense of state, the modern reforms undertaken by past rulers, and experience of negotiation rather than war. For Bourguiba, this history amounted to a national culture with Arabo-Muslim roots but situated at a crossroads of Africa, Europe, and the Middle East, with desert, plains, mountains, and ocean.[2]

Although European influence had been encroaching on the region for centuries, the French Protectorate in Tunisia was not established until the 1880s. During the Protectorate period, the majority of existing political, legal, and economic structures were kept intact, and the French attempted to rule indirectly through them.[3] The nationalist movement that emerged in the 1930s and lasted until independence was officially declared in 1956, marked by a split between those favoring Arab nationalism and those favoring Tunisian nationalism and demands for a constitution. The Neo-Destour party, led by

---

[1] Entelis, "Republic of Tunisia," 509; Willis, *Politics and Power in the Maghreb*, 14–18.

[2] This "historical sense of state" included elements such as provision of public goods and a fairly clear geographic entity with an army to protect it. Modern reforms undertaken by past rulers included abolishing slavery and enacting a *Pacte Fondamentale* (1857) followed by the first constitution in the Arab world (1861) under Muhammad as-Sadiq Bey. This followed a host of other such reforms under Prime Minister Khair al-Dine.

[3] This is in distinct contrast to the French colonization of Algeria, a case not discussed here but that helps highlight the characteristics of Tunisian colonization. See, for example, Willis, *Politics and Power in the Maghreb*, 19–21.

Bourguiba, had formed to guide the independence movement but split in the early 1950s, and followers of Bourguiba ultimately won out (thanks in large part to the involvement of the national labor union, the UGTT) in the struggle against the more conservative wing of the party, led by Salah Ben Yousef.

With independence came the setting up of the state under full Tunisian administration, which included a strong central administration, an army clearly separated from politics, and a single-party system that would remain, despite attempts by those in charge to feign liberalization and political pluralism. Meanwhile, organizations such as the UGTT stayed closely aligned with political parties while also working to preserve a certain level of autonomy as part of a larger process of the development of a genuine civil society.

The other important developments over the 1960s, 1970s, and into the 1980s were economic. By the early 1980s, Bourguiba's statist economic policies had proved themselves clearly unsustainable, and in 1986 the country agreed to accept an IMF loan and structural adjustment program (SAP). Yet, as is well-documented, privatization was accompanied by cronyism and deepening inequality and unemployment.[4] Economic growth resulting from neoliberal reforms benefited middle class families, most of whom lived in the capital city of Tunis and the coastal cities of Sousse and Monastir, at the expense of large swaths of the population based in the interior. Economic changes were also the main driver behind the split between the labor union and the ruling party in 1978, and some of the beginnings of political opposition movements.

In the meantime, another political opposition movement had formed in the late 1970s, this one based in Islam. The Mouvement de la Tendance Islamique (MTI, later renamed Enahda) drew sufficient support to pose a threat to the ruling party, and was soon banned.

---

[4] One of the most acclaimed works on the societal effects of Tunisia's economic reforms during this period is Hibou, *The Force of Obedience*. Other valuable sources include Alexander, *Tunisia: From Stability to Revolution in the Maghreb*, 106–129; Cammett et al., *A Political Economy of the Middle East*, 268–269, 299–302. For a more contemporary analysis of Tunisia's reforms, see Murphy, *Economic and Political Change in Tunisia*; and Zartman, ed., *Tunisia: The Political Economy of Reform*.

When Ben Ali took over from Bourguiba in 1987 via a bloodless coup,[5] he reintroduced political pluralism and legalized all opposition parties under a rhetoric of "change." Yet, as the Islamists gained support, he found excuses to repress political freedom once again – most notably with the growing support of the West in clamping down on Islamist groups. In this context of political repression and economic injustice, the Tunisian uprising of 2010–2011, which led to the TPA, began.[6]

Immediate Attempts to Appoint New Leadership

On January 14, 2011, given that Ben Ali and his party-state had disappeared, there was no clear answer to the question of who should legitimately represent the Tunisian people. On the contrary, various groups of Tunisians were in constant negotiations about who should be in charge. Who should be allowed to serve in what roles now that the former dictator was no longer in charge? Did old regime people have any right to weigh in on decisions about what would happen next? How much legitimacy did the protestors, or the main bodies responsible for the downfall of Ben Ali, have in calling the shots? Indeed, these are fundamental issues that concern any interim government.

Remaining members of the Ben Ali government responded to the crisis by referring to the 1959 constitution, which allowed them to retain their positions as decision-makers. However, protestors on the street believed Ben Ali's absence was the product of *their* courage and efforts, and therefore did not want to accept decisions by anyone who could not claim responsibility for the situation. The prime minister, Mohammed Ghannouchi, in his public announcement the evening of the president's departure, called for the application of Article 56, according to which the president, in case of temporary absence,

---

[5] This event is also sometimes referred to as a "constitutional coup," because of Ben Ali's success in persuading those involved that he should take over as the president given Bourguiba's weakening health, according to the constitution (e.g. Willis, *Politics and Power in the Maghreb*).

[6] For more detail on the relationship between these political economy variables and the Tunisian uprising, see Cammett et al., *A Political Economy of the Middle East*; Diwan, *Understanding the Political Economy of the Arab Uprisings*, 57–79.

delegates his responsibilities to the prime minister. Clearly, these actors were prioritizing an appearance of order and control and working within the legal framework.[7]

Within hours, Ghannouchi and the president of the Chamber of Deputies (or lower house of parliament), Fouad Mebazza, called the Constitutional Council to advise on the appropriateness of the application of Article 56.[8] These experts questioned the application of this article, which suggested that Ben Ali had only temporarily ceded his duties as the president of the republic and had delegated them himself to Ghannouchi. The experts agreed that Article 57, which stated that in the case of "death, resignation or permanent deterrence of the president," the president of the Chamber of Deputies would lead the government. His authority would last for forty-five days and no more than sixty days. Thus, on January 15, Fouad Mebazza assumed the role of interim president. He chose to keep Ghannouchi in the position of prime minister.[9]

On January 17, Mebazza, speaking from the government palace in the Kasbah, announced a national "unity government" (an executive cabinet not dominated by any single ruling party).[10] The defense, foreign, interior, and finance ministers – all members of the Constitutional Democratic Rally (RCD) – retained their posts, along with ten other members of the former ruling party. In addition, the cabinet

---

[7] Interview with former Tunisian politician, January 5, 2015.

[8] Under Ben Ali, parliamentarians were elected, but the "winner takes all" electoral system allowed the Constitutional Democratic Rally (RCD) to dominate every election. The parliament had been changed to a bicameral one in 2005 (following a 2002 constitutional amendment), part of Ben Ali's efforts to feign inclusion/political pluralism (Erdle, *Ben Ali's New Tunisia*, 164–165; Alexander, *Tunisia: Stability and Reform in the Modern Maghreb*, 62–63).

[9] For more discussion of the switch from Article 56 to 57, see Elloumi ("Les Gouvernements Provisoires en Tunisie," 17–25; Ben Romdhane, *Tunisie: La Démocratie en Quête d'Etat*, 203–212). Such sources suggest that these decisions of the first few days were not so much meant to keep the old regime intact at any cost, but rather to maintain a semblance of order, especially given that the permanence of Ben Ali's departure was, like everything else, still unclear. The real debate would not be about who should take over for Ben Ali but whether the 1959 constitution needed to be abrogated (Elloumi, "Les Gouvernements Provisoires en Tunisie," 23–24).

[10] Tunisia has a two-headed executive in which a president holds certain executive powers while a cabinet of ministers (also referred to as the "government") is appointed by the prime minister, who comes from the political party with the greatest number of seats in parliament.

included representatives of three opposition parties: Ahmed Najib Chebbi of the Democratic Progressive Party (Parti Démocrate Progressite, PDP), Ahmed Brahim of the *Ettajdid* (Renewal) Movement, and Mustafa Ben Jafar of the Forum Démocratique Pour le Travail et les Libertés (FDTL, whose Arabic name was Ettakatol). The other members had either resigned from the RCD or were brought in as "national personalities."[11] This cabinet was tasked with organizing free and fair parliamentary and presidential elections within sixty days.

Ghannouchi's attempt at opening the government failed to satisfy the opposition. Three members of the UGTT also accepted posts but then immediately resigned;[12] this was followed by the resignation of Ben Jafar from Ettakatol (the two other opposition party members, Ahmed Najib Chebbi and Ahmed Brahim, remained). The UGTT's secretary general, Abdelsalam Jrad, called for all other political party representatives and "national personalities" to resign as well, claiming the government was not "representative of the people."[13] Other key opposition figures had also been excluded, most notably Moncef Marzouki from the Congrès Pour la République (CPR), who was en route back to Tunis from his self-exile in Paris, and Rachid Ghannouchi (no relation to the prime minister) from the moderate Islamist party Renaissance (Enahda).

On January 20, Ghannouchi's cabinet held its first meeting, during which it decided to recognize all banned political parties, remove state assets from the control of the RCD, and issue a general amnesty for political prisoners (through a bill approved by the minister of justice and ultimately passed by the parliament). The government soon promised an even broader range of political reforms, including freedom of expression, internet access, and the lifting of restrictions on the long-controlled Tunisian Human Rights League (*Ligue tunisien de droit de l'homme*, LTDH).[14] On February 9, the Ghannouchi cabinet and the Chamber of Deputies passed legislation allowing interim President

---

[11] This is referring namely to a young dissident blogger named Slim Amamou, although he had also helped found a political party, the Parti Pirate Tunisien.

[12] Those three ministers were Houssine Dmassi, Abdeljalil Bedoui, and Annouar Ben Gueddor.

[13] Chick, "Why Tunisia's Interim Government May Not Fly with Protesters."

[14] DL 2011-1 through DL 2011-5. According to Emma Murphy, this was "ultimately a precondition for getting a broad rainbow of opposition groups to join the national unity government." See Murphy, "The Tunisian Uprising and the Precarious Path to Democracy," 303.

Mebazza to rule by decree.[15] This enabled Mebazza to bypass the parliament when issuing decrees, effectively dissolving both houses.[16]

Despite these announcements of reforms, protests continued over the heavy influence of the RCD in the new government: the large number of RCD members in the new cabinet and Ghannouchi's position as prime minister. This round of protests, later named Kasbah 1, called for a new constitution and the complete dissolution of the RCD. Security forces tried to halt these protest gatherings while also combatting organized violence. As a result of this large-scale unrest, on January 18, Ghannouchi and Mebazza, as well as the other RCD ministers remaining in the executive cabinet, resigned from the RCD.[17] These events led Prime Minister Ghannouchi to appoint a second provisional cabinet on January 27, replacing twelve cabinet members, including some in key posts.

Still, the unrest continued. Participants of the Kasbah sit-ins continued to object to the presence of members of the former regime in the interim government and to demand the election of a parliament and constituent assembly, among other demands.[18] Clashes between the protestors and the police continued in other towns. Thus, although the Ghannouchi government had attempted to demonstrate its control over events in the country, the chaos continued. Some of those in the government blamed the violence on a "conspiracy" of RCD supporters trying to spread chaos and reclaim power.[19] Government institutions were not always seen as working in cooperation with the protestors. Kasbah protestors described themselves as bravely standing between the army (on the side of the people) and the police (on the side of the regime).[20] On January 25, the army chief, General Rachid Ben Ammar, told demonstrators that the army was "the guarantor of the country,

[15] Following Article 28 of the 1959 constitution.
[16] Later, other state institutions "strongly influenced by the regime" would be dissolved. These included the Constitutional Court, the Economic and Social Council, and the secret police agency "and its umbrella state security department" (*Middle East Journal*, "Chronology," 65, no. 3, 495; Schraeder and Redissi, "Ben Ali's Fall.")
[17] These included Kamel Morjane, Ridha Grira, Ahmed Friaa, Moncer Rouissi, and Zouheir M'dhaffer.
[18] Another demand was for the choice of a parliamentary regime, in a rejection of the powerful institution of the presidency. This debate would reemerge after a constituent assembly had been formed.
[19] Economist Intelligence Unit, *Tunisia – Country Report*, February 2011, 10.
[20] Interview with Tunisian civil society activist, July 6, 2013.

the people and the revolution." Clearly, the battle was not over; no consensus on a way forward had been reached.

Establishing a Way Forward

Finally, Prime Minister Ghannouchi and three other of Ben Ali's ministers stepped down on February 27. Mebazza asked Béji Caïd Essbesi, a former statesman from the Bourguiba era, to take over as the prime minister.[21] On March 3, President Mebazza announced the scheduling of elections for a National Constituent Assembly (NCA) – thus finally ceding to the protestors' remaining key demand and ending the protests – to be held on July 24.[22] The new interim prime minister also gave his first speech, in which he reassured Tunisians that security would be restored and a democratic transition process was underway.

Thus, in the span of approximately six weeks, Tunisia's third interim cabinet had been constituted. This cabinet immediately made several important moves. First, the new prime minister instructed the members of his cabinet to promise not to run in the NCA elections that had just been scheduled. This led to the resignation of two members, Ahmed Najib Chebbi of the PDP and Ahmed Brahim of Ettajdid, who wanted to be eligible to run in the elections. The government also made further arrests of former RCD members, and the Supreme Court announced plans to liquidate the party's assets and funds.[23] During a press conference held on March 7, Caïd Essebsi stressed that his government would prioritize, in addition to organizing the elections, restoration of stability and security. To that end, he announced the dismantling of the political police and its umbrella ministerial subunit, the State Security Department.[24]

---

[21] Mebazza seems to have been the individual who actually requested to call in Caïd Essebsi, based on my understanding from the interviews with Tunisian academics and TPA members (December 22, 2014; January 21, 2015).

[22] Also see Schraeder and Redissi, "Ben Ali's Fall," 16; Murphy, "The Tunisian Uprising."

[23] The arrests included former Interior Minister Rafik Belhaj Kacem, accused of being complicit in the killings of dozens of protestors. See *The Telegraph*, "Tunisia's Interior Minister Sacked."

[24] The political police had been a key part of the internal security apparatus in charge of intelligence and the maintenance of order. Protestors had demanded the dissolution of this body due to its perceived functions of spying on citizens and monitoring dissent activities.

By this point it was also clear that Tunisia's transition would not move forward under the unique control of the individuals in Caïd Essebsi's interim cabinet. Since the start of the uprisings, organizations known as "local councils for the protection of the revolution" had begun emerging around the country. Having started as neighborhood vigilante groups during the chaos of December and January, these councils represented protestors' first attempts to organize around a unified set of demands. Eventually these attempts reached the national level.[25] Under the general leadership of the UGTT and the Tunisian Bar Association, twenty-eight social and political organizations representing the protestors formed a National Council for the Protection of the Revolution (CNPR).

The Council's "principal objective was to control the public decrees issued by the government with the aim of protecting the revolution."[26] It included a wide spectrum of political parties and coalitions (including Enahda) along with the major civil society actors.[27] The CNPR organized "liberation caravans" that brought protestors to Tunis from rural areas such as Sidi Bouzid, Kairouan, and Gafsa (many of them representing families of people who had been killed during the protests) to take part in another sit-in, later called Kasbah 2.

With Kasbah 2 and the formation of the CNPR, the distribution of power between the protest movement and the remaining elements of the old regime began to shift.[28] Immediately after Ben Ali's resignation, the first Ghannouchi government had established via decree-law three interim working commissions.[29] The first, a Political Reform Commission, was initially tasked mainly with reforming the electoral code and a few other parts of the old constitution in time for the elections. Ghannouchi announced its creation on January 15 and appointed

---

[25] See Redissi et al., *La transition démocratique en Tunisie: Les Acteurs*, 189–215. As the next chapter discusses, these local councils would become quite controversial after the TPA was gone.

[26] Elloumi, "Les Gouvernements Provisoires en Tunisie," 47.

[27] Civil society organizations included the UGTT, LTDH, the Bar Association, and the Tunisian Association for Democratic Women (ATFD). Political parties included the small far-right Congrès Pour la République (CPR), the Tunisian Communist Party (PCOT), and Ettakatol.

[28] Murphy, "The Tunisian Uprising," 303.

[29] Importantly, these commissions had been called for by Ben Ali during one of his final speeches. The texts that created them were DL 2011-6; 2011-7; and 2011-8.

constitutional law expert Yadh Ben Achour as the president.[30] However, protestors objected to this decision, arguing that the appointment of a small committee of constitutional experts to revise or rewrite the constitution would not adequately reflect the voices of Tunisian society as a whole.[31] Ghannouchi and Mebazza thus entered into negotiations with the CNPR, which was demanding legal recognition. As a result, the political reform commission was officially merged with the CNPR on February 18. The commission's name was then changed to the High Authority for the Realization of the Goals of the Revolution, Political Reform, and Democratic Transition (Haute Instance pour la Réalisation des Objectifs de la Revolution, la Réforme Politique, et la Transition Démocratique, commonly known as the Ben Achour Commission for its president).[32]

Thus, by April, 2011, Tunisia's first post–Ben Ali provisional government comprised a cabinet of ministers under the leadership of Caïd Essebsi and four parallel commissions,[33] of which the largest, most important, and most high-profile was the Ben Achour Commission. The Ben Achour Commission would establish an electoral management body with regional and local units. These bodies collectively formed the first Tunisian Provisional Administration, or TPA.

The Ben Achour Commission thus represented a compromise between revolutionary (e.g. the CNPR) and existing state forces (essentially, old regime figures). This would become important during the TPA's work as it struggled to balance these various forces. Between his appointment on January 15 and the CNPR's assumption of responsibilities as part of his commission on February 18, Ben Achour had named ten legal and constitutional experts to serve on the Political Reform Commission. With the transformation of the original commission into the larger Ben Achour Commission, Ben Achour added another eight experts, including from law schools outside Tunis.[34]

---

[30] Ben Achour was apparently chosen over Sadok Belaid, for reasons that remain unverified. One interviewee suggested it was because Ben Achour was a cousin of Mebazza. Interview with Tunisian academic, July 10, 2013.
[31] Interviews with Tunisian civil society members/academics, January 12, 2015, and July 6, 2013.
[32] The Ben Achour Commission has also frequently been referenced by the acronym HIROR.
[33] The fourth was added slightly later, and these are described below.
[34] Interview with Tunisian legal scholar and expert core member, December 24, 2014.

The expert core divided itself into five subcommittees, according to members' backgrounds; each subcommittee was tasked with drafting a different legal text.[35] Draft interim laws produced by the expert core were discussed in plenary sessions before going to vote in the advisory council. The council would then debate these drafts, suggest revisions, and ultimately ratify them with a vote. Responsibilities across these two "tiers" within the Commission often overlapped,[36] as the experts sought input from civil society on their draft texts, including from civil society organizations not necessarily represented in the council.[37]

However, the representatives of the twenty-eight organizations who had formed the CNPR and now merged with Ben Achour's experts into the commission were immediately deemed insufficiently representative of Tunisian society. Several decried the absence of youth, women, and people from the regions – the segments of society seen as the main drivers of the revolution – from among those represented. During its first few meetings, the Ben Achour Commission debated ways to address this concern. Eventually, the members decided to require each organization or party represented to add one youth and one female representative to its team. It further decided to task the UGTT and LTDH with using their local chapters and branches to help identify individuals who could serve.[38] The commission soon expanded to include over 150 members, distancing it from its originally intended form and making it harder to manage, but also giving it more "revolutionary legitimacy."[39]

[35] The five committees were for the elections law, the law on freedom of association, a draft constitutional text, a law on the media, and a text on judicial reform.

[36] For a more in-depth explanation of the structure and functioning of this committee, see Ghariri, "El Haia el oulia l'il tahqeeq el ahdaf a-thawra, islah e-siasia, wa intiqalia el demokratie" (The High Commission for Realization of the Objectives of the Revolution, Political Reform, and the Democratic Transition) in "Taqdeem el intiqalia el demokratia vi Tunis baad thalath senuwat" (Presentation of the Democratic Transition in Tunis After Three Years, 11–27).

[37] For example, the drafters consulted the Ligue des Electrices Tunisiennes (LET), a new civil society organization working to raise awareness and capacity around women's participation in elections. Interview with civil society member, July 8, 2013.

[38] Haute Instance Pour la Réalisation des Objectifs de la Révolution, et la Réforme Politique, et la Transition Démocratique, *Moudawalat el-Haiat* (Committee Deliberations), Part I, 37–56.

[39] As documented in the record of the commission's deliberations, bringing people from regions for regular meetings became difficult, especially with the limited funds available to the commission. Managing the committee was also difficult

Balancing Continuity and Change

The final formation of the TPA thus resulted from a sort of trial-and-error process by which an interim cabinet made up of individuals acceptable to protestors filled ministerial posts, and negotiations over the composition of several interim commissions, including a political reform commission tasked with establishing a way forward for the transition. This section discusses the ways in which the individuals who now made up the TPA reflected attempts to manage the transition by balancing continuity and change.

The individual actors working to define Tunisia's interim governance during these early weeks played an important role in balancing or bridging Tunisia's new (or emerging) and old political systems.[40] Mohammed Ghannouchi, for example, would play this bridging role before ultimately leaving the TPA. Although Ghannouchi had been a close affiliate of the former ruling party, he came from a technocrat background.[41] Having started his career in the Ministry of Planning, he became the minister of International Cooperation and Foreign Investment in 1992 and gradually moved up the ranks of the ruling party, the RCD, becoming vice president in 2007. He became prime minister in 1999, although Ben Ali had significantly downgraded this role to a "mere coordinator of government activities and executioner of presidential directives."[42] Thus, by 2011, he was seen as a "tool" for Ben Ali.[43]

---

due to its size and the wide range of groups represented, including many with little or no experience in politics. Finally, perhaps it became difficult to manage simply by virtue of being a totally new structure with no precedent. See Haute Instance Pour la Réalisation des Objectifs de la Révolution, et la Réforme Politique, et la Transition Démocratique, *Moudawalat el-Haiat.*

[40] Elsewhere I have called them "soft-liners" or "regime moderates," in reference to a concept from the "transitology" literature (Henneberg, "Comparing the First Provisional Administrations in Tunisia and Libya"; Henneberg, "Before and After Bin 'Ali").

[41] When Ben Ali became president in 1987, all cabinet posts were given to technically trained professionals in an attempt to facilitate economic reforms and renew the regime's "political and social legitimacy." Of these, Ghannouchi was the "quintessential technocrat" (Erdle, *Ben Ali's "New Tunisia,"* 154), and was continually rewarded for his cooperation with the regime.

[42] Erdle, *Ben Ali's "New Tunisia,"* 151–154.

[43] Arieff, *Political Transition in Tunisia,* February 2, 2011, 14. Ghannouchi was also credited with many of the country's economic reforms, including macroeconomic stability and attracting foreign investment.

Ghannouchi's presence as interim prime minister for the first six weeks of the TPA period reflects the TPA's struggle to balance continuity and stability with revolution and change. Ghannouchi's initial reluctance to suspend the 1959 constitution and organize elections for a National Constituent Assembly may have appeared to many as nothing more than an attempt to retain power. Yet evidence suggests that he and others were instead worried that such a drastic move as abrogating the constitution might create too much instability. Thus, this rather reserved individual, although a close ally of the toppled dictator, seemed to be motivated, informed by his long tenure as a government technocrat, by the need to maintain stability rather than preserving the influence of the old guard.[44]

Ghannouchi was also present for many key decisions that shaped the TPA. For example, he was one of the main interlocutors with the protest movement during the negotiations of early February, and he initiated talks with the opposition parties about forming a unity government in the days following Ben Ali's departure. He was also involved in appointing the heads of the other TPA commissions, along with Fouad Mebazza. Therefore, during his short time in the TPA, Ghannouchi filled an important political role, taking steps to ensure stability and demonstrate a response to the protests, while also negotiating with opposition figures.

Another TPA actor who helped bridge old and new was Fouad Mebazza. Mebazza had a somewhat more political background than Ghannouchi. Born in 1933, he had joined Bourguiba's party, the Neo-Destour (which later became the Parti Socialist Démocratique, PSD, and then the RCD), in 1947, and served in the Chamber of Deputies (lower house of parliament) and various ministerial and ambassadorial posts under Bourguiba. He became a member of the ruling RCD Central Committee in 1988, and returned to the Chamber of Deputies, this time as its president, in 1997.

Mebazza's presence in the TPA as interim president reflects the important role of old-guard figures who actually remained in the TPA. His background as a Neo-Destourian and minister from the Bourguiba era (considered more transparent and less corrupt than under Ben Ali), as well as his extensive experience in government, may have made him appear to revolutionaries more palatable as a

---

[44] Numerous interviewees made this point.

decision-making partner than Ghannouchi. He was also acceptable as a former regime member because he was effectively powerless within the TPA; his job was merely to sign the decree-laws passed by the Ben Achour Commission.[45] Thus, Mebazza represented the TPA's ability to incorporate some elements of the former regime while still retaining most decision-making power in the hands of reformers, revolutionaries, and radicals.

Finally, there was Béji Caïd Essebsi. The name Caïd Essebsi was a familiar one to students of Tunisian political life during the first several decades following the French protectorate (ca. 1956–1987). For people who had come of age during the Ben Ali period, though, he was a new figure. Born in 1926, Caïd Essebsi had held several ministerial posts under Bourguiba and had been a key member of the Social Democratic Party (PSD – the party of Bourguiba) until joining a break-away movement called the Social Democratic Movement in the late 1960s.[46] As a result of his criticism, Caïd Essebsi was forced out of the government in the early 1970s. He rejoined in the 1980s at the invitation of Bourguiba, who had begun to feel renewed pressure to liberalize.[47] Caïd Essebsi served in various positions (including foreign affairs minister from 1981 to 1986) and moved up the ranks of the RCD under Ben Ali. He was once again shut down and forced into less powerful roles when he became too critical or appeared as too much of a threat to the president.

Caïd Essebsi has been described as "charismatic" and "diplomatic," and with more political savvy than his predecessor, Ghannouchi.[48]

---

[45] Interview with Tunisian academic, December 6, 2014.

[46] This opposition party, the Social Democratic Movement (or Mouvement Démocratique Sociale, MDS), was formed by Bourguiba's ally-turned-critic Ahmed Mstiri in 1978. It was the second main such offshoot of the PSD; the first was the Movement for Popular Unity (Mouvement pour la Unité Populaire, MUP), formed in 1979 by Ahmed Ben Salah (Bourguiba's one-time minister of planning).

[47] See Ben Aicha, "Béji Caïd Essebsi, un vieillard tunisien, ancien dictateur, encore assoiffé de pouvoir." This pressure came in the form of general strikes (the first major one occurring in 1978) and the "bread riots" of 1983 – the second social flare-up due to the government's economic reforms (and other factors affecting the economy).

[48] See Schraeder and Redissi, "Ben Ali's Fall," 15. Interviewees mentioned how he spoke to the people and told them what they needed to hear; how he even sat on the Kasbah with the young protestors despite his advanced age. Interview with Tunisian academic, December 22, 2014.

This contributed to his being accepted by protestors as interim prime minister despite his past associations with authoritarian presidents. For example, one young activist said that protestors were at first suspicious of Caïd Essebsi due to rumors circulating that he had helped falsify electoral processes under Bourguiba.[49] However, there seemed to be little evidence of this, and his eloquence and apparent experience sufficed for them to trust him. Like Mebazza, Caïd Essebsi's association with the less corrupt and more revered of the two past presidents, about whom he had also recently published a book, may also explain his suitability for the post.

Importantly, Caïd Essebsi's powers were also limited, but he nonetheless made several substantive contributions to the TPA. For one thing, he represented the administration's *provisional* nature. He possessed a keen understanding of the importance of not being perceived as a dictator. This led him to emphasize publicly, as well as firmly within his own government, that all the ministers who had become part of Ghannouchi's unity cabinet would promise not to run in the NCA elections, helping assure his and his government's credibility. In addition, Caïd Essebsi demonstrated a genuine commitment to moving away from authoritarian rule. This was reflected in his willingness to cooperate with the other institutions of the TPA and his efforts to manage the government with maximum effectiveness.[50] In sum, Caïd Essebsi encapsulated the TPA's ability to convince people of its legitimacy while also serving as an effective provisional administration.[51]

In addition to representatives of the opposition, several ministers who served in the interim cabinet of the TPA were considered independent experts and generally trusted to help fill the critical job of keeping Tunisia stable and preventing a return to authoritarian rule. Several fit the category of "technocrats." Ben Ali had expressly tried to fill the executive cabinet with such types in an attempt to bolster party legitimacy; it was thus somewhat logical that, being nonpartisan, they could transition into similar roles under the TPA. In short, during the first weeks following Ben Ali's departure when Tunisians needed to

---

[49] They were also initially disappointed to see an octogenarian at the helm of the government, despite the uprisings having been led by the youth. Interview with Tunisia activist, July 6, 2013.

[50] Interview with TPA cabinet member, October 28, 2014.

[51] As later chapters will demonstrate, Caïd Essebsi was much less universally accepted following his return to politics in 2013.

establish who would be in charge, several not-too-revolutionary individuals guided the process. Although their profile largely resembled the
old guard, their presence reflected the TPA's more moderate side, and
they played a critical bridging role.

Other TPA leaders were perceived as independent and fair (as
opposed to corrupt, political, or overly aligned with the old regime)
either because of their past as a regime critic or their ability to bridge
between the old and the new. The best example of a TPA leader who
gave the interim government credibility due to his stature as an independent expert was Yadh Ben Achour, who led the political reform
commission, an institution central to the TPA.[52] Born in 1945 to a
family from La Marsa, a relatively affluent suburb of Tunis, Ben
Achour came from a well-known family. His father was a distin-
guished religious scholar, and Ben Achour held several of his own
credentials as a legal scholar, including advanced degrees in public
law and prestigious academic appointments.[53] He had a history of
scholarship in Islamic political theory that "sought to find a synthesis
between tradition and modernity."[54] This search for compromise and
consensus was a defining characteristic of Ben Achour – some commissioners even described him slightly "naïve"[55] in this regard – and it
carried over into the work of the TPA as a whole.

In addition to his scholarly credentials, Ben Achour had a history of
dissidence. Most famously, in 1991, as a member of Tunisia's Constitutional Court, Ben Achour refused to support a proposed constitutional amendment that would effectively block the LTDH from
operating.[56] It was this type of courage and principled behavior that
defined this type of independent actor.

---

[52] It is important to note that this book's focus on certain actors is not meant to
diminish the role of the many others who contributed during this critical, chaotic
period. The actors discussed here were selected to represent certain features.
[53] On his family, one interviewee said, "His father was a mufti, his grandfather was
a very well-known Muslim theologian.... It was a well-cultivated, aristocratic
family." Interview with Ben Achour Commission member, July 3, 2013.
[54] Interview with Tunisian academic, December 22, 2014.
[55] Interview with Ben Achour Commission member, January 21, 2015.
[56] The 1992 law set forth a classification of associations, including "general
associations" such as the LTDH. By stating that an association "cannot refuse
membership to any person who is committed in his principles and his decisions,"
and by forbidding political party leaders to hold positions of leadership on the
boards of general associations, the law allowed RCD loyalists to infiltrate
League membership in every section, flood votes, and thereby control its

Given that Ben Achour's political reform commission soon morphed from a small group of legal experts to something much bigger and more diverse, it was fortuitous that he was so well-suited for the job. In addition to being respected for his intelligence and his principled history, Ben Achour was seen as calm, moderate, and fair. His expertise was of course critical, given his close work with the expert core working to draft new legal texts. And, as referenced above, Ben Achour had a mind for compromise, facilitating the strategy of consensus which would permeate throughout the work of the TPA. In sum, the technocratic, independent expert, or bridging and balancing profile of these individuals who populated the TPA, helped demonstrate its competence and independence, giving the interim government its credibility and acceptability before the Tunisian people.

Setting Up Interim Institutions

Yet finding individuals to guide decision-making during the immediate post-uprising period was only one of the daunting tasks before the TPA. Another was setting up interim governing structures and restoring faith in law and institutions so that Tunisia could return to relative stability and an electoral process could be carried out. Did the TPA have the "right" to pass laws, for example? If so, which laws and decisions should take priority? And how should the process of transition be organized and managed, especially given the absence of any Tunisian precedent?

The TPA faced a hybrid state system as it began its work: many parts were functioning, but many, including the court system and the legislature, were not. It therefore had to create new institutional mechanisms to carry out several of its tasks while continuing to acknowledge "revolutionary" demands. As illustrated with the formation of the Ben Achour Commission, these new, temporary institutions were different from the existing constitutional order, state administration, and legal texts because they represented an "institutionalization of the revolution."[57] In so doing, they transferred significant power into the hands of citizens.[58]

---

management (Norton, *Civil Society in the Middle East*, 138; Hibou, *The Force of Obedience*, 98–101).

[57] See Ben Hafaiedh and Zartman, "Tunisia: Beyond the Ideological Cleavage," in Zartman, ed., *The Arab Spring: Negotiating in the Shadow of the* Intifadat.

[58] Interview with Tunisian academic, July 10, 2013.

Thus, Tunisia's new interim authorities had to decide whether to preserve, revise, or dissolve the political institutions that were in place when it formed. In outlining a new institutional order, the first principle upon which the TPA insisted was "continuity of the state."[59] On March 23, it passed a decree-law[60] on the organization of public powers, which described the new general powers of the executive, legislative, and judicial branches of the government.[61] This document became known as the *"Destour Sagheer,"* or little constitution.[62] This preservation of some form of the existing order reflected more than a mere attempt to avoid chaos. It also reflected an important decision about how governing should happen, by allowing for new rules to be written while affirming that the government would remain a constitutional republic.

Alongside the Political Reform Commission, Ghannouchi announced the formation of a National Fact-Finding Commission on Corruption and Embezzlement (henceforth the Amor Commission) on January 17 as an attempt to appease protestors (again, it had been called for by Ben Ali in his last speech). He appointed Abdelfatah Amor, a Constitutional Law expert, to be its head.

As per the decree-law that created it, the Amor Commission comprised two parts: a technical committee and a general committee.[63] The technical committee of the Amor Commission included twelve people: accountants, auditors, finance experts, lawyers, and judges of both genders recruited through recommendations from the various organs within the judiciary and the financial sector. The general council was made up of representatives of civil society and academics. Unfortunately, and unlike in the Ben Achour Commission, the relationship between the two committees was not optimal. Members of the general

---

[59] See Ben Hafaiedh and Zartman, "Tunisia: Beyond the Ideological Cleavage," 56.

[60] This term is basically the equivalent of an "ordinance." See *Oxford English Dictionary* online, Second Edition, accessed August 5, 2016, www.oed.com/, "Ordinance."

[61] The law, DL 2011-14, specifies that it should be valid until a constituent assembly was elected and a new public powers law is passed (Article 18), and that the president should retain his functions until a constituent assembly was in place (Article 8).

[62] Coupe and Redissi (in Lust, ed., *The Middle East*, 13th ed., 798) use the term "transitional constitution."

[63] DL 2011-08. Also noted in Redissi et al., *La transition démocratique en Tunisie: états des lieux*, Vol. 2 , *les thématiques*, 31–32.

committee/council complained about wanting to be more involved in the investigation process and sometimes accused the technical committee of hiding documents. Several quit.

The commission's formal responsibility, according to the decree-law, was to study general guidelines for a future anti-corruption strategy; to uncover cases of corruption and embezzlement committed between 1987 and 2011; and to collect and verify information, documents, and testimonies permitting the investigation of these claims and prepare their transmission to judicial authorities.[64] In practice, the Amor Commission received complaints of corruption filed by citizens and investigated them using its technical expertise and the evidence it had collected from the state. Ultimately, the commission had to adjudicate each complaint by determining whether it was sufficiently valid to be sent through the judicial system.

The third of the three commissions put into place by Ghannouchi in January, 2011, was a fact-finding commission on state abuse. Ghannouchi invited Tawfik Bouderbala, a lawyer and former president of the Tunisian Human Rights League (LTDH), to serve as the president.[65] According to the decree-law that created it, the commission (henceforth the Bouderbala Commission) was meant to investigate complaints of abuse by the state during the revolutionary period and document those committed. However, the decree-law defined the "revolutionary period" as lasting from December 17, 2010 (when the uprisings started), until "the completion of its objective"; it did not specify a concrete end date. Ultimately, the Bouderbala Commission decided to stop receiving complaint files submitted after October 23, 2011, and to only consider complaints about abuses committed during the period from December 17, 2010, to the end of February, 2011.[66] This imposed a definite end to and limited the scope of its work.

---

[64] See DL 2011-08, Article 2 and 3.
[65] Originally Lazher Karoui Chebbi was appointed to head this commission, but he demurred and was instead nominated as interim justice minister. Interview with commissioner, November 6, 2014; Mrad and Moussa, *La transition démocratique à la lumière des expériences comparées*, 155.
[66] As far as I can surmise, this was selected as the end date because it coincided with the end of the Kasbah protests. The French version of the commission's report also states that the period from March to October was relatively calm compared to the months prior, despite continued isolated incidents of violence (UNDP, *Résumeé du rapport de la commission d'investigation sur les abus enregistrés au*

Like the other commission presidents, Bouderbala formed his committee in an "open" manner, consulting with major civil society organizations such as the Tunisian Association for Democratic Women and
the LTDH.[67] The final composition of the commission included psych-
ologists, journalists, lawyers, academics, two doctors, and one judge.
Several sources note the high proportion of women in the commission,
especially in comparison to the other commissions (fourteen out of
nineteen members, although two women would quit.)[68]

The Bouderbala Commission visited the families of those who had
been killed or individuals who had been injured to hear and record
their testimony. It also investigated individuals suspected of having
issued the commands to commit the abuses. Commissioners thus
visited and interviewed officials from the ministries of interior, defense,
and health and officials from the President's Office and members of the
Presidential Guard.[69] They also visited hospitals, prisons, and courts to
collect evidence and testimonies. Additionally, the commission investigated accusations against the state, most notably the use of snipers in
carrying out some of the killings committed during the revolution.[70]
Finally, as with the Amor Commission, some commissioners received
experts and officials from other countries to provide guidance and
training on collecting, documenting, and reporting facts in transitional
justice contexts.[71] They even organized a trip to Morocco to learn from
the Instance d'Equité et Reconciliation (Equity and Reconciliation
Commission) there.[72]

The culmination of the commission's work was a long report
(ca. 1,000 pages), heavy on text about the types of abuses committed,

cours de la période allant du 17 décembre 2010 jusqu'à l'accomplissement de
  son objet, 53).
[67] Redissi et al., *La transition démocratique en Tunisie: les thématiques*, 31–32.
[68] The two women who quit were Bochra Bel Haj Hmida and Slahdinne Jourchi.
  Three men quit as well.
[69] UNDP, *Résumé*, 58–63.
[70] The commission found that the government had not used snipers per se but had
  ordered internal security forces to shoot specified targets from high-up building
  tops during peaceful protests (UNDP, *Résumé*, 54).
[71] The concept of transitional justice and its relevance to the TPA is discussed more
  in the next chapter. Here, the term refers broadly to the process of dealing with
  injustices committed by the former regime.
[72] UNDP, *Résumé*, 15. It should be noted that this Moroccan Commission's actual
  independence and effectiveness is debated. See, for example, Linn, "'Change
  with Continuity.'"

details on the victims, and the people who should be held responsible for them, as well as tables and statistics. It breaks down the findings by time period as well as governorate and type of abuse, and notes that the largest proportion of victims were youths. The report also includes recommendations about compensation for victims and mechanisms for transitional justice. The Bouderbala Commission also organized all the information it had collected into a database that included victims' personal and medical information (e.g. autopsy reports), photos and videos, and more. In 2014 the database was sent to the National Archives.

About a month after establishing the three commissions called for by Ben Ali (political reform, corruption investigation, and abuse investigation), Ghannouchi began considering the need for reform in the media sector. In consultation with other journalism experts and critics,[73] Ghannouchi created a National Authority for the Reform of Information and Communications (INRIC), signed into law on March 2.[74] INRIC was intended to support transition in the media sector, as barriers to freedom of expression had suddenly been lifted but no central authority or set of accepted professional principles or ethics existed. Kamel Laabidi, a journalist living in exile and "known for his defense of freedom of the press and the dignity of journalists," was chosen as its head.[75]

After having returned to Tunisia and taken on the role of heading INRIC, Laabidi went about composing his team. He solicited nominations from the journalists' union, the judges' association, and other relevant civil society organizations known for their militancy against repression of free and independent speech, and then selected the commissioners from among those nominations. INRIC's final composition included five independent journalists, one judge, one university professor, and a blogger.

These eight commissioners were supported by academics and journalists who acted as consultants on an as-needed basis.[76] Thus, like the Amor Commission and the Ben Achour Commission, INRIC had a

---

[73] Chouikha was received by Ghannouchi about a month after the flight of Ben Ali to discuss the process of media reform, and their collaboration led to the creation of INRIC and the appointment of Laabidi as its head (interview with INRIC member, November 6, 2014).

[74] DL 2011-10.

[75] Chouikha, "La difficile entreprise," 2.

[76] Chouikha, "La difficile entreprise," 2.

two-tier structure, with a relatively small expert core at the center and a wider advisory council around it, comprising mostly academics and journalists.[77] Two members, one for personal and one for professional reasons, resigned before INRIC finished its work.[78]

Ghannouchi's interim government had foreseen that INRIC would play an authoritative or executive role, but Laabidi persuaded the relevant interim ministers that INRIC's primary responsibility should be to study and document the current state of the journalism sector in Tunisia and issue recommendations for media reform. The commission would also study how equivalent processes in other countries that had successfully transitioned away from authoritarian rule had occurred. After starting its work, INRIC also decided that it would develop a procedure for issuing licenses to new radio and television stations.[79]

These four commissions (the Ben Achour Commission on political reform, the Amor Commission for investigation of corruption, the Bouderbala Commission for investigation of human rights abuses, and INRIC for media reform) reflected the highly innovative nature of the institutions created by the TPA. Lastly, the TPA (through the Ben Achour Commission) created an independent electoral management body, which became known as the ISIE (Instance Supérieure Indépendente pour les Elections).[80] Creating the ISIE was critical, given the TPA's central task of organizing democratic elections. Members of the Ben Achour Commission[81] elected from among the individuals

---

[77] Only the Bouderbala Commission, which had a single, slightly larger group, differed in structure.

[78] Interview with INRIC member, December 12, 2014.

[79] The nine criteria for licenses were to serve public interest; uphold diversity of the broadcasting scene; independence from the legislative branch of government and from political and religious organizations; absence of foreign funding or foreign presence on the board of directors; employment of a professional team of journalists; a clear and detailed financial and operations plan; support and preserve plurality and diversity in the public sphere and "participate in the cultural renaissance of Tunisia"; participate in protecting society from media monopolies; and not be combined with an advertising or communication institution (INRIC, *General Report*, 119).

[80] The decree-law establishing the Ben Achour Commission gave it the responsibility for creating such a body, which it did by adopting yet another decree-law (DL 2011-27), which was signed by Mebazza on April 18 and announced by Caïd Essebsi on April 26.

[81] It is important to note that candidates from the government, and individuals with ties to the former regime or from established political parties, were not allowed to serve (DL 2011-27, Article 10.) As later chapters will discuss,

who nominated themselves or others to serve on the ISIE; these individuals then voted human rights activist Kamel Jendoubi to be the committee's head. The newly appointed members also elected a vice president and a secretary-general.[82] The final composition followed a breakdown of various professions: three judges, four lawyers, one notary, one accountant, one communications expert/journalist, one information technology (IT) expert, one expat, two professors, and two representatives of nongovernmental organizations (NGOs) specialized in human rights.[83]

Each of these commissions played an instrumental role as independent mechanisms for the development of a new political system, yet they also faced many challenges. They faced not only, as the resignations of several commissioners indicate, internal tensions but also enormous time pressure and were constantly fending off public criticism. The next sections discuss some of the ways in which the TPA dealt with these challenges.

Securing Legitimacy

Although various decree-laws gave the TPA legal cover, there was no guarantee that the Tunisian people would respect its authority. The TPA was not elected, and it did not have control over the armed forces in the country. In other words, it had no traditional source of legitimacy.[84] This section presents the key strategies that emerged as the TPA began working and the strategies it used to ensure the Tunisian people

decisions around how to treat individuals associated with the outgoing regime are critical for interim governments (also see Boduszynski and Henneberg, "Explaining Divergent Pathways of Post-Arab Spring Change").

[82] Like the Ben Achour Commission, the ISIE had a vice president and a third executive chief, a secretary-general. The vice president was Souad Triki and the secretary-general was Boubaker Bethabet (Carter Center, *National Constituent Assembly Elections in Tunisia*).

[83] There is inconsistent documentation of the ISIE's composition. If we take the website of ISIE 2 as the final authority, then the composition is as described here, which is a little different from what the decree-law creating it specified.

[84] The most frequently cited authority on legitimacy of the state is Max Weber, who typologizes three sources of legitimacy: traditional, charismatic, and legal-rational (Weber, "The Types of Legitimate Domination," in Roth and Wittich, eds., *Max Weber: Economy and Society*). Scholars generally agree that as time goes on, permanent governments rely on a mix of strategies and sources of legitimacy to stay in power. The TPA didn't have any such precedent, so it had to improvise.

would respect its authority and its decisions. It discusses the ways the TPA sought to use legal mechanisms to guide its work, the ways it adapted as conditions changed to ensure full effectiveness, and critically, given the history of only partly concealed exclusion under Ben Ali and Bourguiba, the ways it ensured the inclusion of different sectors of Tunisian society. The TPA also found ways to work with civil society, build on Tunisia's historical traditions, and use democratic procedures where possible in an attempt to garner the support of the Tunisian people. Each of these strategies brought inherent tradeoffs and challenges.

First, given that it had no precedent and no bylaws or standard operating procedures to guide its work, the TPA had to constantly adjust its methods and approaches. For instance, the dissolution of the state institutions that had been so dominated by the ousted president was done through legal mechanisms in a clear effort to legitimize the TPA.

The decision to create the Ben Achour Commission rather than perform constitutional revisions via a committee of experts was also codified in a decree-law. For some, the creation of this commission marked the beginning of what would become the "transition," because it began the process of political reform through new instead of existing institutions and frameworks. The decree-law that created the Ben Achour Commission also gave it a certain legitimacy by documenting its authorities and responsibilities *before* the arrival of interim prime minister Caïd Essebsi, thus freeing it from his domination.[85] And both the prime minister and the Ben Achour Commission, of course, were "legal" only until new elections were to be held. In these ways, the TPA gained legitimacy by adapting existing legal mechanisms to the extent possible and necessary.

While the strategy of using legal mechanisms to justify its actions was effective, the provisional nature of the TPA meant that the laws it wrote could also be changed.[86] The TPA took advantage of this flexibility to adapt its own work as it moved forward. For example,

---

[85] Interview with Tunisian academic (December 6, 2014). The independence of this commission was critical given the risk that a new head of state (even if interim) would seek to dominate other state institutions as Ben Ali had.

[86] Some interviewees used this to explain why Tunisia, unlike Libya or Syria, immediately took legal steps to fill the void created by Ben Ali's departure, rather than taking up arms (Interview with TPA member, November 13, 2014).

the initial regulations for the NCA elections, written over the course of late March, April, and May, 2011, stated that anyone with a national ID card was a potential voter. A few weeks before the elections, however, the ISIE realized that this provision could jeopardize the transparency of the electoral process, due to the high number of ID cards of the deceased in circulation. Therefore, shortly before the elections, the ISIE created a new, separate mechanism to prevent this.[87] This reflects an agility unique to first interim governments.

The TPA also showed its flexibility during the early process of expanding the Ben Achour Commission. As noted above, the original sixty or so members in their first meeting decided that each organization represented, including political parties, needed to add one youth and one woman to its representative team. Eventually, however, it became clear that not all organizations could meet these criteria, for various reasons.[88] In order not to stymie its work, the Ben Achour Commission decided to permit exceptions to its own rules.[89] In these ways, the TPA showed its adaptability to the fluid, unusual, and difficult circumstances it faced.

The TPA also occasionally showed its flexible side in less constructive ways. All six decree-laws the Ben Achour Commission adopted – on the ISIE, political parties, and associations, as well as an electoral code and decrees on audiovisual and print media – were discussed within the Ben Achour Commission before going to vote, with the expectation that Caïd Essebsi's government would sign them into law without alteration. Yet when the law on associations appeared in the official national journal after having been signed, commissioners were surprised to discover that it had been altered.[90] Although no members

---

[87] Interview with TPA member (November 6, 2014). An American journalist with extensive experience in Tunisia noted that doing things through laws and legal mechanisms was a Tunisian-government tradition.

[88] For example, in cases of very rural or under-resourced districts, it was impossible for many parties to find women willing and able to run.

[89] One Ben Achour Commission member (interview, January 14, 2015) faulted this chaotic start to the fact that the original composition had been so hastily decided upon, without any clear plan or criteria.

[90] The drafters had intended for the law to include two sanctioning mechanisms for associations that violated the law, with one more strict than the other depending on the severity of the violations. The Ben Achour Commission as a whole had passed it as such. But when the law was issued, it included only the less strict mechanism, rendering it less harsh on violators (and more liberal or flexible in terms of what associations were permitted to do). (Interview with Tunisian legal

of the Ben Achour Commission raised significant protest, in hindsight, this seems to be a surprising deviation from the processes otherwise adopted and accepted for the period during which the TPA was in charge. This example attests to the unprecedented, and therefore often fluid or unclear, processes used by Tunisia's first interim government.

Meanwhile, members of the TPA knew that the Ben Ali and Bourguiba regimes had sustained themselves by excluding certain political groups, most notably the Islamists, and recognized the importance of demonstrating that it would not continue such practices. However, the TPA lacked explicit criteria for allowing people to become part of its decision-making structures. It had not been democratically elected: each of its institutions had been created as interim bodies with clear, specific functions, with members being selected for their reputations as independents, their representativeness of Tunisian society, or their technical skills. This opened it up to accusation of exclusion and unfairness.

The TPA thus found various ways to show that it was being as inclusive and representative as possible. The decision to abrogate the 1959 constitution and organize elections for a constituent assembly that would be reflective of the entire population constituted the first step. As illustrated in the discussion of interim institutions above, the TPA also worked to involve a wide range of voices in the drafting of transition texts and to represent specifically the segments of society that had been marginalized under Ben Ali or had been instrumental in bringing him down. It also used inclusiveness as a principle for making decisions that would affect the country's future.

The TPA's strategy of inclusion was most visible in the Ben Achour Commission. This commission adopted this same idea of bringing different forces together when it formed subcommittees. The composition of these subcommittees was meant to reflect, for example, feminist movements, secular movements across the ideological spectrum (though they were mostly leftist but still with diversity among them), and Islamist movements.[91] This example shows how the TPA attempted to be inclusive and balanced, down to its lowest levels.

expert, December 23, 2014.) As will be discussed in Chapter 3, this had repercussions in later phases.

[91] Haute Instance Pour la Réalisation des Objectifs de la Révolution, et la Réforme Politique, et la Transition Démocratique, *Mudawalat*, Part I, 404–405.

In creating such institutions, the TPA also showed great awareness of the importance of civil society's role in a democracy of balancing the powers of the state. One example of this was the way associational life was incorporated into the structure of the Ben Achour Commission and the other TPA commissions. Many of these organizations such as the UGTT which, as discussed elsewhere, had played instrumental roles during the revolution and then in forming the structures of the TPA, continued to be active both in and outside the TPA and in later phases.

This inclusion of civil society is noteworthy because – as with the TPA leaders described above – it helped create for Tunisians outside the TPA an impression of an interim government that truly represented them. This was more than a mere impression – civil society representatives in the TPA actively recruited "ordinary" Tunisians, focusing on marginalized segments of society (namely interior regions and women). Moreover, due to a shared history of being targeted by the regime, an important network was in place when Ben Ali fled, which would help the TPA more rapidly form and carry out its work.[92]

The Ben Achour Commission also voted on another article of the electoral law that explicitly addressed balance and exclusion: Article 18, the "gender parity principle." This article stated that parties were required to present candidate lists where every other candidate was a woman. Like with the general electoral system decision described above, this decision by the TPA reflected more than just a strategy of inclusion – it also reflected the values of the majority represented in the Ben Achour Commission.[93] Nonetheless, these decisions all show how the principle of inclusion was at work within the Ben Achour Commission and how it ultimately helped the TPA achieve its goals and become accepted.

As another example of inclusion, Tunisians consider the 2011 uprising as being driven by the country's large disaffected youth population.[94] For this reason, including youth voices was another sub-strategy the

---

[92] See Henneberg, "Before and After Bin 'Ali."

[93] The women's organizations represented, with the largest being the Association Tunisienne des Femmes Democrates (ATFD) and the Association de la Femme Tunisienne pour la Récherche et le Développment (AFTURD), are the best examples of theses values. Several "national personalities" also identify this way.

[94] See Russo and Santi, *Non ho più paura: Tunisi, diario di una rivoluzione*, 49. Here I do not intend to ignore the recognized role of other groups, notably women and organizations such as the UGTT and the Bar Association.

TPA deployed to secure its legitimacy. It took steps to ensure adequate youth representation in the Ben Achour Commission, the interim Caïd Essebsi government, and the ISIE, among others.

The TPA also saw the need to prepare a new generation for a future era of democratic politics. Thus, several political parties set up specific mechanisms and/or supported policies that would promote youth inclusion. For example, during the debate over the electoral code, some parties favored a law that would produce a high level of youth representation in the NCA. Many newly created parties also found explicit ways to involve and empower youth.[95]

Attempting to be broadly, but not unboundedly, inclusive worked as a strategy for being accepted but also presented challenges. Some analysts noted that after the revolution, a fear arose among the older generation of opposition activists of being pushed aside by the rising youth.[96] And despite the TPA's efforts to reach out to the youth, a significant youth boycott of the NCA elections, widely thought to be due to a persistent distrust of politicians that had carried over from the Ben Ali era, occurred.

In addition, although independent figures like Ben Achour and large national organizations like the UGTT and LTDH acted as catalysts for the work of the TPA, they and the decisions by the TPA about legitimate representation were constantly attacked. As described above, during its initial meeting on March 17, the hastily formed Ben Achour Commission determined that its composition was unsatisfactorily representative of Tunisian society. There was general agreement that it should include more youth, women, and people from the regions, as these groups were considered leaders of the revolution. Thus, the original members crafted a plan in which the two most representative organizations from among their ranks, the UGTT and the LTDH, would go to their local sections and recruit youth and female members

---

[95] A representative of Ettakatol, who mentioned the party's support for an electoral law favoring high youth representation in the NCA, also emphasized during an interview the party's historic emphasis on inclusion of and support for youth (interview, January 29, 2015). Newer parties, namely *Jabhat al Aslah*, also claimed to put youth in decision-making positions (meeting with party members, June 27, 2013).

[96] Interviews and meetings with Tunisian activist and international democracy assistance worker, January 6, 2015 and February 2, 2015.

to join.[97] Yet a clear vetting process never seems to have been established. This caused several people to demand explanation for why *they* couldn't also join the commission, creating headaches for its leaders.[98]

Another downside of including such a diverse set of legitimate representatives in the TPA was the challenge of working as a unified group. Trying to manage this amalgamation of groups and individuals nearly drove Ben Achour to quit several times.[99] Moreover, because many youth and regional representatives joined its ranks as part of the expansion process, suddenly many people with little experience in politics were voting on the content of legal texts and other national issues. Some suggested that such members might be vulnerable to manipulation by political parties, and/or subject to the biases of the experts who had been tasked with drafting the texts and presenting them to the wider council.[100] In addition, they, like all the members, were serving on the commission as volunteers. Though a small budget had been provided for bringing them from their homes to Tunis twice a week to meet with the committee and vote on the draft laws, the full cost as well as the difficulty of travel and imbalance of experience meant that retired people residing in the capital who had a history of

---

[97] This discussion went on over the course of several sessions of the commission, as members continued to invoke the importance of representativeness – of Tunisia's regions, of its women, and so forth – as a source of the commission's legitimacy, even as membership expanded. The final composition, reached by the end of March, was not totally satisfactory to all (only twelve regional representatives were included, which some found insufficient (Haute Instance Pour la Réalisation des Objectifs de la Révolution, et la Réforme Politique, et la Transition Démocratique, *Mudawalat*, Part I, 90), but the commission went on to discuss, draft and vote on the electoral law anyway.

[98] Interviews with TPA member, Tunisian academic, and civil society activist (November 14, 2014; July 6, 2013; July 10, 2013).

[99] Interviews with Tunisian academic and Ben Achour Commission member July 6, 2013, and November 18, 2014. Ben Achour even described the structure of which he was in charge as: "a circus ... unmarked territory where one could find extremely rude political parties, national organizations not intending to negotiate with anyone, and uncontrollable national personalities." (Ben Achour in Mrad and Moussa, eds., 156) (my translation). Also, interestingly, one of the organizations most credited for helping the revolution succeed, the UGTT, prides itself on having always brought together a widely diverse set of members (interview with former UGTT leader, November 12, 2014). Yet this same asset, according to some Tunisian academics (July 10, 2013) rendered it impossible for the UGTT to field a candidate for the NCA elections.

[100] Interview with Tunisian academic, December 16, 2014.

political activism became more active participants than youth from the regions.[101]

In addition, sometimes members of the Ben Achour Commission challenged one another's claim to be "independent." Though Ben Achour's independence was generally accepted,[102] the independent status of the vice president and spokesperson was more controversial. Although these officers were elected by their fellow commission members, they found themselves confronted at least once by other members who felt they had been unfairly excluded from these positions.[103] Similarly, the Islamist Enahda party opposed the process of elections for the members of the ISIE, feeling itself outnumbered by leftists who had a different understanding of independence than Enahda's.[104] Thus, the commission's efforts to be inclusionary and operate using democratic processes did not always satisfy everyone.

The notion of representation or inclusion within the Ben Achour Commission may have been compromised when certain parties quit. In May, Enahda walked out in protest over the postponement of elections. In late June, Enahda again withdrew from the Commission in protest over an article of the political parties' law limiting the amount of funds a party could raise from foreign sources.[105] The party justified its departure by claiming that only an elected assembly, and not the Ben Achour Commission or any other part of the TPA, had legitimacy to be writing such laws.[106] For some commissioners, this move jeopardized the "spirit of consensus" upon which the commission was supposed to be operating. Though Ben Achour tried to persuade those who walked out to rejoin the commission after their departure in June, they never returned. Moreover, by the end of the period in which the commission worked, campaigning for the elections had begun, which meant that many political party representatives were also absent. Thus

---

[101] Interviews with Ben Achour Commission members, January 14, 2015 and January 21, 2015.
[102] Interview with member of the expert core, July 1, 2013.
[103] Interviews with Ben Achour Commission members, November 13, 2014, and January 21, 2015.
[104] Interview with Ben Achour Commission member, January 28, 2015.
[105] Economist Intelligence Unit, *Tunisia – Country Report*, July, 2011.
[106] Although most written documentation doesn't mention CPR, some Ben Achour Commission members said CPR would always follow Enahda in these withdrawals. Interviews, November 18, 2014, and January 29, 2015.

the issue of legitimacy and representation, at least within the commission, was never fully resolved.

The challenges of this strategy thus capture an inherent contradiction within the TPA. On the one hand, "transition to democracy," which was one of its purported missions, is a gradual process, partly because it requires overcoming mentalities that have developed over several generations.[107] At the same time, laying the groundwork for a democratic transition would require the TPA to adhere to democratic constraints (such as term limits), thereby limiting its capacity for overseeing that long-term, gradual change. As the next chapter details, the TPA would face such a challenge in many other areas as well.

The TPA also adhered to the principle of individual rights and liberties. The preamble of the decree-law creating the Ben Achour Commission declared respect for human rights as among the commission's main principles. The notion of freedom of consciousness was reflected in the very first decree-law the TPA passed issuing a general amnesty for political prisoners. The TPA also recognized how dearly Tunisians clung to their new freedom of expression, given the decades-long experiences of state dominance over the media sector – hence the creation of INRIC. Several members of the TPA also looked to international standards set through documents like the Universal Declaration of Human Rights (UDHR) to guide the reforms they were drafting.

The TPA additionally drew on historical traditions, both political and nonpolitical, to legitimize its existence and its work. For instance, the issuance of the *Destour Sagheer* (or little constitution) immediately after the abrogation of the existing constitution in January, 2011, reflected important segments of Tunisia's state-building history. Indeed, the constitution of 1861, drawn up by Tunisia's Ottoman Beys following a series of declarations, culminating in what was called the *Pacte Fondamentale* meant to guarantee certain groups' rights, was the

---

[107] The official name of the Ben Achour Commission included the term "democratic transition," as did the document discussed below known as the "September 15th document." As an example of the long-term nature of these changes, one outside expert and long-time advisor on human rights advocacy in Tunisia noted that true judicial reform in Tunisia would involve training of a whole new generation of judges. Author meeting, April 1, 2015.

first of its kind in the Muslim world.[108] The importance of such a document therefore influenced the TPA's decision to issue a placeholder constitution, the *Destour Sagheer*, while it worked on establishing and then carrying out the steps for writing a new one.

The *Pacte Fondamentale* and the constitution of 1861, in fact, reflect a long-standing trend of pushing for reform and modernization in Tunisian state-building and nation-building (described in the opening section of this chapter). This history – of which Tunisians tend to be proud – was at the forefront of TPA leaders' minds as they sought to determine the steps that would direct Tunisia's future.

Part of modernity meant emphasizing Tunisia's "openness" as a Mediterranean country rather than an Arab country, which was traditionally based on an *ulama*, or community. One strategy for promoting openness was fostering good relations with both Maghrebian and European neighbors and emphasizing social and economic development through investment in education in order to avoid becoming externally dependent on any foreign power.[109] The TPA carried on this historical tradition. The Caïd Essebsi cabinet in particular (with its prime minister a statesman who had come of age during the nation-building period) strove to form good relations with Western donors and generally avoided combative foreign policies. Even the other independent commissions – the two investigation commissions and the commission for media reform (INRIC) – set aside time to receive trainings from international experts with experience in relevant issues and reforms.

Other decisions during the first interim government also reflected the country's historical tradition of pushing for modernity and reform. Members of the TPA felt Tunisia's strict separation of the military from politics – a principle established under Bourguiba, which even Ben Ali, despite his military background, didn't alter – was preserved through the TPA's emphasis on making decisions through legal mechanisms. Its rich associational life also became important in several instances, including the formation of the CNPR and then the role of the UGTT and LTDH in helping expand the Ben Achour Commission. And members of the TPA, in recalling the importance of civil society

[108] A good reference on Tunisian modern history is Perkins, *A History of Modern Tunisia.*
[109] Alexander, *Tunisia: Stability and Reform in the Modern Maghreb*, 68–73.

(including the syndicates) throughout Tunisia's history and up through the first provisional government, noted how it helped lead opposing or polarized forces toward moderate solutions, thanks to its history of dialogue and negotiations.[110]

A final important part of this history of modernity and reform is the role of women in Tunisian society and economy. The Personal Status Code was an early (1957) piece of legislation under Bourguiba that empowered women vis-à-vis some of the customs relating to marriage and the family sanctioned by Islamic law.[111] Along with the emphasis on inclusion, this recognition of the need for legal mechanisms to protect and encourage women's participation in public life helped justify the Ben Achour Commission's – and by extension, the whole TPA's – adoption of Article 18 and the parity principle of the new electoral code mentioned above.[112]

Members of the TPA also drew on the use of dialogue, another acclaimed Tunisian tradition. Many TPA leaders of the various commissions insisted on the use of negotiation and dialogue in order to mitigate the high level of uncertainty they faced, calling such methods "the historical Tunisian way" and "part of the political culture."[113] Others invoked the way listening became a key tactic within the TPA: Members of the Bouderbala Commission noted, for example, that their listening served as "the first comfort [the victims] had," suggesting a first step toward dialogue and reconciliation to overcome the injustices

[110] Interview with TPA member, November 14, 2015.
[111] As with the *Pacte Fondamentale* and the constitution of 1861, the Personal Status Code was the subject of much controversy between supporters of Bourguiba and Neo-Destour and more traditionally minded people (including women) and religious authorities (Perkins, *Historical Dictionary of Tunisia*, 110–111). For a discussion on impacts of the Personal Status Code, see Masri, *Tunisia: An Arab Anomaly.*
[112] Another historical event – the drafting of a constitution by an elected constituent assembly, as had occurred in 1956 – at first glance seems like a potential candidate for a historical precedent or tradition from which the TPA drew inspiration. However, this assembly – which appointed Bourguiba as president of the republic, and *not* on an interim basis – was not very representative of the Tunisian population or its will, having been elected without universal suffrage after the Neo-Destour forced the Bey to decree it (Willis, *Politics and Power in the Maghreb*). Therefore, I have decided not to include it as an example of how the TPA used historical traditions as a strategy for legitimacy/survival.
[113] Interview with Ben Achour Commission member, November 14, 2014.

of the past.[114] This idea of bringing all sides to the table represented something "Tunisian," and ultimately made the TPA more acceptable to the population.

The TPA's effort to gain people's trust was a critical part of its strategy of legitimizing its work by demonstrating accountability to the public. Some members of the TPA used techniques like sharing the reports they wrote following visits to communities.[115] Most commissions, notably the wider council of the Ben Achour Commission, made their sessions open to the public. The TPA was criticized by some for not thinking enough about democratic accountability – for example, some legal experts outside the Ben Achour Commission expert core argued that the electoral code drafted by the TPA should have emphasized more local governance and decentralization so that elected officials would be more accountable to the Tunisian people.[116] On the whole, however, these efforts helped the TPA accomplish its goal and become accepted as an interim government, because they represented a break from the more authoritarian past.

Finally, TPA members were also acutely aware of the need for international support of their actions. One official in the Ministry of Foreign Affairs said the ministry's task was to persuade international partners that the Caïd Essebsi government was sincere about trying to implement democratic reforms and help the government become truly democratic.[117] This was in the interest of forming strong relations with Western partners and also receiving economic assistance. Tunisian politics and economy have always been sensitive to the international context because its territory and population are relatively small.[118] However, under Ben Ali, many Tunisians had grown increasingly suspicious of the motives of Western governments: thanks to Wikileaks and the Internet, there was a growing awareness that the United States and its allies (especially after September 11, 2001) were ignoring repression of individual liberties in exchange for Ben Ali's cooperation

---

[114] Redissi et al., *La transition démocratique en Tunisie: les thématiques*, 42. Others from the interim cabinet emphasized the importance of listening to the grievances of certain groups, such as youth. Interview with TPA member, January 26, 2015.
[115] Interview with TPA member, January 26, 2015.
[116] Interview with Tunisian legal expert/academic, December 16, 2014.
[117] Interview with TPA member, October 28, 2014.
[118] Alexander, *Tunisia: Stability and Reform in the Modern Maghreb*, 68.

in the war on terror and repression of Islamists.[119] Given these histor-ical tensions as well as the newfound freedom to publicly express one's faith without fear of repression, the actors of the TPA knew they needed to be wary of Western hypocrisy in this regard. They strove to achieve a delicate balance between acknowledging the tension and appealing to Western donors.

Claiming electoral legitimacy was of course more difficult for the TPA. The TPA's independent commissions were often accused of being illegitimate for this reason. TPA members sometimes defended this absence of electoral legitimacy by arguing that, in a society unaccus-tomed to free and fair elections, asking average citizens to vote for the TPA's members would amount to nothing more than a popularity contest, and would not necessarily result in a qualified administra-tion.[120] The Ben Achour Commission and the ISIE also did use demo-cratic methods internally, such as holding elections for executive officers.[121] And in general, their commitment to organizing national elections was accepted as the only way forward, although people had to be reminded of this at times.[122] In sum, the TPA – even if not always consciously or perfectly – adopted a wide variety of strategies to ensure the Tunisian people of its genuine intentions to respond to their demands and manage transition toward a new democratic republic.

Building Consensus for a New Political System

The various members of the TPA drew their legitimacy as individuals from different sources. As mentioned above, many had reputations as independent critics or dissidents against the authoritarian regime. Others had credentials as competent leaders (Caïd Essebsi in particu-lar, who had a long history as a statesman under Bourguiba[123]) or

[119] Russo and Santi, *Non ho più paura : Tunisi, diario di una rivoluzione*, 23. I consulted an English-language draft of this manuscript.
[120] Interview with TPA member, December 12, 2014.
[121] For example, the members of the Ben Achour Commission elected the members of the ISIE; both of those TPA institutions also elected their own leaders such as presidents (ISIE only), vice presidents, and spokesperson (Ben Achour Commission only).
[122] As described elsewhere, the institutions and individuals of the TPA were being constantly protested on a small scale.
[123] As mentioned at the start of this chapter, many consider that under Bourguiba, especially up until 1975, the state brought many benefits to the country.

technocrats, or were considered important representatives of Tunisian society.

However, although each member brought his or her own qualities and assets to the TPA, their views and opinions were not uniform. Within each TPA commission or group, there was no immediate method for reaching an agreement. For instance, the eighteen members of the expert core of the Ben Achour Commission instinctively realized that, because of these different ideologies and interests, they would need some kind of strategy to move forward. Thus emerged the principle of consensus.

For the TPA, operating on the basis of consensus meant achieving general agreement on each decision as well as trying to place collective or majority interests over individual ones. This principle of consensus that guided the work of the Ben Achour Commission and, ultimately, the entire TPA, was sometimes described by observers as a "spirit" (*"ésprit de consensus"*); others described it as a "decision-making tool" necessary "in a revolution like ours, without a leader."[124] In other words, many saw this strategy as the natural, and maybe the only, method available.

These experiences represent the collective spirit of the TPA that emphasized cooperation, negotiation, and compromise over competition and reaching broad agreement on decisions before putting them to vote. It also involved – particularly for the more "political" members of the TPA, but for all those with a history of wariness of certain other groups – establishing trust in one's opponents and thus a general acknowledgement of the common desire to contribute to a better Tunisia.

Contributing to this collective spirit and emphasis on consensus and cooperation over differences was the tradition of civil society activism, alluded to above.[125] This is partly due to the limitations on political pluralism and the range of acceptable views and the banning of most

---

[124] Interviews with Tunisian academic and TPA member, October 24, 2014, and November 14, 2014. On the leaderless-ness of the uprisings, see Ben Hafaiedh and Zartman, "Tunisia: Beyond the Ideological Cleavage," International Crisis Group, *Tunisia's Way*.

[125] An important feature of Tunisian associational life is that it expanded and altered dramatically after January 14, 2011. This section focuses only on organizations that existed before the revolution; organizations that emerged after will be discussed later.

political parties under Bourguiba and Ben Ali.[126] These limitations forced many individuals with political interests in opposition to those of the ruling party to find other ways to associate with each other. Between 1956 and 2011, young people wishing to become politically active joined student unions, labor unions, professional associations, and other such associations where they could advocate for political causes, even though the state found ways to limit associational activity without formally banning it.[127] Thus, during the formation of the TPA, many activists were organized in associations rather than political parties (the associations and political parties often attempted to collaborate, to varying degrees of success.)

One of the most well-known organizations in Tunisian society is the General Tunisian Workers' Union (UGTT). The UGTT had played a critical role in the uprising;[128] it also contributed to TPA recruitment by reaching broadly and deeply into Tunisian society to solicit representatives for the Ben Achour Commission. This in turned demonstrated to the Tunisian public that the TPA was representative of the people, not made up of elites from the capital or individuals tied to the former regime. Its long relationship with the ruling party, particularly under Bourguiba, also meant that it would be closely involved with all the negotiations that occurred during the TPA – from the first Government of National Unity formed by Mohammed Ghannouchi on January 15 to the NCA elections. This relationship also meant, however, that the UGTT suffered its own internal turmoil during this period.[129] Nonetheless, so solid and durable was this organization that it would reappear as a mediator during later phases.

Along with the labor union and other professional associations such as the Bar and Judges' Association, the regime had permitted a degree of freedom for other associations to form around common political

---

[126] Willis, *Politics and Power in the Maghreb*, 128–135.
[127] For example, the regime would find ways to infiltrate organizations such as the Bar Association with PSD/RCD members, appoint its president, or legally restrict their capabilities in other ways. See Gobe, "Of Lawyers and Samsars"; Gobe and Ayari, "Les Avocats dans la Tunisie de Ben Ali: Une Profession Politisée?"
[128] See Willis, *Politics and Power in the Maghreb*; Coupe and Redissi, "Tunisia," for an overview.
[129] For a discussion of this internal turmoil, see International Crisis Group, *Popular Protests in the Middle East and North Africa: Tunisia's Way*, 4–6, and Ben Hafaiedh and Zartman, "Tunisia: Beyond the Ideological Cleavage," 60.

interests. Like their professional counterparts, the Tunisian Human
Rights League (LTDH) had a long history of struggle against the
authoritarian regime. It had formed in the 1970s, partly through
international influence,[130] and fought continuously for the protection
of political dissidents – including Islamists – against torture and repression. It had suffered from the use of similar tactics by the regime to
coopt it, to the point where it was nearly shut down and forced to form
a separate organization in exile.[131] Over the decades, the LTDH had
managed to remain more cohesive than the judges' associations, and
was thus one of the central organizations to join the protest movement
and, later, the Ben Achour Commission.

These two organizations represent an important (albeit inconsistent)
capacity of Tunisian civil society that helped further some of the
promised reforms of the 2011 uprisings: bridging Tunisia's two social
divides, class and religion.[132] Despite the country's long-standing tension between the upper-middle classes of the Tunisian Sahel (middle
coastal area) and the poorer miners and farmers from the interior, the
UGTT incorporated workers of different classes.[133] Likewise, the
LTDH, although largely comprised of elites, had historically defended
the rights of Islamists against the abuses of the regime.[134] Owing in
large part to Ben Ali's harsh repression of free political expression and
organizing, the determination of the UGTT, LTDH, and other organizations to achieve enhanced freedoms was renewed with the opportunities provided by Ben Ali's departure and the emergence of the TPA.

---

[130] Dwyer tells, for example, human rights movements formed in Egypt, Tunisia,
and Morocco in the 1970s, drawing on the 1948 Universal Declaration of
Human Rights as well as the work of the Arab Human Rights League (Dwyer,
Arab Voices). For a good general discussion of the history of the LTDH, also
see Erdle, 252–253, and Waltz, *Human Rights and Reform*, 134–139.

[131] This was the Committee for the Respect of Liberty and Human Rights in
Tunisia (CRLDHT, also abbreviated as CNLT [Conseil National pour les
Libertés en Tunisie], formed in 1998), originally led by Moncef Marzouki.

[132] As the next chapter illustrates, it would not be accurate to say that TPA
participants were uniformly inclusive or able to overcome these social divides.

[133] For observers like Hèla Yousfi, the UGTT's ability to act as a mediator,
presumably due, at least in part, to its historical role in shaping Tunisian
national identity, was critical in this phase. She sees the UGTT as a uniquely
important vehicle for continuing to stand up for all Tunisians. See Yousfi,
L'UGTT: Une passion tunisienne. Enquête sur les syndicalistes en révolution.

[134] As mentioned above, Tunisia's urban elites tend to identify as secular, while the
lower classes from rural areas are more likely to support Islamist ideologies. See
Waltz, "Tunisia's League and the Pursuit of Human Rights."

The civil society activists involved in the TPA had cooperated for decades in their struggle for more freedoms under Bourguiba and Ben Ali. During those years, they had gradually begun to realize that their various causes were linked, and unionists, human rights defenders, lawyers, judges, and women rights' groups merged into a larger network.[135] Because Islamists during the 1980s, 1990s, and 2000s were becoming increasingly repressed, tortured and persecuted, many of these activists also began collaborating in different ways with them, despite their more secularist inclinations.

These actors brought experience not only in activism but also in pushing for genuine democratic change (fighting for women's rights, an end to torture, constitutional reform, etc.) despite attempts by past regimes to suppress this activism. Many exhibited an idealistic, almost romantic vision of overcoming the omnipotent dictatorship that drove their work. Without this group of individuals who had spent decades fighting for this lofty goal – one described it as akin to "believing in a myth" – the TPA as such may never have come into being.[136] It was this hope that motivated those individuals, and when the terrain finally *was* ready for their licit and accepted participation, they were not only present but also critical in continuing to present a vision of a new, more democratic Tunisia.

This vision underlying the TPA's emphasis on consensus was not unique to the TPA members representing civic associations. Like the independent associations, Tunisian political parties had suffered from decades of regime restriction and manipulation. Some scholars argue that these parties' failure to form a unified front while the dictator was in power, due to ideological and tactical/strategic disagreements, explains their inability to respond to the downfall of the authoritarian

---

[135] As mentioned, they also formed relationships with opposition political party members. Christopher Alexander, in his work published shortly before the Tunisian uprising began, noted about this network (made up of what he calls "agents of change"): "Building the kind of opposition that could produce more substantive change will require time and some courageous risk-taking. It will require risk-taking not by desperate people who have nothing to lose, but by people who may, in fact, have a good deal to lose. [These] … 'agents of change' … have valuable experience building organizations, formulating a message, and navigating Tunisia's authoritarian labyrinth." Alexander, *Tunisia: Stability and Reform in the Modern Maghreb*, 122–123.
[136] Interview with a Tunisian Ben Achour Commission member, January 16, 2015.

regime.[137] During the TPA period in Tunisia, however, a close look at the range of behaviors and contributions of the various political parties, existing and new, reveals a more complicated dynamic. Throughout the period, parties played varying roles according to their strategies, ideologies, and personalities. The first six weeks under the TPA created a new strategical divide among opposition parties: whether to enter into an interim government that was still seen by many as a continuation of the old regime or remain on the side of the "revolutionaries." Three political parties – PDP, Ettajdid, and Ettaktol – were invited into Mohammed Ghannouchi's first national unity government formed on January 15. Ettakatol accepted the invitation and sent ministers to work for the new government but then resigned immediately to rejoin the protest movement; the other two accepted but withdrew with the arrival of Caïd Essebsi at the end of February, due to his requirement that anyone planning to run in the NCA elections could not serve in his cabinet.[138] Most other major opposition parties eventually sent representatives to the Ben Achour Commission.

Eventually, Ettakatol, Ettajdid, and the PDP sent representatives to the Ben Achour Commission as well. The parties thus became reunited in their cooperative, consensus-based efforts to begin the process of democratic reform.[139] Like independent associations, political parties' oppositionist history prior to the TPA, and the preexisting relationships among them, would influence the formation and inner workings of the TPA and, as later chapters will discuss, had both immediate and lasting effects.[140]

---

[137] See Haugbølle and Cavatorta, "Will the Real Tunisian Opposition Please Stand Up?" A cohesive opposition can aid in democratic transition by mobilizing protestors and presenting a unified block to negotiate with the former authoritarian regime. For further empirical discussion of this idea, see, for example, Bratton and Van de Walle's 1997 study of sub-Saharan African cases of attempted transition from the early 1990s. Bratton and Van de Walle, *Democratic Experiments in Africa*.

[138] As was written into DL 2011-14 about the organization of public powers.

[139] However, they soon became divided again, this time over a different strategic issue: whether or not to participate in the drafting of the laws on associations, political parties, and media.

[140] For some history on the collective work of the Tunisian opposition prior to 2011, see Hajji, "The 18 October Coalition for Rights and Freedoms in Tunisia."

Organizing Elections

One of the first debates in the Ben Achour Commission was the type of electoral system that would be used for the NCA elections. The type of electoral system – proportional representation or majoritarian, with the many varieties each type offers – would have important implications for the composition of the new governing body. Although the question of which electoral system would best capture the interests of Tunisians was implied, each voting member of the commission also, of course, had his or her own interests in mind.

An electoral system was thus chosen through a process in which the experts first presented the various electoral system alternatives to the wider council in the Ben Achour Commission, following which the wider council would vote, and the final text of the electoral code was drafted and passed. The electoral system that was ultimately adopted – proportional representation with remainders – was chosen because it would allow for the largest number of different groups in the NCA.[141] By advantaging small parties, this system was meant to create an assembly that included the highest possible diversity of voices and to avoid domination by one party.[142] Whether the final decision was reached because the number of representatives of small parties in the Ben Achour Commission outweighed the number of representatives of big parties or because the majority of the commission believed in an inclusive constitution-writing process is not clear. Regardless, the resulting electoral system was another way the TPA's strategy of inclusion played out.

As part of establishing the transition process, the TPA also needed to define the mandate and competencies of the NCA. In August 2011, as the country was approaching the first post-revolution elections, several political parties began to call for a referendum to define via popular vote the mandate of the NCA. This call for a clear mandate resonated with interim Prime Minister Caïd Essebsi, who expressed support for the idea.[143] On the other hand, members of the TPA had their chief

---

[141] Four different experts from the Ben Achour Commission legal expert core made this point, in various ways, during interviews (July 3, 2013; December 11, 2014; December 23, 2014; January 6, 2015).

[142] See Carey and Reynolds, "The Impact of Election Systems," 39–40. The repercussions of this decision are discussed in more detail in Chapter 6.

[143] Interview with TPA member, November 18, 2014.

goal – successful elections – within sight, and leaders such as Ben Achour knew that a referendum would cause significant delay. They feared that if the elections were delayed a second time – they had already been postponed once, back in May, from the originally-promised date of July to October – the TPA might be accused of clinging to power, thus undermining its legitimacy.

Ben Achour proposed a compromise solution. In mid-August, he gathered the political parties represented in his commission, including those who were calling most forcefully for a referendum, to draft a document specifying the mandate of the NCA. Twelve parties (of which eleven would sign[144]) worked together for a month and finally arrived at a statement declaring their commitment to abiding by the electoral codes that had been passed in the previous months. The document, which was referred to as the September 15th document, also outlined the process of transferring power to the NCA and asserted that the NCA's mandate should be fulfilled within one year. Finally, the document stated parties' agreement to "continuing the search for consensus between political parties, in order to better run the transitional period after the elections for the NCA."[145] This process and agreement were satisfactory for political parties to go ahead with the NCA elections.

Ben Achour called the statement "short but precise," and, indeed, it gave little clear direction.[146] It stated that the elected Assembly was to be in place for one year, and that it would appoint an interim president, prime minister, and head of parliament to govern during the period while the constitution was being written. Following these appointments, Caïd Essebsi and Mebazza, along with the rest of the cabinet, would cede their positions to the new interim government. Drafters could not reach an agreement on whether the NCA should have legislative powers; this question was left unaddressed in the document. In short, determining a process for electing a new interim government was fraught with challenges, but the TPA by-and-large managed to overcome them. Again, however, these choices would have implications going forward.

---

[144] Although Enahda signed the document, the CPR refused. The party that had most loudly called for a referendum but ultimately signed on to the agreement was the PDP (interview with TPA member, November 18, 2014).
[145] Interview with TPA member, January 29, 2015.
[146] Byrne, "Tunisia Clinches Deal on Road to Democracy."

Conclusion

The TPA formed against a backdrop of widespread discontent with the Ben Ali regime and a legacy of exclusion and repression. It also formed under a cloud of suppressed social cleavages, all produced as part of the prior autocrats' goals/pillars, focus on unity, modernity, and reform.[147] In its initial days, moderate-leaning members of the Ben Ali government negotiated with protestors and ultimately created an amalgamation of interim institutions led by individuals with a reputation for independence and/or experience. As this new administration sought to establish its own legitimacy, develop a transitional roadmap, and organize elections, it used a variety of strategies and tactics and took a host of actions and decisions necessary to carry out its mandate.

The behaviors and struggles of the TPA (and to an extent, its successor interim governments, as later chapters will show) reflect how they were caught between an old system that had been rejected and a new system that was only vaguely defined. For instance, while some actors, such as Mohammed Ghannouchi, were forced out of the TPA due to their association with the outgoing regime, others took measures to ensure the decision-making structures during this period was not too revolutionary in composition. The decision to preserve Fouad Mebazza's role – which was, in fact, mandated by the 1959 constitution – reflected such attempts. Similarly, the presence in the TPA of many "independent" (as opposed to revolutionary) personalities, the efforts to ensure different parts of the TPA would check and balance each other, and the TPA's overall emphasis on consensus-based decision-making, reflected this ultimate prioritization of balancing the old and the new. In many ways, the TPA – perhaps by virtue of the unique period during which it governed, which was simultaneously open-ended and heavily constrained – would be more successful at striking this balance than its successor, the NCA. This is the subject of the next chapter.

---

[147] See Perkins, *A History of Modern Tunisia*.

3 | Impacts of the Tunisian Provisional Administration

The Tunisian Provisional Administration's formation, structure, and actions had many implications for the subsequent process of change. The TPA had organized elections for a National Constituent Assembly (NCA), written rules for those elections, set up and overseen the elections, and outlined a roadmap for steps to follow. Yet the events of the subsequent months were far from what the TPA had anticipated. Rather than swiftly drafting a new constitution and organizing elections for a permanent government, the elected assembly installed a government, known as the Troika, under which violence and political polarization mounted, and reforms stalled. The chaos became so threatening that civil society actors intervened in order to restore the process. Luckily, thanks in part to the models of inclusion and the "bridging" individuals the TPA had introduced into Tunisian governance, stability was restored and a new constitution and new permanent government were ushered in.

This chapter shows how many of the events and much of the work of the second interim government in Tunisia were directly linked to or produced by the behaviors, traits, and decisions of the TPA. The chapter begins by explaining how – in line with the previous chapter – the TPA was not operating in wide open territory; rather, it faced many constraints by nature of its role as a first interim government. These included pressure to quickly hand power to an elected government, thus forcing it to work quickly; the need for care as it tried not to overstep its mandate, thus constraining its decision-making ability; and a host of constraints created by the legacies of the outgoing autocracy and inexperience with democratic governance, including its own lack of preparation. The chapter then describes the series of events and actions under the NCA, each with its own echoes of what had come before.

Constraints

The first constraint the TPA faced was time. The TPA needed to reassure Tunisians that its existence did not reflect an intention to govern indefinitely but rather to organize genuine elections as fast as possible. This placed it under great pressure, as the task was not an easy one. The challenge was illustrated by controversial decisions such as the postponing of elections to October. Naturally this created a backlash, yet the organizers of those elections felt they had no choice.[1]

The TPA also needed to be careful about defining its own mandate. Caïd Essebsi presented his government as one of technocrats with only one mission: get to the elections. Members of the TPA were thus working under a strict set of conditions. Although the TPA knew it could not neglect the country's dire security situation and its looming economic reforms, it could take only limited actions toward addressing these issues.

Meanwhile, the TPA was working under conditions that most established governments rarely face. Economic and security conditions across the country were in shambles. Carrying out the basic functions of a government (such as delivery of public services and general management of the economy), despite the strong state administrative system, was extremely challenging.[2] Moreover, daily protests over the lack of jobs and various other grievances continued, often rendering operations of the TPA even more difficult.[3]

In addition, the Tunisian media and Tunisian peoples' right to express themselves freely had gone from one extreme (severely curtailed) to another (completely unregulated). For those with public responsibilities, this sudden change created further challenges. Media scrutiny of the independent commissions was often done in an unprofessional way, putting pressure on TPA members and distracting them from their legislative, investigative, or operational tasks. The commissions of Tawfik Bouderbala and Abdelfatah Amor, for example, which

[1] Interview, Independent High Electoral Authority (ISIE) member, December 12, 2014.
[2] Interviews with TPA members, October 28, 2014, and November 6, 2014.
[3] At least two interviewees who were members of the TPA, one as part of the ISIE and the other as part of the Caïd Essebsi cabinet, described regular protests outside their ministry or commission office. Interviews with TPA members, October 28, 2014 and November 14, 2014.

had been tasked with investigating wrongdoings of the state, faced such an outcry from certain implicated groups – namely the police or corrupt members of the former regime who were being brought to trial – that members sometimes even feared for their lives.[4] And the Ben Achour Commission often struggled to reach final decisions and declarations before information was leaked to the press.[5] Thus, from beginning to the end, the TPA suffered "revolutionary" pressure that challenged both its legitimacy and its logistical ability to carry out tasks.

The TPA was challenged by its provisional nature in still another way – lack of preparation. Generally speaking, members of the TPA had not been trained to do the tasks they were suddenly being called upon to do.[6] That is, despite their technical expertise, most individuals in the TPA had little experience in the particular roles in which they served. For example, the members of the Independent Commission for Investigation of Corruption (Amor Commission) had never had the opportunity to work genuinely – not just superficially – on anti-corruption measures, programs, or reforms. Another issue was lack of experience with democratic institutions. Because there was no history of ensuring free and fair elections, availability of qualified staff for the Independent High Electoral Authority (ISIE), for example, was limited.[7] The Amor Commission staff similarly did not have the capacity to process all eleven thousand complaints about corruption it received before the NCA elections, leaving the majority of them to be handled by the future judicial system.

Moreover, although effectively belonging to the state, the various independent commissions did not have specific state resources other

---

[4] At least one TPA member said he was personally threatened (interview, November 6, 2014). In relation to media unprofessionalism, others noted, for example, that certain commissioners were falsely accused by the press of being Islamists (interview, October 31, 2014).

[5] See Haute Instance pour la Réalisation des Objectifs de la Révolution, la Réforme Politique, et la Transition Démocratique, *Moudawalat el-Haiat*.

[6] Even the technocrats in the Caïd Essebsi cabinet had either never before had the chance to serve in government, because of their oppositionist histories, or they had served but, as the previous paragraph mentions, had no experience managing "revolutionary" situations.

[7] As one ISIE member said, "We were preparing and learning at the same time." (Tavana, "Preparing to Draft a New Social Contract," 3–4 and 12). One Amor Commission member also phrased it similarly: "It was research and practice at the same time." (Interview, November 12, 2014).

than the minimal budgets devoted to them.[8] Although the Caïd Essebsi government tried to provide adequate material resources to the commissions, the intense time and psychological pressure as well as limited funds from the state meant their members were often pulled in all directions.[9] Several commissions had to rely on international NGOs for certain supplies, including the printing of their reports.[10] Thus, in the midst of all the scrutiny, threatening, and public criticism described above, the members of the TPA were forced to accomplish difficult tasks they had never done before, without remuneration and with limited resources, often alongside their regular jobs.[11]

Finally, the TPA faced the challenge of trying to organize democratic elections in a country where few genuine democratic institutions existed. Tunisia had seen elections under both Ben Ali and Bourguiba; however, due to limitations on freedom of competition, association and media, a strong electoral infrastructure was absent. This frequently caused conflicts among individuals with different ideas about tolerance for diversity and pluralism. It also created challenges on a legal level: as one constitutional expert put it, due to the lack of reliable demographic data, historical voting patterns and other societal data, it was difficult for the Ben Achour expert core to write an electoral law.[12]

But the largest challenge the TPA had to overcome in terms of effects of authoritarianism was its history of excluding segments of the population from full participation in politics and the economy. Under Ben Ali and, especially in his later years, Bourguiba, two main forms of exclusion had been practiced: exclusion of certain socioeconomic and regional groups and exclusion of opposition political movements, especially religious ones. Both forms of exclusion were ultimately the products of a decades-long process of nation-building that had begun

---

[8] DL 2011-6, 2011-7, and 2011-8; multiple interviews with TPA members.
[9] Interviews with TPA members, November 14, 2014; December 11, 2014. Also see Tavana, "Preparing to Draft a New Social Contract," 9–10.
[10] Occasionally, this lack of resources even compromised members' privacy. For example, commissioners had no choice but to contact the individuals with whom they were consulting as part of their investigations with their private mobile phones.
[11] Tavana documents similar stories about the challenges faced by the ISIE, which included, among others, a lack of funds, experience, and time that created confusion and may have ended up duplicating efforts. Tavana, "Preparing to Draft a New Social Contract."
[12] Interview with a Tunisian legal expert, January 12, 2015.

with the independence struggle and developed into a distinct regional and socioeconomic disparity and a single-party or state-dominated political system.[13]

This legacy of exclusion created a dilemma for the TPA. First, as alluded to in the preceding chapter, a proud national identity helped foster a belief that Tunisia, with its relatively educated population and large middle class, was equipped to turn its revolution into a genuine transition toward democracy. Yet that same revolution had brought to the surface the clear economic disparities that authoritarian leaders had tried to hide. The TPA was thus caught in a position of needing to build on its educated, reform-minded elites while also not wanting to exclude the marginalized groups of the interior, especially because they were considered as having led the revolution.

In addition, although the various opposition movements that had emerged over the previous decades were unified in their stance against a one-party state, they had also experienced much tension among themselves, especially between those who identified as Islamists and those who identified as secularists.[14] Several examples of cooperation among the opposition, such as the 18 October collective of 2005 or the defense of Islamists by the Tunisian Human Rights League (LTDH), had been historically paired with examples of competition.[15] Some analysts even propose a tension between those dissidents who stayed inside Tunisia and those who went abroad.[16] Ben Ali's departure abruptly left political opposition movements and dissidents without a common enemy, and the TPA was tasked with unifying them around a common goal. In short, the history of exclusion under authoritarianism – in addition to a shortage of time, resources, and democratic infrastructure or experience – constrained the TPA's decisions, and it was forced to continuously demonstrate its intention to

---

[13] See, for instance, Alexander, *Tunisia: Stability and Reform in the Modern Maghreb*; Hibou, *The Force of Obedience*.

[14] See Haugbølle and Cavatorta, "Will the Real Tunisian Opposition Please Stand Up?"

[15] The 18 October Collective is referenced in Chapter 2. For example, long-time members of the Islamists by the Tunisian Human Rights League (LTDH) cite how, while the LTDH worked with Islamists and even included them in their ranks, they never felt that Islamists were committed to human rights principles in the same way. Interviews with Ben Achour Commission members, January 21, 2015, and January 29, 2015.

[16] Interview with a Tunisian activist, January 16, 2015.

be inclusive while also trying to reconcile various competing and conflicting tendencies.

Formation of the National Constituent Assembly and Troika

Amid all these constraints, elections for a National Constituent Assembly (NCA) took place. The elections of October 23, 2011 represented a historic event, but they did not relieve Tunisia's interim authorities of their challenging duties. The newly elected members of the NCA were constrained by a different set of factors, directly relating to the TPA's limitations, especially its inability to address necessary reforms or to force its successor, the NCA, to abide by principles of inclusion and consensus as it had. Overall, the NCA/Troika period directly reflects the ways first interim governments are both critical to any transition process, and are at the same time severely constrained.

The NCA held its first meeting on November 22. Its first task was to select an interim president for the period of constitution drafting, and then to form a government. Enahda had won the most seats, and although some parties called for a broad unity government, Enahda instead formed a troika coalition government with two secular parties who got the second- and third-most seats, Congrès pour la République (CPR) and Ettakatol.[17]

The NCA also had to draft its own bylaws. This process took nine weeks and involved high levels of internal tension, leading to accusations in the media of purposefully stalling or being highly inexperienced. In the bylaws, finally passed on January 20, 2012, the body gave itself power to legislate.[18] This led the NCA to quickly surpass its one-year mandate, even though the parties represented within it, including Enahda, had signed the September 15th agreement stating that the constitution was to be written within one year.

The troika coalition of Enahda, CPR, and Ettakatol filled the positions of prime minister, president, and head of assembly, respectively.

[17] In fact, al-Aridh a-Shaabia, or the Popular Petition party, had won more seats than Ettakatol, but some of these seats were contested. Rather than forming a coalition among parties whose members would constitute a majority in the parliament, leaving those outside the coalition to form an opposition, a unity government would have distributed ministerial portfolios across all the largest parties represented in the assembly.
[18] Proctor and Moussa, *Tunisia's Constituent Assembly's By-Laws*, 15–16.

It then agreed upon a cabinet of ministers to replace that of Caïd Essebsi. This arrangement was formalized in an organic law,[19] passed in December 2011, which replaced the organization of public powers law (the *Destour Sagheer*, or mini constitution) that had been issued by the TPA in March of that year. Another major change to the competencies of government institutions specified in the law was the role of the judiciary. While the March law had stated that the judicial branch would continue to operate according to the provisions in place, the December law stated that an interim judicial reform commission would take charge of the sector. While these decisions did not contradict the process of change foreseen by the TPA, they would bring many unexpected consequences.

With the election of the NCA, the extent of the TPA's influence on its successor interim government as well as on the longer-term transition from authoritarian rule to a more democratic government became clear. First, in terms of representation, a broad comparison of the actions taken in the TPA commissions with those of the elected NCA delegates suggests that the former group was more effective and perhaps more democratic than the latter, despite the former's lack of electoral legitimacy. The Ben Achour Commission's constant interaction with civil society, as opposed to accusations that the NCA was disconnected from the people, provides another example.

The constraints and challenges for the NCA/Troika were captured in the conflicts with which it dealt. Nearly every issue became an arena for political jostling, which often led to delays of key reforms. It was also clear in the divergent attitudes among individuals and groups during the period. As discussed below, the NCA/Troika would ultimately need outside assistance to overcome its internal stalemate.

This important change between the first and second interim governments in Tunisia seems to have been due to a variety of factors. Several people believed, for example, that the Ben Achour Commission was more democratic than its successor, the NCA/Troika, because it was

---

[19] *Oxford English Dictionary* (2nd ed., 2000) defines "organic law" as "constitutive; that establishes or sets up; stating the formal constitution of a nation or other political entity." This is thus different from a decree-law in that it is made as an order through the executive, and an ordinary law, which is not necessarily adopted to establish institutions or powers outlined in a constitution.

made up of people who were "prepared to accept differences."[20] Others have suggested that the "democrats" from the TPA no longer had a common cause now that the authoritarian regime was gone.[21] In addition, Tunisians' inexperience with truly democratic processes may have meant that not only was the electorate during the NCA elections unfamiliar with how to choose the candidates who would best represent them, the elected delegates themselves often got caught up in petty concerns at the expense of concrete policy debates. What is clear is that, although the NCA came to being through elections organized by the TPA, the TPA had little influence over it.

Drafting a New Constitution, Polarization, and National Dialogue

As discussed in Chapter 2, the TPA had to grapple with what has always been the largest divide in Tunisian politics: national identity.[22] The complex question of the relationship between a modern, secular government and the Muslim Arab culture of the people had been at the heart of political battles since the time of independence.[23] With the departure of the old regime and especially the legalization of Enahda on March 1, 2011, these repressed debates reemerged in the public sphere.

The TPA made a mild attempt to channel this conflict, but its effectiveness was minimal. Early in April, when the new electoral law was nearly complete, the wider representative council of the Ben Achour Commission formed a subcommittee to draft a Republican Pact (*Ahd Joumhouri*) to aid in the constitution-writing process by providing a broad outline of the new country's new social contract.

---

[20] Interviews with Ben Achour Commission members, January 19, 2015 and November 13, 2014.
[21] Interview with a civil society activist, January 6, 2015.
[22] See, for example, Mezran, *Negotiation and Construction of National Identities*, 107–138.
[23] This is mentioned briefly in the historical background given earlier. Although Bourguiba defeated Ben Yousef in the modern-versus-traditional struggle that played out during the nationalist revolution, those who wished to see Islam play a larger role in society and politics did not go away, giving Ben Ali a pretense for his constitutional coup in 1987. As has been well-documented elsewhere, tolerance for an Islamist vision contending for power with the secular elite did not last long (e.g. Perkins, *A History of Modern Tunisia*; Willis, *Politics and Power in the Maghreb*; Coupe and Redissi, "Tunisia").

When introducing this project to his commission, Ben Achour presented it as based on historical precedent (the original NCA of 1956 had drafted such a pact),[24] intended to "determine the principles and roles of a democratic competition."[25] Others described the project as "a common platform, a pact among the parties, civil society ... to have everyone engage a common code of values."[26] It was, therefore, a key next step in moving forward with a post-authoritarian transition.

But the process of drafting such a pact was difficult for several reasons. First, the leaders of the Ben Achour Commission frequently felt the commission had more urgent matters to deal with, and the project often got sidelined. Second, as would be the case with many issues the commission encountered, the Republican Pact became a platform for cross-accusation among opposing political parties. For example, while parties such as Ettakatol and the Nationalistes Démocratiques believed such a pact must be written before any elections took place, Enahda and CPR argued that it could only be written by an elected body. Moncef Marzouki of the CPR accused the other members of the Ben Achour Commission of introducing the pact in order to stall the elections.[27]

The pact represented the first chance for the sensitive issue of national identity to rise to the surface. Under the authoritarian rulers, national identity had been used as a strategy for control. No one had experienced living in a Tunisian system where diversity of opinions was permitted: previously, Tunisians were forced to choose between buying into the ideas of the state – which, since independence, had been to emphasize the country's "openness" and "modernity," embrace secularism, and de-emphasize the Arabo-Muslim identity – or remaining silent. Because it was such a deep-seated and emotional issue, the TPA's efforts to reach a consensus on national identity would prove insufficient. Thus, addressing the question of a national identity that all Tunisians could accept was a heavy-duty task that the TPA could not resolve but only manage until the NCA took over.

---

[24] See Haute Instance pour la Réalisation des Objectifs de la Révolution, et la Réforme Politique, et la Transition Démocratique, *Moudawalat el-Haiat*, Part I, 243.

[25] Quoted in Ben Hafaiedh and Zartman, "Tunisia: Beyond the Ideological Cleavage," 56.

[26] Interview with a Ben Achour Commission member, January 14, 2015.

[27] See Chaker, "Les Conseils pour la Protection de la Révolution," in Redissi et al., *La Transition Démocratique en Tunisie: Les Acteurs*, 189–215.

These issues only became more fraught with controversy in later phases and even led to violence. The frequent attacks on security forces during the NCA period, and an attack on the American Embassy in September 2012, reflected a continued inability of the government to assert control, leading to heightened criticism of the Troika/NCA government.[28] Many accused the leading party of the Troika, Enahda, of being tied to the radical Islamist groups that were claiming responsibility for the attacks.[29]

This controversy helped lead to the formation of a new political party, Nida Tounis, or "call for Tunisia," in April 2012. This new party, driven by Béji Caïd Essebsi, "cast itself as a necessary counterweight to the political force of Enahda and the Troika government" and "was formed in opposition to what its leaders describe as 'instances of disturbing extremism and violence that threaten public and individual liberties, as well as the security of citizens.'"[30] It formed under a slogan of restoring dialogue and consensus. Although many would come to accuse the party of representing the old regime, for others it represented a return to security and order – ultimately reflecting the deep divisions over state and national identity within Tunisian society.

The NCA also largely disregarded the text of the Republican Pact that was agreed upon by the TPA. Instead, the issue of identity became a major source of controversy within the assembly. Just as the old authoritarian rulers had done, delegates tried to manipulate the issue to their advantage – in other words, to use national identity as a strategy for control. Frequently, delegates, lacking a technical expertise, felt more comfortable discussing values and identities, or tried to use those issues as a way to control the agenda. These members would find, for instance, a way to bring up controversial issues such as the reference to

---

[28] Cavatorta and Merone, "Post-Islamism, Ideological Evolution and 'la Tunisianité' of the Tunisian Islamist Party al-Nahda," 31.

[29] Rachid Ghannouchi, the party leader, made statements during this period suggesting that the party was aligned with some of the groups accused of carrying out the attacks. For example, he said that the newly formed anti-Islamist party Nida Tounis supporters were more dangerous than Salafists (Ghilès, *Tunisia: Secular Social Movements Confront Radical Temptations*). One of these groups, the Leagues for the Protection of the Revolution, was sometimes accused of being Nahda's militia.

[30] Quoted in Tavana and Russell, "Previewing Tunisia's Parliamentary and Presidential Elections," 9.

sharia (Islamic law) in the constitution even during discussions over seemingly unrelated issues, such as a proposed development project.[31]

On August 31, 2012, the first draft of new constitution was announced. Several of its articles were highly criticized and debated, largely because of how they were perceived vis-à-vis the question of national identity.[32] Resolving the NCA's internal disputes was made all the more difficult by the increasing political polarization plaguing the country. In October, the General Tunisian Workers' Union (UGTT) initiated a national dialogue meant to accelerate the constitution-writing process and restore stability.

But the violence and the political polarization continued. On October 18, a high official from the newly formed opposition party Nida Tounis, Lotfi Naguedh, was killed during clashes between his party and activist organizations in Tatouine. Former TPA Prime Minister (and now increasingly active political figure) Caïd Essebsi called the death an "assassination," although Enahda officials stated that he had died of a heart attack.[33] On February 6, 2013, an NCA delegate from the far-left Democratic Patriots Movement party, Chokri Belaïd (who had also been a member of the Ben Achour Commission), was assassinated outside his home. Although the Troika government responded by reshuffling the cabinet and replacing the prime minister, it continued to face strong criticism from opponents, who accused it of mismanagement and leading the country astray.[34]

On April 22, the NCA announced a new draft of the constitution, but certain articles continued to cause controversy and public protests.[35] Civil society organizations such as the UGTT – who had been present in the TPA-continued to try and mediate talks between the competing political forces. Meanwhile, more high-profile incidents surrounding freedom of expression and the role of Islam in

---

[31] Author meeting with a researcher on NCA, July 10, 2013.

[32] Two examples of such debates were over the mention of sharia (Islamic) law as a source of guidance for legislation, and wording over the protection of rights of women.

[33] Ghilès, *Secular Social Movements Confront Radical Temptations.*

[34] After Belaïd's assassination, Prime Minister Ahmed Jebali resigned after suggesting that Nahda should form a technocratic government (a proposal the party refused). He was replaced by Ali Larayedh.

[35] A second draft had been announced on December 14, 2012.

society occurred.[36] Such tensions, of which the country had already had a taste under the TPA, were now exploding out of control.

In June 2013 the Troika government announced a fourth draft of the constitution, but it was so controversial that it prompted at least a dozen opposition members of the NCA to quit. Meanwhile, unrest and discontent with the Islamist government in Egypt, which had been elected within months after the NCA, was growing. A new major protest movement (*tammarod*, or rebellion) began in Egypt, and on July 3, the military removed the elected Muslim Brotherhood president Mohammed Morsi from power. The next several weeks in Tunisia saw heightened anticipation. Would this be a lesson for Enahda? Would Tunisians, also unsatisfied, stage a *tamarrod* movement against their elected government? Then, on July 25,[37] a second left wing political leader, Mohammed Brahmi from the Front Populaire (FP) party, was assassinated outside his home. This event represents the height of the chaos and divergence from the TPA's original roadmap during the subsequent interim phase.

After Brahmi's assassination, several NCA delegates, angry about the ineffectiveness of the government and the assembly, staged a sit-in outside the Bardo Palace in Tunis, where the assembly worked. They called for the dissolution of the NCA. On August 6, the NCA formally suspended its work, while a dialogue mediated by the UGTT between the political parties regarding the contentious articles in the draft constitution continued unsuccessfully. The deputies staging the sit-in resigned, and tens of thousands of citizens joined them in protest, which became known as the Bardo sit-in. Meanwhile, unsettling attacks by Islamist militants continued. These attacks, along with the coup in Egypt, a weakening economy, and other pressures gradually cornered Enahda into a choice between losing political credibility or

[36] For example, on March 11, a feminist activist known as Amina posted a topless picture of herself on Facebook in support of women's rights, leading to her arrest. Refusals by school and university administrators to admit students wearing the niqab (religious female face covering) also sparked violent attacks claimed by Salafists. These incidents reflect the larger debate about whether and how freedom of speech should be limited, and tensions over the separation of church and state. The chaos and violence as well as the controversy that ensued also demonstrate the near-anarchical state of the country.

[37] This day is symbolic for the founding of the first Tunisian Republic in 1956. Rumors at the time were that a movement was calling for a Tunisian *tamarrod* on that day (interview with a civil society activist, July 8, 2013).

distancing itself from its religious base by condemning groups claiming to act in the name of Islam.[38]

Immediately after the Brahmi assassination, two of the largest unions in the country, the business-owners' union UTICA (Union Tunisienne de l'Industrie, du Commerce, et de l'Artisanat), and the UGTT, issued a joint call for a new national dialogue. They were soon joined by the Tunisian Human Rights League (LTDH) and the bar association. Together, these four organizations, known as the Quartet, became the mediators of a national dialogue. This process, which began in September 2013, guided the leaders of all involved political parties through the draft constitution, article by article, until they reached an agreement on the text.

At the end of September, Enahda agreed to step down as the leading party of the ruling government coalition. Ali Laarayedh, the Enahda prime minister, resigned. In October 2013, cooperating parties agreed on a new roadmap, and the NCA deputies resumed work. Talks stalled again later in the fall because political parties could not agree on a figure to replace Laarayedh. Finally, in December 2013, they agreed on Mehdi Jomaa, a nonpartisan engineer who had been serving as the minister of industry.

Over the next six months, the atmosphere remained rocky, as several militant attacks occurred, including in the Chambi mountains near the Algerian border as well as in major cities like Sfax and Jendouba. Several high-level security officials from the Ben Ali era, who were widely considered complicit in the torture, surveillance, and other forms of repression that had occurred under that regime, were also acquitted in military tribunals, or their sentences shortened.[39] As explained below, this provoked an uproar among those working to build a transitional justice process, and caused disillusionment in the general public about prospects for democratic freedoms.

Jomaa had appointed a technocratic government meant to rule only until a new president and parliament were elected. Meanwhile the

---

[38] See Merone, "Enduring Class Struggle in Tunisia."

[39] For instance, Rafik Belhaj Belgacem, Ben Ali's former interior minister and head of presidential security, was granted appeal by a military court on April 12, 2014. Several members of the parliament demanded a retrial in a civilian court. Another former head of presidential security, Ali Seriati, had his sentence reduced by a military court the following month (*Middle East Journal*, "Chronology," 68, no. 4, 628).

constitution-writing process resumed, with Enahda conceding one of its principle demands (to include a reference to Islamic sharia law in the constitution). On January 26, 2014, the final draft of the constitution passed in a near-unanimous vote within the NCA. With that, the country was finally ready to hold elections for a new permanent parliament and president.

Although it is difficult to pinpoint a single cause, the negotiations that constituted the 2013 National Dialogue, under the auspices of the so-called Quartet, were a turning point in Tunisia's political trajectory.[40] As reflected in the 2015 awarding of the Nobel Prize to this Quartet, the success of the National Dialogue led to the adoption of a new constitution. Perhaps it was because of the coup in Egypt, which prompted Enahda to cooperate rather than risk being overthrown as the Muslim Brotherhood had been; perhaps it was due to the joining of forces of four organizations representing large and complementary swaths of society.[41] Or perhaps the third political assassination in less than one year prompted political and societal leaders to put their differences aside – for instance, the head of UTICA remembers calling Houcine Abassi, head of the UGTT, the moment she heard the news to say that it was time to unite in order to save the country.[42] The National Dialogue likely succeeded due to a combination of all these (and maybe other) factors.

Importantly, the National Dialogue and final phase of constitution-writing recalled the experiences of the TPA in several ways. For one thing, the expert core of the Ben Achour Commission – who were, after all, experts in constitutional law – had worked hard to develop a draft for the NCA to work from, and had offered to give support to the NCA early on. The NCA rejected these offers. Eventually, however,

---

[40] It should also be noted that throughout the later part of 2012 and all of 2013, the UGTT took the lead in trying to help overcome the political crisis that was deepening within the NCA (see Yousfi, *L'UGTT, une passion Tunisienne*).

[41] The number of lawyers in the country can be estimated at around 6,000 (Gobe, "Of Lawyers and Samsars," 46). The UGTT's membership, recorded in the same year at 517,000, dwarfs this (Ghilès, *Secular Social Movements Confront Radical Temptations*). Assuming the membership of the LTDH falls somewhere between these two, the organizations and professions may cover somewhere close to 750,000 Tunisians.

[42] Interview with a civil society member, February 2, 2015. Cooperation between the workers' union and the business-owners union is notable because those two groups should theoretically be in opposition.

the NCA became aware of its need for expertise, and began engaging with many of the Ben Achour Commission experts (also members of the Tunisian Association for Constitutional Law).[43] At this time, the influential role of the representative organizations such as the UGTT, LTDH, and the Bar Association also reappeared. And finally, the "technocrat" government of Mehdi Jomaa, if not in its actual composition, recalled the role of the 2011 Caïd Essebsi cabinet in its apolitical and circumscribed function of getting to new elections.

In sum, the TPA's failure to reach broad consensus on the issue of national identity may have contributed to the violent acts that eventually brought down the Troika government. The TPA's approach to governance, however, did seem to have an important, indirect influence on events. This is most clearly manifest in the National Dialogue process. Overall, the TPA had recognized the need to address the issue of national identity but was unable to address it sufficiently. Thus, the NCA carried an electoral legitimacy that the TPA did not but was much less effective – at least until it began to draw on the TPA's "democratic" features.

Reforming Institutions

Alongside the interim commissions described in Chapter 2, the TPA took – or did not take – several decisions about existing institutions and the functioning of the state apparatus more generally. The ad hoc and transitional nature of the TPA's decisions meant both that its decisions could have a major impact on the transition process, and posed challenges for this decision-making process. This section presents the ways the TPA dealt with these challenges and how this helped set the stage for attempted reforms in the NCA/Troika period.

For instance, the TPA had kept more or less intact the executive and judicial branches. Once Caïd Essebsi became interim prime minister, the structure of the executive cabinet was maintained, but the scope of its authority had been reduced. Ghannouchi and then Caïd Essebsi also helped preserve the position of president of the republic, although the president's powers had, similarly, been significantly reduced. Although the presidency had been a frightening force under Ben Ali, the TPA

---

[43] Interviews with TPA members, January 12, 2015 and December 9, 2014.

retained the executive solely to ensure the running of the state administration, and to keep a sense of order.[44]

The TPA dealt with the judicial branch of government similarly, but
for different reasons. Because the judiciary under Ben Ali was dependent on the executive, there was widespread recognition within the TPA
that the entire judicial branch was in need of a major reform.[45] Yet the
TPA's organization of public powers law (*Destour Sagheer*) contained
only one statement about the judiciary: "The judiciary would be
organized, managed, and would carry out its competencies according
to the rules and laws in place."[46] A Ministry of Justice, with jurisdic-
tion over the Tunisian court system, continued to function as part of
the TPA, with its minister acting in a purely provisional manner and
according to a purely provisional legal framework. Apart from this, the
TPA took no other action toward judicial reform, although a subcommittee within the expert core of the Ben Achour Commission
attempted to draft a text to that effect. As such, the institution of the
judiciary was neither revised nor used by the TPA.[47]

Alongside this retention of certain institutional frameworks, and as a
means of securing legitimacy in the eyes of the "revolutionaries," the
TPA also acted early on to effectively dissolve several institutions
perceived as tools for repression under the old regime.[48] For instance,
two major institutions related to the media and freedom of expression,
the Ministry of Information and the Tunisian External Communications Agency (Agence Tunisienne des Communications Externale,
ATCE) were intended to be dissolved; they had served as instruments

---

[44] One Tunisian academic explained that it was probably also acceptable to keep
him because his powers were so limited (interview, December 6, 2014).
[45] The president appointed all members of the constitutional court, for example,
which "assess(ed) legislative constitutionality" (Coupe and Redissi, "Tunisia,"
800). Beginning in the mid-2000s, the Ben Ali regime consistently thwarted all
organized attempts by justices to protect their independence. The Supreme
Magistrates Council, also headed by Ben Ali, was established to "watch over the
appointment, assignment, promotion, and transfer of judges" (Erdle, *Ben Ali's
"New Tunisia,"* 171).
[46] DL 2011-14, chapter 3, Section IV, Article 17.
[47] Coupe and Redissi call it "barely functioning" during the period.
[48] As Chapter 2 explains, when Mebazza was given powers to rule by decree on
February 9, this effectively dissolved the parliament; it, along with several other
institutions, including the Economic and Social Council and the Constitutional
Council, were officially dissolved with the first decree-law on organization of
public powers of March 23, 2011 (DL 14-2011).

for media censorship and limiting freedom of expression as well as maintaining Ben Ali's positive image abroad.[49]

As a result of its decisions to create new institutions and dissolve or merge others, the structural arrangement of the TPA was fluid. The fact, for example, that the Ben Achour Commission could monitor the decisions of the Caïd Essebsi cabinet by calling the members in for questioning – to which those members would always respond – was not specified in the decree-law that created it. The creation of an independent commission to advise on media reform (INRIC), but not on the other legal texts the expert core of the Ben Achour Commission was drafting, also appeared to be a somewhat ad hoc decision. Moreover, several individuals acted in either a full or consultative role,[50] or else were invited to join or work with more than one commission.

Moreover, because the Ben Achour Commission was created and made official before Caïd Essebsi became interim prime minister, he was unable to control or dominate it. On the contrary, it tried to control him![51] For example, although Caïd Essebsi did little to suggest that he was trying to use his position as interim prime minister to hold on to power, he was reluctant to honor ISIE's request to postpone the NCA elections from July to October. In the end, however, because he had no power over the Ben Achour Commission and the ISIE, he conceded.[52] This flexibility of the TPA's institutions would become important not only for the work of the TPA itself, but also during later phases.

The decree-laws that created the independent commissions required the state to furnish the necessary means – including information – for them to accomplish their tasks, while also deeming them not part of any hierarchy of authority.[53] Caïd Essebsi, by and large, cooperated

---

[49] It is not clear that the Tunisian External Communications Agency (ATCE) was actually dissolved (see Reporters without Borders, "Reporters without Borders in Tunisia: A New Freedom that Needs Protecting," INRIC, *General Report*, 150).

[50] One such individual was constitutional law professor Kais Saed, who, in fall 2019, became Tunisia's second post-uprising president (see Chapter 6).

[51] Interview with a Tunisian academic, December 6, 2014.

[52] And perhaps because the others persuaded him of the value of postponing.

[53] See, for example, Hafidha Chekir's description of the Bouderbala Commission in Redissi et al., eds., *La Transition Démocratique en Tunisie: Les Thématiques*, 29–31.

with this system and obliged the ministers of his cabinet to do the same. It provided each commission with one vehicle, office space, and one or two functionaries to perform administrative tasks such as note-taking.[54] Nonetheless, each commission reported experiencing at least one incident of resistance by the Caïd Essebsi cabinet: members of the Ben Achour Commission, for example, described "passionate" debates with interim ministers over their actions or the laws being drafted.[55] Others complained about the scarce resources provided to them, although this is likely a reflection of the limitations of the resources available to the Caïd Essebsi cabinet itself rather than resistance to commission activities per se.

In some cases, other parts of government staged more resistance to the new independent institutions. For example, many security agents from the Ministry of Interior clung to secrets, posing obstacles for the Bouderbala Commission.[56] And various parts of the judicial system were hostile to the Amor Commission, accusing it of taking over its work or creating a parallel justice.[57] In other instances, new and old institutions cooperated without difficulty: INRIC, for example, worked closely with the National Broadcasting Office, the National Internet Agency, and the National Frequency Center.[58] On the whole, members of the TPA and all its institutions note that the shared goal of moving the country forward and not returning to autocratic rule dominated over those individuals or groups of individuals who tried to stand in its way.

Media reform serves as a prime example of how the TPA struggled to strike this balance, and how its shortcomings affected the next phase. Under the TPA (and under the Troika), many new media outlets were forming and, given their lack of experience, journalists and other media actors often acted quite unprofessionally: spreading rumors, making alliances, or hampering the Ben Achour Commission's work

---

[54] For example, the ISIE made budget requests that went through the Ministry of Finance. Interview with a TPA member, November 14, 2014.

[55] Interview with a Ben Achour Commission member, November 13, 2014. The main example was the debate over Article 15 of the elections law.

[56] Redissi et al., eds., *La Transition Démocratique en Tunisie: Les Thématiques*, 41.

[57] Interview with a Ben Achour Commission member, November 18, 2014.

[58] INRIC, *General Report*, 191–200; Chouikha, "La difficile entreprise," 4.

by leaking draft decrees or statements before they were complete.[59] However, like its control over national identity, repressing freedom of expression had been an important tool for state control under Ben Ali and Bourguiba; thus any member of the TPA who tried to control the media in any way risked being accused of trying to take this new-found freedom away.[60]

Countless incidents occurred during the TPA period that reflected the media's immaturity. Unsubstantiated articles were published, for example, accusing members of Ben Achour's expert core of being sympathetic to or part of Islamist groups.[61] The newspaper *Essabah* reported in May that the Ben Achour Commission had failed to reach an agreement with the government on the contentious Article 15 of the elections law, just as an agreement was being reached.[62] One observer summarized it nicely, stating: "Whether it was political parties or activists from newspapers … liberty of expression was being confused with what were more like insults … we weren't accustomed to [this] freedom of expression."[63]

The difficulty for the TPA was twofold. On the one hand, it had to demonstrate that it recognized the role of independent media in democratic governance. On the other hand, it was also responsible for keeping daily life generally under control; it thus had an interest in not letting the media stir up too many suspicions or fears. Although the TPA initiated the development of long-term measures for setting standards for a both free and ethical media, the tradeoff once again of being an interim government was that it would have little influence over the long term.

The media had little experience with freedom of expression, and practiced politicians were unused to such an environment. This led

---

[59] Redissi et al., *La Transition Démocratique en Tunisie: Les Acteurs*, 211; Interviews with TPA members and Tunisian legal experts, December 12, 2014 and December 22, 2014.
[60] Under Ben Ali, controlling the media was not only a way to limit domestic criticism, it was also a way to prevent the international community from learning about the conditions in the country.
[61] Interview with an expert core member/Tunisian academic, October 31, 2014.
[62] Ben Achour, "Témoinage à propos de la Haute Instance pour la réalisation des objectifs de la révolution, la reforme politique, et la transition démocratique," in Mrad and Moussa, eds., *La Transition Démocratique à la Lumière des Expériences Comparées*, 158.
[63] Interview with a Tunisian legal expert, December 22, 2014.

them to sometimes revert to the practices they were accustomed to, even if these were not those to which they aspired. For example, INRIC was charged with recommending certain radio and TV stations for an official license based on its review of their applications and its understanding of independent media. Although the commission was meant to be independent, interim Prime Minister Caïd Essebsi demanded several times to preview the list of TV stations, implying that he should "approve" them before the list went public. INRIC asserted its independence and was ultimately able to publish the list without the government's intervening.[64]

Politicians were also unused to taking criticism. During one press conference, for instance, a persistent questioner made Caïd Essebsi so angry that he tried to grab her microphone.[65] A lack of competent advisers contributed to politicians' feeling ill at ease with media reform during this period.[66] These incidents reflect the TPA's struggle to abandon past ways and build a new order.

Members of INRIC and the subcommittee of the expert core working on media reform also recall the fierce resistance to the proposed reforms (such as the creation of the audiovisual media regulation body known as the HAICA) staged by the owners of private TV stations, many of whom were cronies of Ben Ali.[67] Even journalists who had been known for speaking out against the dictatorship failed to keep up with the changing rules. In one instance, a dissident station called *Radio Kalima* tried to take advantage of the TPA. INRIC recommended that any outlet that met certain internationally held standards should receive a license as long as it followed a certain application process. However, *Radio Kalima* insisted that as an outlet that had always defended free speech, it should be exempt from these

---

[64] Interview with an INRIC member, December 12, 2014; INRIC, *General Report*, 123. The report and the interview offer slightly different accounts of the incident: the report simply mentions that the prime minister's office pressured INRIC to delay its announcement of the television stations that would receive permits until after the elections.
[65] Interview with a Tunisian journalist, January 15, 2015.
[66] Interview with an INRIC member, December 12, 2014.
[67] Interviews with an INRIC member and expert core member, December 12, 2014 and December 24, 2014. They particularly note Nesma TV and Hannibal TV.

processes, maintaining that it did not need to uphold standards set by INRIC.[68] When the INRIC refused to grant it a license as a private radio station, *Radio Kalima* launched an attack against the commission. But the media, like other sectors, were beginning to be governed by rules that applied equally to everybody, regardless of their history, and INRIC persuaded Caïd Essebsi of this. Even after this incident, however, the TPA's struggle to protect media standards from personal agendas continued.

INRIC also worked closely with the subcommission of the expert core of the Ben Achour Commission to draft new audiovisual and print media laws as well as a decree-law passed in May 2011 about access to public documents.[69] The print media law replaced the repressive Press Code of 1975, essentially changing the legal basis for a publication from permission based on the authorities' discretion (*régime d'autorisation*) to one in which any media outlet was recognized provided it did not violate certain standards (*régime de declaration*). The main innovation of the audiovisual media's new law was the creation of an independent authority to monitor audiovisual media (la Haute Autorité Indépendente de la Communication Audiovisuelle, or HAICA).[70] However, although this decree-law foresaw a certain role for the HAICA in safeguarding media independence, things would play out differently.

In its final report, INRIC evaluated the new media legislation drafted by the Ben Achour Commission against international standards for

---

[68] INRIC's *General Report* also describes the pressures INRIC faced from the Tunisian Union of Free Radio Stations, which issued a statement in which it accused INRIC of "adopting 'favoritism and courtesy' as the only standards for distributing permits." The union wrote a letter to the former prime minister asking him not to adopt the recommendations of INRIC. However, on September 26, 2011, the union issued another statement stating that, "despite some differences with INRIC and some reservations," it supported INRIC and "condemned all attempts at defamation and all insult campaigns targeting INRIC with the aim of weakening it and hindering its work." The union said in the same statement that it was "surprised at the transitional government's procrastination and its lack of impartiality in implementing and approving INRIC's recommendations" (INRIC, *General Report*, 122–123). This is another example of the constant challenges to the TPA manifest in the domain of media reform.

[69] The laws governing print media and those governing audiovisual media are separated in Tunisia.

[70] The print media law and audiovisual media laws drafted by INRIC are DL 2011-115 and DL 2011-116, respectively.

free media and expression. It also discussed the state of the media sector since independence, offered suggestions for overcoming the culture of self-censorship and other consequences of the decades of repression it had experienced, and made recommendations for enhancing the role of public bodies such as the Tunisian External Communications Agency (ATCE), journalism training institutes, and the national broadcasting, internet, and radio frequency offices in supporting free media. Finally, the report described democratic countries' experiences with media monitoring and compared the Tunisian experience of media monitoring since the uprisings, and particularly during the October 2011 elections.

Despite its tensions with other parts of the TPA, INRIC was generally able to carry out its work as an independent commission playing a consultative role for those working on reform.[71] Yet the commissioners became increasingly frustrated as this changed under the Troika. For instance, the two interim laws governing audiovisual and print media were largely ignored in subsequent phases.[72] As a result, controlling the media and developing a regulated sector comprised of public and private media outlets that also self-regulated according to ethical standards became even more difficult in the NCA/Troika phase.

When the Troika came to power, it made unilateral appointments to the directors of state media outlets.[73] The Troika government's practices were so reminiscent of the way the media had been coopted under the former regime that thousands of journalists staged a huge eighty-day strike in front of the national TV station. The Troika government also ignored INRIC in other ways: for example, when in 2012 it organized a National Consultation on media reform, it neglected to recognize the recommendations INRIC had been working for over a year to develop, invited only journalists INRIC had already identified as having cooperated with the former regime, and did not consult INRIC in any form. In short, INRIC felt the Troika government had no intention of reforming the media sector according to international standards of freedom of expression and free speech.[74] For this reason, INRIC decided to fold prematurely, on July 5, 2012.

---

[71] Interview with an INRIC member, December 12, 2014.
[72] Interview with a Tunisian journalist, January 15, 2015.
[73] Chouikha, "La difficile entreprise".
[74] Interview with an INRIC member, December 12, 2014.

Moreover, the reforms for the audiovisual media sector envisioned by the TPA would stall under the Troika in a process that somewhat paralleled judicial reform. The drafters of the decree-law on governance of the audiovisual media sector had envisioned an independent body to govern those media, (the HAICA). Although the drafters of decree-law had thought carefully about a composition that would preserve the commission's independence, the Troika government suffered from extensive controversy over the members it nominated, delaying its creation until May 2013.[75] Once in place, the HAICA was subject to criticism and accusations of being a new authoritarian government in disguise. Each time the HAICA condemned or punished a certain station, it was publicly attacked and accused of bias.[76] In addition, because the law's drafters failed to specify that it should set a term limit for the heads of national media the HAICA appointed, the position became more vulnerable to politicization.[77] These were examples of issues the TPA had either not anticipated or did not have the capacity to prevent.

The TPA also struggled with but ultimately reached a compromise over the issue of gender parity. Due to the historical importance of women's rights in Tunisia, many passionate voices within the Ben Achour Commission urged the incorporation of the gender parity principle, or a requirement to alternate the candidates on each party list by gender, into the elections law.[78] However, other voices staged significant opposition: some of the more conservative representatives from the interior may have been opposed in principle, and many smaller or newer parties were concerned about finding an adequate number of female candidates. Enahda too initially hesitated to give support but changed its position when it realized the gender parity rule would help it politically.[79]

Some parties did not achieve full gender parity but were still allowed to compete in the NCA elections. Moreover, during the Ben Achour

---

[75] Chouikha, "La difficile entreprise."
[76] Blaise, "Interview avec Riadh Ferjani."
[77] Interview with a TPA expert core member, December 24, 2014.
[78] For more discussion, see Marks, "Women's Rights Before and After the Revolution," in Gana, ed., *The Making of the Tunisian Revolution*, 235; Petkanas, "Emerging Norms," 359–360.
[79] Interviews with TPA members, November 13, 2014; January 6, 2015; January 29, 2015.

Commission debates, there had been many advocates for "zipper parity," or the requirement to alternate male-female candidates down each list ("vertical parity") and across the heads of lists ("horizontal parity"). This regulation was agreed upon in principle but not adopted in the law, and of the final lists that competed in the NCA elections, only 7 percent had women at the head (the final composition of the NCA was 30 percent women).[80]

Meanwhile, the TPA struggled to deal with institutions related to the security sector. The army was left intact because it had refused Ben Ali's orders to fire on the protestors, arrested the head of the President's National Guard, and secured the airport for Ben Ali's safe passage out of the country.[81] Yet the directors of eleven security agencies were dismissed, causing confusion among the operational ranks of the security services and creating a vacuum that then fueled further resentment of security forces and, in turn, a further reluctance on their part to work.[82] Though initially welcomed, the dissolution of the political police and State Security Department had similar effects, particularly because they were not accompanied by the necessary restructuring within the Ministry of Interior. A final change to the security sector was the legalization of unions for security personnel, which had the effect of helping engage the public in the political debates over the reforms of the sector.[83]

In contrast, the issue of electoral reform evolved somewhat differently under the TPA. Within the Ben Achour Commission, a healthy debate occurred over the type of electoral system that should govern the NCA elections. However, the issues went beyond this to include debates over other articles within the electoral law; the creation of an electoral management body and the process of organizing the proper

[80] Petkanas, "Emerging Norms," 360.
[81] Schraeder and Redissi, "Ben Ali's Fall," 13. Several sources also mention how under Ben Ali, the internal security forces, including the National Guard and the Presidential Guard, received a large allocation of resources relative to the military (e.g. Willis, *Politics and Power in the Maghreb*, 104; International Crisis Group, *Popular Protests in North Africa/The Middle East: Tunisia's Way*, 11).
[82] Mahfoudh, *Security Sector Reform in Tunisia*, 3–4.
[83] Mahfoudh lists the eleven agencies whose directors were dismissed and notes that these dismissals "took place in multiple stages across consecutive governments." He also explains how the new unions of security sector personnel "became active players in political life and involved themselves in political choices, including who would be chosen as Minister of Interior." Mahfoudh, *Security Sector Reform in Tunisia*, 6.

electoral infrastructure; and the institutionalization of all these procedures. More so than in other sectors, the TPA was able to manage these
issues in a constructive way.

Other than specifying the responsibilities of the elected positions of
president, vice president, and secretary general, the decree-law man-
dating the ISIE gave little guidance as to how the ISIE was to structure
its operations.[84] Under the guidance of an expert on media law, the
ISIE formed seven committees, one for each of the following areas:
administrative and financial affairs; legal affairs; training; voting for
Tunisians abroad; public relations; information technology; and external relations. The ISIE recruited people from outside the commission to
staff these committees. The ISIE also established thirty-three Independent Regional Authorities for Elections (Instances Régionales Indépendentes pour les Elections, IRIEs), one for each electoral district,[85] as
well as several local commissions (Instances Locales pour les elections,
ILEs). The IRIEs were composed of individuals drawn from local civil
society organizations and professional associations, as well as lawyers
and judges. It took essentially the entire month of July for the ISIE to
name all regional and local commissioners.[86]

Because the ISIE had no precedent to follow, it became almost an
incubator for the development of an electoral management system. Its
members spent considerable time learning what was required to
develop a free and fair electoral system with an independent electoral
management body, including how to allocate its limited resources. This
learning entailed, of course, mistakes, which would have an impact on
the TPA, the electoral process and outcomes, and, therefore, subsequent phases.

The ISIE demonstrated its inexperience in several ways. It struggled
to properly educate voters about both the registration process and the
voting process: although it had opened a website and Facebook page,
for example, the information presented on these pages about the
process was incomplete.[87] Such shortcomings may have influenced

---

[84] Tavana, "Preparing to Draft a New Social Contract," 5–6.
[85] Twenty-seven domestic and six abroad.
[86] For more detail on the Independent Regional Authorities for Elections (IRIEs)
   and Independent Local Electoral Authority (ILEs), see Carter Center, *National
   Constituent Assembly Elections in Tunisia.*
[87] Carter Center, *National Constituent Assembly in Tunisia*, 25–26, 35–36. The
   report also describes one such incident where the ISIE decided to ban political

voter turnout. The ISIE also failed to take simple steps to speed up the vote-counting process and to warn the public that the results would not be announced immediately, heightening anxieties.[88]

Finally, the ISIE learned that a very rigid application of the elections law didn't always produce the best results. As per the law, the ISIE tried to ensure that the head of each party list was allotted three minutes of air time on a public TV/radio station to announce its campaign.[89] However, the ISIE did not anticipate that the high number of lists registered, as well as the refusal of private stations to participate in the airing of those statements, would place a great burden on public TV and radio stations.[90] Moreover, the law stated that no voters were to receive assistance of any kind during the casting of their ballot. But because ISIE staff (and staff of the local branches, the IRIEs) applied this to illiterate voters as well, many ballots during the NCA elections were cast in error.[91] Because of the limited timeframe within which the ISIE was working, these types of considerations could not be corrected; they could only be taken into account for future elections.

The members of the ISIE were to serve only until the NCA was in place, according to the decree-law that created it. However, the need for institutionalizing an electoral management body to oversee future elections soon became clear.[92] Thus, a second ISIE, known as ISIE 2, was established. It would learn from the mistakes of the TPA's ISIE in late 2014 when it oversaw the elections for a new parliament and president.

advertising during a certain portion of the campaign period but announced the decision at such late notice that it was difficult for all parties to follow. Naturally, this created controversy.

[88] Author meeting with an international electoral assistance worker, July 10, 2013 and interview with a civil society activist, July 8, 2013.

[89] DL 2011-35.

[90] Chouikha, "L'instance supérieure indépendante pour les élections et le processus électoral tunisien: Un témoignage de l'intérieur," 175–176.

[91] Author meeting with an international electoral assistance worker, July 10, 2013. Approximately 20 percent of the Tunisian population is illiterate (World Bank, World Development Indicators, cited in Cammett et al., eds., *A Political Economy of the Middle East*, 175).

[92] Notably, Hubler tells how the experience of establishing an electoral management body in Egypt to ensure independent elections after President Mubarak resigned was comparatively more difficult. See Hubler, "Election Management Bodies in Transitioning Democracies," 64.

Under the NCA/Troika, the process of selecting the members of ISIE 2 became, like the creation of the HAICA, a forum for political jockeying to create an acceptable representation of political parties. As with the HAICA, this caused great delays in the establishment of a new ISIE, which in turn delayed the elections.[93] However, when ISIE 2 was finally appointed, observers noted that it was more professional and experienced than ISIE 1.[94] Like ISIE 1, ISIE 2 also had to organize elections within a tight timeframe, but it had learned the importance of building an effective communications strategy. It even worked with an American NGO to develop a manual for dealing with illiterate voters.[95]

In this sense, the process of institutionalizing a reformed electoral system was less erratic and difficult than in other sectors. For example, members of the Amor Commission for the investigation of corruption complained that they wished they had received chances to build on their experiences and acquired knowledge as the reform process continued.[96] Similarly, the HAICA did not have a predecessor to learn from or build on, because the INRIC (which created it) had played an explicitly consultative role. Thus, the ISIE laid significant groundwork during its tenure under the TPA (including lessons about things *not* to do) for a future electoral infrastructure. Although it committed mistakes in the process, which would lead to some imperfections during the NCA elections, by and large it represented a firm step on the path to electoral reform.

Despite these mild influences over media, electoral, and other forms of institutional reform, the TPA's efforts around the September 15th document and defining the role of the NCA showed the stark

---

[93] The extensive debates within the NCA over various constitutional articles had already delayed the appointment of two ISIE members.

[94] Author meetings with TPA members and Tunisian academics, July 1, 2013 and October 24, 2014.

[95] During the 2014 elections, voters still were not allowed to receive assistance, but illustrated posters about the voting process were to be hung in every polling station, and the ISIE had also produced posters and videos about the voting process. See International Foundation for Electoral Systems, *Tunisia – First Round Presidential Elections: Frequently Asked Questions*, 6–9.

[96] Interviews with commissioners, November 18, 2014 and December 16, 2014. A new commission for evaluating corruption claims (including those the Amor Commission had not had time to finish) was appointed, but the government consistently resisted providing the commission with adequate funding, allegedly due to a lack of political will.

limitations of its influence in later phases. Once in place, the NCA's first task was to write its bylaws (*règlements d'interieur*), at which point it decided to give itself legislative authority. As noted above, this expansion of its own powers, in addition to intransigence during debates over constitutional issues, meant the NCA's deadline of November 2012 would pass long before its work was done. The delegates justified this exceeding of their time limit by claiming that the September 15th document was not legally binding.[97] The NCA ignored the lesson from the TPA that an effective interim government (or provisional administration) needs to be just that – provisional – despite the tradeoffs in power and capacity this may entail. This failure to demonstrate a true commitment to being provisional would cost the NCA/Troika government its legitimacy – as 2012 gave way to 2013, it came under increasing accusations of trying to hold on to power, in addition to being unfit to govern.

Beyond basic institutional reform, the TPA had tried to maintain control through the use of a functioning state apparatus. Historically in Tunisia, a strong, well-functioning state has been a source of pride and an aspect of national identity, yet had also been used as excuse to repress free society, including Islamists.[98] Now the balance between state and society – once dictated by the notion that the state had a tutelary role in helping the country develop[99] – had all of a sudden been thrown into question.

Hence, TPA structures like the Ben Achour Commission took on a quasi-revolutionary government role, with their high proportion of radicals (having been derived from the CNPR, which was originally quite radical), their forceful demands (such as the ability to control the work of the Caïd Essebsi government), and their insistence on representation of youths and people from the interior. At the same time, the TPA exhibited a generally accepted recognition of the need

---

[97] Interview with a Tunisian legal expert, December 23, 2014. According to the interviewee, various NCA delegates and Troika politicians claimed that the September 15th document was "only political, not legal." Another Tunisian constitutional law expert said the NCA was very protective of its "sovereignty" (interview, January 12, 2015).

[98] Beatrice Hibou does not discuss this directly but implies it in her analysis of the term "policing state" (Hibou, *The Force of Obedience*, 279–281). Steffen Erdle also includes a useful discussion of how this worked in practice (Erdle, *Ben Ali's "New Tunisia,"* 305–307).

[99] Alexander, *Tunisia: Stability and Reform in the Modern Maghreb*, 36–37.

for a state-like actor, an established central authority – in other words, it demonstrated a commitment to the state. This organization of the TPA, albeit almost accidental, reflected its position caught in between an old system and a new one.

This had pros and cons. For one thing, the new opportunity for non-state and nonpartisan actors to have a voice in governing introduced a wealth of experiences and new perspectives into the TPA's decision-making. It led to innovations like the HAICA and the ISIE. On the other hand, the TPA's insistence on retaining some authority in central ministries and other state institutions, even when they had been severely weakened, made it hard to accomplish certain goals. For example, TPA members were so focused on day-to-day security issues that addressing comprehensive security sector reform – a clear need given the role of the state security apparatus in Ben Ali's repression – was nearly impossible.[100]

Overall, the TPA found itself walking a tightrope between maintaining authority and a commitment to the state while not appearing overly authoritarian as it tried to ensure law and order and provide services. As it sought to guide reform processes in the media, security, electoral, and other sectors, it managed to both set precedents and come up against its own limitations.

Dealing with Questions of Transitional Justice

Finally, two critical issues addressed by the TPA that had an impact in later phases were judicial reform and transitional justice. Transitional justice refers to the processing of former officials for human rights violations and financial crimes as well as the political exclusion of party officials complicit in such crimes. The central goals of transitional justice include pursuing perpetrators of past crimes through the court system, truth seeking, reparations for victims, and institutional reform.[101] Judicial reform refers here to more broad efforts to render the judicial system democratic and independent. The TPA's activities in these areas were again important, but limited, and the impacts of its actions in later phases reflected this.

---

[100] Mahfoudh, *Security Sector Reform in Tunisia*, 8–9.
[101] Gray, "In Search of Righting Wrongs."

As with other reform issues, transitional justice and judicial reform under the NCA/Troika reflected the impact of what the TPA could and could not do. Despite the negotiations that took place between Ghannouchi and Mebazza and the National Council for the Protection of the Revolution (CNPR) over January and February 2011, which resulted in the resignation of Ghannouchi, the constitution of an interim cabinet without the Constitutional Democratic Rally (RCD), and the restructuring of the Ben Achour Commission, the question of involvement of former regime members in political life was not entirely resolved under the TPA. The process of replacing RCD members who had been serving at all levels of the government, such as in state organizations and government civil service positions, took place gradually, especially at the middle and lower levels of management.[102] This slow pace of change in leaders provoked continuing sit-ins and protests outside governorate offices, often organized by the local councils for the protection of the revolution.[103]

Moreover, not all individuals with ties to the government of Ben Ali were fully excluded. After all, people like Mebazza (who had been the head of the Chamber of Deputies) or the chief of the armed forces, General Rachid Ben Ammar, had been Ben Ali appointees or had only resigned from the RCD in January 2011 because of the Kasbah protests. Businessmen with ties to Mebazza and Caïd Essebsi also retained influence.[104] In late March 2011, Caïd Essebsi announced that the person who had been acting as interim interior minister, Ferhat Rajhi, would be replaced with Habib Essid, who had been a junior interior minister under Ben Ali.[105] This decision caused significant controversy. Thus, individuals who represented the former regime – even though they were allegedly appointed "in the general interest" – remained a part of the TPA.[106] In sum, individuals and interests of the former regime were still represented in the TPA, even if only in pockets.

---

[102] Economist Intelligence Unit, *Tunisia: Country Report*, June 2011, 4.
[103] Redissi et al., *La Transition Démocratique en Tunisie: Les Acteurs*, 200, n. 27.
[104] Economist Intelligence Unit, *Tunisia: Country Report*, June 2011, 13.
[105] Rajhi subsequently defended himself on a website called "Scandali," the "context, form, and tone" of which were harshly criticized. The incident reveals the fragility of the political situation and more specifically, the question of the legitimacy of government representatives. See Abderrazak, "Effets dévastateurs et révélateurs suite à la polémique soulevée par les affirmations explosives de Farhat Errajhi."
[106] Arieff, *Political Transition in Tunisia*, June 27, 2011, 11.

The TPA took some immediate steps toward the prosecution of high-level officials from the Ben Ali era. Several family members and close associates of Ben Ali had been arrested in the early days after January 14, and the TPA, especially the Amor Commission, studied cases in other countries of how such figures are tried and punished.[107] Moreover, partly as a result of the work of the Bouderbala Commission, several police and figures from the Ministry of Interior were convicted of having committed crimes during the uprisings (such as killing or injuring peaceful protestors).[108] These initial steps represented a clear intention of the TPA to halt the injustices practiced under the Ben Ali regime, and thus found general support among the population.

The Bouderbala Commission had also investigated and documented all claims of violence by the state during the revolutionary period, and the recommendations in the commission's final report touched on the issue of reparations for victims. These recommendations included the creation of a Truth and Dignity Commission (TDC) to investigate all crimes since 1955. However, the Bouderbala Commission had a limited, defined mandate, which was to investigate, collect information, and document it. It was not to make decisions about what the victims with whom it dealt were owed. Some commissioners felt frustrated by these limitations – noting, for example, that reparations/indemnities were dispersed in uneven or unfair ways, particularly in regard to women.[109] In these ways, the TPA moved the country toward setting up permanent transitional justice mechanisms, albeit in a restricted way.[110]

The Amor Commission also dealt with questions related to transitional justice and prosecution of former regime officials for their crimes. This commission was both helped and hurt by its independent, nonjuridical nature. Because Tunisians had never known such an

---

[107] Interview with a Tunisian academic, December 16, 2014.
[108] Interview with a Tunisian legal expert, December 22, 2014.
[109] One commissioner explained, for example, that the commission was unprepared for dealing with cases of sexual abuse, which occurred particularly against women, although many women were also hesitant to come forward. Interview, December 19, 2014. Gray also discusses the delicacy of reparations for female victims (Gray, "In Search of Righting Wrongs").
[110] In the French summary of its report, the Bouderbala Commission recommended a more comprehensive reparations scheme, saying it should include people killed "other than by live ammunition" and benefit "all victims from the period, without distinction" (UNDP, *Résumé*, 71; my translation).

apparatus, they weren't sure whether to trust it. The commission also suffered from accusations of being tied to the old regime, especially since Ben Ali had in fact created it.[111] Many Tunisians thus remained suspicious of the Amor Commission. (On the other hand, because it was not part of the actual judicial system – whose independence had been so compromised by the former regimes – Tunisians had reason to trust in the Amor Commission and the process it was trying to set up.) Developing working relationships with other parts of the judicial system was also challenging, because some of these judicial institutions felt that the work of the Amor Commission called their competencies into question.[112]

The Amor Commission was further challenged by the "explosion of information" about acts of corruption and embezzlement committed by the former regime.[113] This meant that it could not deal with all the complaints that had been filed by time of the October 23 elections. It also worked to draft an interim law about indemnification and protection of victims and witnesses around corruption charges; however, this text was not approved by the Caïd Essebsi government.[114]

The Amor Commission produced three main results. First, it processed between four thousand and five thousand of the approximately eleven thousand complaints of corruption filed, which contributed to the return of some assets to state coffers.[115] Second, it laid the groundwork for a more permanent anti-corruption commission by drafting Decree-Law 2011-20, which was signed into law in November. One commissioner even said, "Decree-Law 120 was a source of inspiration for the constituent assembly [the NCA], because they adopted its principles in the new constitution."[116] Finally, the Amor Commission published a report describing its activities and findings.

Under the Troika government, many of the officials from the Ministry of Interior and other government agencies who were arrested and

<hr>

[111] As one political-transitions expert noted, the creation of "investigation commissions" was a classic authoritarian trick meant to calm disquietudes. Interview with a Tunisian academic, December 6, 2014.
[112] Interview with an Amor Commissioner, December 16, 2014.
[113] Interview with an Amor Commissioner, December 16, 2014.
[114] Interview with an Amor Commission member, December 11, 2014.
[115] One commissioner even said that "about 28 billion TD was resuscitated from Leila Ben Ali (Trabelsi)'s bank account, which went back to national treasury." (Interview, November 18, 2014).
[116] Interview with an Amor Commission member, December 16, 2014.

convicted of committing crimes in 2011 were given light sentences or even released from jail. Moreover, in December 2013, following a national consultation on transitional justice organized by the Troika government, the NCA passed a transitional justice law that sent those convicted before military tribunals to be tried.[117] In April 2014, those who had been tried were all acquitted due to lack of evidence (much evidence had been hidden or destroyed in the flurry of the days around January 14).[118] These events led to widespread disillusionment as they suggested that the persecutors of past crimes would never be prosecuted.

When it came to families of martyrs, this felt especially unjust. Those Tunisians – mostly parents of the youths who protested in December 2010 and January 2011 – would never have an answer to their only question: "Who killed our children?"[119] Although a modification to the December 2013 law was passed in May 2014,[120] the complexity of establishing these processes reflects the difficulty of knowing in a transitional situation who should be held responsible for what crimes, and under what justice system they should be tried.[121]

The Truth and Dignity Commission (TDC) that had been recommended by the Bouderbala Commission was legally created through the December 2013 transitional justice law. Like with the Bouderbala Commission's recommendation on reparations, this was an important step in the transitional justice process and therefore one of the TPA's

---

[117] DL 2013-53.

[118] Interview with an Amor Commission member, December 16, 2014.

[119] Meeting with Tunisian legal expert, December 22, 2014.

[120] The amendment stated that people accused of *such* crimes – those that could be considered human rights abuses according to international standards – should be tried before civil, rather than military, courts. Meeting with a Tunisian legal expert, December 22, 2014.

[121] See Ben Aissa, "Pouvoir judiciaire et transition en Tunisie" (unpublished). Ben Aissa elegantly presents the complexities of disentangling transitional justice and democratic transition by assessing the constitutionality of the transitional justice law of December 2013 in light of the new constitution, which was passed *after* it (January 2014). His analysis shows that the success or failure of any transitional justice process – which is meant to serve a larger process of democratic transition – depends on the answers to the questions of how to confront the past: how to determine who should be held responsible for crimes committed under the dictator, how to punish them, and how to accord reparations to victims. Thus, the fate of the process is in the hands of those who determine the answers to those questions – and if such actors have any reason to hide the truth about the past, the whole democratic transition may fail.

more concrete impacts. However, once again, the process of establishing the TDC entailed the selection of a group of people theoretically meant to be independent, which quickly turned it into a political issue. The launching of the commission's work faltered multiple times throughout 2014, as politicians and civil society members protested the NCA's selection of commissioners, and several commissioners resigned due to personal and partisan disagreements. The law also placed the TDC under the purview of the newly created Ministry of Justice and Human Rights, which became another locus of political bickering as opponents accused each other of trying to dominate the issue. This only served to further delay effective implementation of the TDC.

In the middle of these debates, Troika President Marzouki unilaterally launched an investigation, purportedly in the name of transparency and in the spirit of the new truth-seeking body, into journalists complicit with the former regime. However, because Marzouki's investigation itself was not transparent, it lacked credibility and hampered the transitional justice process.[122] Indeed, one journalist remarked that Marzouki's "Black Book," meant to blacklist journalists for their crimes under Ben Ali, was so poorly and hastily compiled that the first journalist to interview him about it was actually one of the journalists it listed![123] Such criticisms suggest that this was a purely political move, rather than in the genuine interest of furthering transitional justice. The episode also highlights how the absence of transitional justice mechanisms can theoretically permit unjust convictions and prosecutions.[124]

In addition, the TPA and its successors had to decide whether and how to reincorporate former RCD members into politics.[125] For the

---

[122] Tolbert, "Tunisia's Black Book: Transparency or Witch-hunt?"

[123] Interview with a Tunisian journalist, January 15, 2015.

[124] Ben Aissa ("Pouvoir Judiciaire") also notes that the NCA's delay in passing DL 2013-53 on transitional justice was difficult to understand given that it did not have the same issues of legal uncertainty that constrained its predecessor, the TPA, and that it had stated its willingness to launch a comprehensive transitional justice process in the first law it passed, the organization of public powers law of December 2011.

[125] The process of taking such decisions in a transitional context is also sometimes referred to as "vetting." See Lamont, "Transitional Justice and the Politics of Lustration in Tunisia"; Boduszynski and Henneberg, "Explaining Divergent Pathways of Post-Arab Spring Change."

TPA, this entailed deciding which former party members were eligible to run in the NCA elections. The question sparked a fierce and lengthy debate. Those in the expert core who wrote the first draft of the law meant to govern the elections had excluded from eligibility any member of the RCD during the previous ten years. But many members of the Ben Achour Commission felt strongly that the law should be broadened to exclude anyone who had been a member of the RCD under all twenty-three years of Ben Ali's rule. They felt that excusing any former party members would be inappropriate, given that they were all complicit in the unjust policies and actions of the ruling regime. Those in favor of the shorter period argued that the regime's[126] most outrageous abuses had only been committed during the last ten years of Ben Ali's rule, and that delimiting the period in this way would avoid prohibiting too great a proportion of the population from participating in the electoral process.

The final compromise solution, codified in the "famous" Article 15 of the 2011 elections law passed by the Ben Achour Commission, was a temporary mechanism for addressing what commissioners saw as a long-term aspect of transitional justice.[127] It defined people who were ineligible to participate in the elections not by the years during which they had been party members but by their role in the party, and it was temporary because it applied to the NCA elections only.[128] As such, Article 15 represented an attempt to punish members of the

---

[126] "The regime" should not necessarily be synonymous with the RCD, but President Ben Ali had manipulated laws and institutions in such a way that the RCD controlled governmental decision-making. Therefore, the argument was that on the one hand, one could have been a party member without *actually* having committed abuses of power, especially prior to 2001; on the other hand, to be a party member was to openly buy into/be complicit with the nondemocratic nature of the system.

[127] Interview with a Ben Achour Commission member, January 29, 2015.

[128] Article 15 specifies: "May not be candidate: all persons having assumed a position of responsibility within the government during the era of the fallen president, except those who were not members of the RCD, and all persons having assumed a position of authority within the RCD structures. The relevant responsibilities are set by decree following propositions of the Haute Instance: All persons having supported the candidacy of the fallen president for a new term in 2014. A list to this effect will be established by the Haute Instance" (DL 2011-35). However, experts criticized the article for not specifying procedures for individuals to challenge a decision placing them in one of those three categories, and that it "failed to notify banned persons" (Lamont, "Transitional Justice and the Politics of Lustration in Tunisia"; Lamont, "The

former regime without abandoning the TPA's strategy of inclusion, while also delaying the decision of dealing with former regime members outside that particular electoral process.

This postponement allowed the law to become yet another battle-ground for the Islamists and secularists in 2012 and 2013.[129] It differed, however, from the political jockeying that was occurring over other issues in that it gave voice to a common desire among victims of past repression, whether or not they identified as Islamists, to punish their repressors.[130] This instance of unity across ideological divisions could have led past victims to take sweeping revenge on their persecutors by targeting people based on their associations, rather than their actions (as is often the case in transitions).[131] And indeed, Enahda proposed in December 2013 a political exclusion or "lustration" law that would ban from government anyone who had been an RCD member for the full twenty-three years of Ben Ali's rule.[132]

The NCA ultimately did not pass the proposed lustration law. The TPA's decision to write a law for only the first elections and to delay the longer-term transitional justice decisions ended up being favorable to the transitional justice process. By taking more extensive decisions about categorically excluding RCD members from politics, the TPA could have prevented the cooperation that occurred later under the National Dialogue. Therefore, the TPA's self-restraint in trying to influence transitional justice of later phases proved in this sense to be a wise strategy.[133]

Scope and Boundaries of Transitional Justice in the Arab Spring," in Sriram, ed., *Transitional Justice in the Middle East and North Africa*, 92–93).

[129] See Gray, "In Search of Righting Wrongs."

[130] Lamont, "Transitional Justice and the Politics of Lustration in Tunisia."

[131] See Shain and Linz, eds., *Between States*, 97; O'Donnell and Schmitter, *Transitions from Authoritarian Rule*, 28–32; Lust, *Voting for Change*, 2.

[132] Lamont uses the term "lustration" "in reference to the vetting of individuals against the records of the former regime for membership in former ruling parties and other organizations associated with the maintenance of the former regime's political, economic, and social order. If found to be members of these parties or organizations, such individuals are excluded from either public service or electoral politics. As such, like lustration in post-Communist Europe, lustration in Tunisia is primarily aimed at excluding persons from transitional processes on the basis of past affiliations, which may not necessarily mean that an individual has committed a criminal offense."

[133] See Boduszynski and Henneberg, "Explaining Divergent Pathways of Post-Arab Spring Change."

These questions of how to try former regime members accused of crimes, the nature of reparations for the victims, and the nature of punishments for complicit party members were all linked to questions of broader judicial reform. Although various institutions of the TPA, notably the Amor Commission, had worked on recommendations for strengthening the independence of the judiciary, almost all decisions were left for successors to the TPA. This process, too, became heavily politicized under the NCA/Troika.

One of the TPA's first step toward judicial reform was through the organization of public powers decree law of March 23, 2011, which suspended the Constitutional Council. Although it did not suspend the Supreme Magistrates' Council (both councils under Ben Ali were supposed to guarantee the independence of the judicial system but in practice had been a tool of the president),[134] the NCA, under guidance from the TPA, did. Yet the Troika government's minister of justice soon restored the council, before the provisional authority meant to replace it according to the organization of public powers law passed in December 2011 could be formed. The necessary law for forming such an authority was finally passed in May 2013 due to relentless pressure from the judges' associations.[135] Yet like the Truth and Dignity Commission, the actual formation of the new council and the starting of its work was delayed by continuing political competition and crises, and was still being set up when the new constitution was passed.[136]

In addition, the new Justice Minister Nourdine Bhriri, of the Nahda party, dismissed eighty-two judges "who were claimed to be incontrovertibly linked to the Ben Ali regime" soon after he was appointed. This move caused great uproar among judges' associations as well as the human rights community because it was not made through

---

[134] Erdle (*Ben Ali's "New Tunisia,"* 170–172) describes how both councils under Ben Ali lacked independence from the executive branch – for one thing, they were headed by the president; the president also handpicked members of the former.

[135] Author meeting with a Tunisian legal expert, December 22, 2014. This was despite the rivalry between the two judges' organizations, the Syndicat des Magistrats Tunisiens (SMT) and the Association des Magistrats Tunisiens (AMT), which may have contributed to the delay.

[136] This, therefore, represents a deviation from the "roadmap" set by the NCA/Troika, because this provisional judicial authority was meant to be in operation and working toward guaranteeing judicial independence until the new constitution was passed. The TDC was only legally established with the passage of the transitional justice law DL 2013-53 in December 2013.

agreed-upon procedures.[137] Instead, as with Marzouki's "Black Book," it represented an attempt by figures holding power during the NCA/Troika period to dominate the transition process.

Despite some cautious steps by the TPA toward transitional justice mechanisms and judicial reform, and despite the favorable outcome on the political exclusion issue, some feared that certain opportunities for transitional justice may have been lost. Much has been written about the importance of truth commissions in helping a society overcome its torn past.[138] This includes both listening to victims' stories as part of the healing process and helping them understand what happened.[139] Building a clear "inventory of the past" also helps prevent the mistakes and crimes of the regime from being repeated by future governments. Yet such tasks require a collective dedication to certain nonpolitical goals; such a mentality was predominant in the TPA but immediately gave way to serious political competition under the Troika/NCA. Moreover, as discussed above, although the mentality of moving forward via consensus, cooperation, and compromise was somewhat restored with the National Dialogue and Jomaa government, and although this helped initiatives like the TDC and Supreme Magistrates Council move forward, the call for taking an "inventory of the past" faded away. By the end of 2015, the new permanently elected leaders of the country – many of whom were closely tied with the Bourguiba regime – were urging national conciliation by turning away from the past and looking to the future.[140]

Conclusion

In every aspect of its work, the TPA left a legacy for its successors. This was true even in areas where it didn't do anything! Sometimes, it launched aspects of transition from authoritarian rule that became institutionalized, such as the independent electoral commission (ISIE). Other times, when the TPA chose not to take any decisions, it left more

---

[137] Institute for Integrated Transitions, *Inside the Transition Bubble*, 21.
[138] See, for example, Gray, "In Search of Righting Wrongs."
[139] See, for example, Chekir, "La Commission d'établissement des Faits et la Justice Transitionelle," in Redissi et al., eds., *La Transition Démocratique en Tunisie: Les Thématiques*, 42.
[140] Meeting with Tunisian legal expert, December 22, 2014 (including the term "inventory of the past").

of a "blank slate" for its successor. In still other instances, the TPA took decisions or modeled behaviors that were sometimes ignored, then reappeared, occasionally via individuals from the TPA who had modeled them.

The ways in which this impact occurred reflect the simultaneous challenges and opportunities any first interim government will face. Although it was operating within numerous constraints, including limited time, resources, and experience, the TPA managed to organize Tunisia's first democratic elections, which gave way to subsequent phases of transition. And although it faced a plethora of challenges and struggled to balance authoritative decision-making with principles and strategies of inclusion and abiding by democratic principles, it also shaped processes of judicial and political reform going forward.

Despite the challenges and limited reform efforts described above, particularly around transitional justice, the country was abuzz with excitement when, on October 4, 2014, official campaigning for the presidential and parliamentary elections began. On October 26, Tunisians went to the polls to elect the first post–Ben Ali parliament (until then, all legislating bodies had been interim, even if one had been elected), and on November 23 and December 28, they elected a new president over two rounds of voting. Nida Tounis won and formed a coalition with Enahda, which had gained the second-highest number of seats. Béji Caïd Essebsi – who had played such a central role during the period of the TPA – was elected president.

The five years that followed in many ways bore the mark of the TPA. As described in Chapter 6, those years were launched in 2014 with the new constitution and the election of the first full post-uprising government, and they closed with the election in fall 2019 of a new president and parliament to replace them. But going into those elections, Tunisia was fraught with conflict and on the brink of a crisis. The consensus politics that characterized the TPA and were reintroduced during the later part of the NCA phase continued but also burdened the new government. Meanwhile, the space left for former regime members such as Caïd Essebsi and others to participate in Tunisia's new political system, while the result of choices made during the period of the TPA, severely compromised Tunisia's ability to bridge the old and new systems.

4 | The Libyan National Transition Council

This chapter describes the formation and work of the Libyan National Transition Council, or NTC. Unlike the Tunisian Provisonal Administration (TPA), the NTC became an interim government even as the *ancien régime* was still in place, rather than filling a complete vacuum as in other situations of authoritarian breakdown. It formed soon after the antiauthoritarian protests began and aimed to coordinate the defeat of the Qadhafi government and oversee day-to-day governance. The NTC needed to establish itself as a legitimate body that could ensure the representation of the Libyan people by facilitating democratic elections. In so doing, it took many actions and decisions, including recruiting membership, organizing itself, securing international assistance, developing a roadmap, coordinating the defeat of Qadhafi, and preparing for and overseeing elections. Each of these acts would have repercussions in the transitional phases to come.

Undertaking to coordinate the overthrow of a longstanding authoritarian government and the installation of a new democratic one presented enormous challenges. These included finding ways to match and defeat loyalist forces, fending off internal challengers (i.e. those who did not want to accept the NTC's decisions), and scrambling to find ways to effectively govern, given the chaotic conditions of the present and the authoritarian legacies of the past. These challenges also shaped and constrained the NTC's work.

Several themes emerge from this analysis. First, the Council was plagued by lack of cohesiveness and a clear, shared vision. Its work and decisions often reflected the fact that it was driven largely by the need to fill a leadership and governance void – that is, to fulfill the basic functions of a state and manage the armed struggle against the Qadhafi regime[1] – rather than a plan to build a new, democratic Libya. This left space for many actors pursuing an individualist, rather than a shared,

---

[1] Chorin, *Exit the Colonel*; Cole and McQuinn, eds., *The Libyan Revolution*.

agenda, to insert themselves. Second, like the TPA, the NTC often took decisions or actions out of perceived necessity, given the circumstances, but that would have implications out of its control. And finally, several decisions the NTC both did and did not take would lay the groundwork for the problems that would arise later on.

Historical Backdrop

In 1517, when the Ottomans first occupied parts of North Africa, the territory that would eventually become Libya comprised roughly three provinces: Cyrenaica in the east, whose features and influences came from the east; Tripolitania in the west, which had been part of the Roman Empire; and Fazzan in the south, which was mainly desert inhabited by nomads. Ottoman attempts to penetrate the interior and set up a bureaucratic administration that began in the mid-nineteenth century, like the Italian invasion seventy-five years later, were met with fierce resistance.[2] The religious order called the Sanusi movement that formed in Cyrenaica in the mid-nineteenth century brought basic governance structures to and a sense of identity among the tribes of the east, but with the end of World War II and Italy's defeat, the British took control of Tripolitania and Cyrenaica, while the French took control of Fazzan, both under military administrations.

When the French, Italians, and British collectively decided in 1949 to keep the three provinces unified as an independent Libyan state, a National Assembly convened by United Nations Commissioner Adrian Pelt produced a constitution granting substantial powers to the provincial governments.[3]

---

[2] For more on the Ottoman and Italian occupations, see Ahmida, *The Making of Modern Libya*; St John, *Libya*; Vandewalle, *A History of Modern Libya*. An excellent source on how these experiences contrasted with parallel occupations in Tunisia is Anderson, *The State and Social Transformation*. Because this background to the narrative is meant to be very general, it does not mention many details, such as the brief period of administration by the British, the short-lived agreement known as the *Legge Fondamentale* granting locals certain powers, periodic alliances between Cyrenaica and Tripolitania, or the important resistance to Italian occupation led by Omar Mukhtar.

[3] One proposal wanted to place each province under a separate trusteeship but granting them independence was more in line with French and British interests, as it would allow for air bases and potentially oil bases to be established there.

The leader was King Idris al-Sanusi, the heir to the Sanusi order, who ruled with little connection to his subjects.[4] Because the country had been formed without any historical sense of a unifying national identity, and because its new king failed to promote one, no strong sense of state, with a government able to extract resources and provide for its citizens, developed. Instead, the "most politicized and coherent group" in Libya became the military.[5] In September 1969 several officers formed a Revolutionary Command Council and staged a coup that overthrew King Idris. The country's new leader became twenty-seven-year-old Colonel Moammar Qadhafi.

Scholars often divide Qadhafi's forty-two-year-reign into three periods.[6] In the first, which lasted roughly from 1969 to 1975, he engaged in experimentation, including large amounts of state spending. Starting in 1973, however, he famously and systematically dismantled any modern state governance institutions that existed, attempting to rule under an ideology of "people's rule" (*Jamahouriya*). This system soon turned into one of highly personalistic rule, and ultimately his increasingly brutal repression of any form of dissent created an environment of atomization and distrust.[7] He took a hostile position toward the West, in an attempt to mobilize support for his revolution (after all, he had come to power under the banner of Arab Nationalism, modeled after the Egyptian revolution led by Gamal Abdel Nasser). His actions drove foreign powers to impose sanctions that badly damaged the economy, weakening his legitimacy.[8] Moreover, his strategy of harboring or

[4] Although the discovery of oil in 1959 and subsequent rapid economic growth strengthened the central government vis-à-vis the provincial governments and re-introduced a role for certain political actors outside the King's circles, the influx of funds nonetheless freed the palace (which already enjoyed substantial power) from the need to extract resources from the population and develop central state bureaucracy.
[5] Vandewalle, *A History of Modern Libya*, 45.
[6] See, for example, Martinez, *The Libyan Paradox*; Vandewalle, *A History of Modern Libya*.
[7] Qadhafi published his *Green Book* in 1977, which outlined his vision for "participatory government" based on Basic People's Congresses. He also created special "revolutionary" committees following a coup attempt in 1976 to monitor anti-revolutionary behavior. Committee members essentially acted as informers. As many scholars have noted, the result was a system controlled by the Qadhafi family or affiliated tribes and high levels of mistrust among the general population (in addition to other detrimental effects).
[8] These actions included, famously, the alleged sponsoring of terrorist attacks in Europe and bombings of two commercial flights in the late 1980s.

sponsoring terrorists as a way of defying the West became difficult once the global war on terror began.[9]

Qadhafi's third period was his "reform" from roughly 2000 to 2011, during which he introduced new institutions for economic development (some headed by figures who would become central actors during the period of the NTC).[10] During this period, relations with the West warmed, with Qadhafi agreeing to dismantle nuclear programs and to no longer harbor terrorists (providing an excuse to crack down even more harshly on the Islamist groups that opposed him).

Some scholars argue that this period highlights how susceptible Qadhafi had become to outside influences, for example, by needing to secure foreign oil contracts.[11] Open reactions to the regime's systematic bloody repression of opposition, such as the 1996 massacre of 1,200 prisoners in the Abu Salim prison in Tripoli, began pushing to the surface. On February 17, 2006, a major uprising was staged in Benghazi, in which the families of the Abu Salim massacre victims demanded their remains.[12] Although the Libyan government still managed to mobilize against protestors, the stage for events of 2011 was nearly set.[13]

Formation of the National Transition Council

The NTC formed against this historical backdrop following the outbreak of a historic protest movement on February 15, 2011. As mentioned in Chapter 1, these street protests began somewhat

---

[9] As several scholars assert, Qadhafi's opening and warming vis-à-vis the West was motivated by several factors, but chief among them was the threat of an American-led invasion such as the one in Iraq of 2003 (Martinez, *The Libyan Paradox*; Pargeter, *Libya: Reforming the Impossible?*).

[10] Some reform attempts had started as early as 1990.

[11] Martinez adds that the declining legitimacy of Qadhafi's *Jamahouriya* ideology helped increase the popularity of Western culture, but this heightened feelings of marginalization among Islamist opposition groups that had become active in the 1990s. Martinez, *The Libyan Paradox*.

[12] Another form of opposition to the Qadhafi government was in attempted coups, which some sources claim to have numbered at over fifty (Al-Toraifi, "Mustafa Abdel-Jalil on Libya's Revolution").

[13] For a detailed description of the attempted economic reforms undertaken by the regime beginning in 1999, and the obstacles they faced, see Pargeter, *Libya: Reforming the Impossible?* Pargeter attributes the 2006 protests to the population's frustrations with these undelivered promised reforms.

spontaneously in advance of a planned "Day of Rage," which appeared to be the result of pent-up resentment toward the government following decades of unfair policies and harsh repression of dissent, as well as perhaps inspiration from what had occurred in Tunisia a few weeks before.

As the movement grew and the response of the regime remained uncertain, communities in eastern Libya, whose uprisings appeared to be substantially threatening the regime, debated how to organize. In al-Baida, the minister of justice, (or secretary general of the General People's Committee of Justice, in the nomenclature of Qadhafi's *Jamahouriya* system), Mustafa Abd-al Jalil, resigned from the post he had held since 2007 and formed an organizing committee. Qadhafi's prime minister, Umar al-Baghdadi al-Mahmoudi, then called him by telephone; during that conversation, Jalil said that the protestors "sought 'a ceasefire, removal of the mercenaries, and a space to express their aspirations.'"[14]

Jalil and members of his committee soon began meeting with leaders of other local councils in the east, such as the one of about fifteen members (primarily lawyers, judges, and academics) that also formed in Benghazi at roughly the same time, and which became known as the Benghazi Council.[15] Through these meetings, the February 17 Coalition – less of a coalition and more of a spontaneous coming together of protestors – formed a small council of representatives from different eastern towns, which became the National Transition Council (NTC). The Benghazi Council soon chose a representative, Abdel Hafez Ghoga, to act as a delegate to the NTC. Representatives from other regions began doing the same.[16] Mustafa Abd-al Jalil soon emerged as NTC's chairman, and Ghoga his deputy.[17]

---

[14] Cole and McQuinn, eds., *The Libyan Revolution*, 33–34.
[15] Key individuals from that council were Kamel Hodeifah, Salah Ghazal, and Jamal Bennour.
[16] Presumably these representatives were selected through some kind of consensual process, as holding elections for representatives was not possible due to time and security constraints.
[17] According to the Economist Intelligence Unit, this was decided by March 1. See Economist Intelligence Unit, *Libya – Country Report*, February 2011. Cole and McQuinn also note that, others such as Abdelfatah Yunis were considered for the role of chairman, but in the end Jalil was chosen because a judge was preferable to a military leader. Cole and McQuinn, eds., *The Libyan Revolution*, 35.

Other local councils were also forming in towns around the country, especially as various towns became liberated (or wrested from the physical control of the government). Together all these groups also began coordinating the military effort as well as the delivery of public services.[18] For instance, the Benghazi council served as a transfer point for bringing materials in from or getting people out for medical treatment to Egypt.[19] These moves thus reflected an awareness of the need to, first, institutionalize the protests so their demands could be articulated, and second, ensure the provision of basic services in the face of a delegitimized regime.

Meanwhile, threats from the regime to use violence against protestors intensified, and the government cut the internet. But the NTC was rapidly gaining support from high-ranking representatives of the regime, as individuals such as Libya's permanent representative to the United Nations, Abd al-Rahman Shalgham and his deputy, Ibrahim Dabbashi, defected to the Council. Several of these defections were motivated by a nationally televised speech delivered by Saif al-Islam on February 20. Some NTC figures like Jalil had hoped that Saif al-Islam (Qadhafi's "reformist" son) would support them in a negotiation to remove Moammar Qadhafi from power, but the speech put that hope to rest. Although Saif al-Islam promised to start delivering on planned reforms, and although he criticized the security forces and admitted that the killing of protestors had been a mistake,[20] he also made clear that the regime would not relent in its fight against the opposition. The

---

[18] These groups tended to organize themselves according to local leadership dynamics. For instance, the International Crisis Group reports: "Cities' representatives to the NTC normally were decided by local councils in consultation with elders, militia leaders, and other prominent personalities, although the exact nature of the process in each case is unclear." International Crisis Group, *Divided We Stand*, 8.

[19] Benghazi council members apparently also served as especially critical links between the NTC and the other local councils. Interview with NTC member, November 9, 2014.

[20] This criticism may have been meant as an attack on his brother Saadi, who was in charge of the security forces. The speech contained several signs of the Qadhafi family's uncertainty over how to respond to the protests. For example, as Bell and Witter describe, he sometimes "ramble[d] and appeared desperate . . ." (although, they also concede, he was firm that the events of Tunisia and Egypt were not about to be repeated). Bell and Witter, *Roots of Rebellion*, 29.

standoff between the NTC (and the protest movement it claimed to represent) and the regime had fully begun.

Others who would end up taking on key NTC posts had been close to the regime but also defected right at the start of the uprisings. Benghazi native Ali Issawi, Qadhafi's ex-finance minister, had been the Libyan ambassador to India when the uprisings began; he resigned on February 21 to return to Libya and support the opposition movement. He became the head of foreign affairs for the NTC. Mahmoud Shamam was the NTC minister for media/information. Ali Tarhouni, who, like Shamam, had been living in exile as a professor at the University of Washington, became the NTC minister for oil and finance.[21]

The NTC quickly issued a set of demands on behalf of the protest movement, including fulfilling the government's promises since 2007 of a constitution and some limited reforms. The Council soon raised the protest movement's demands to include Qadhafi's removal from power and a full amnesty for revolutionaries. On February 22, it published a formal statement, or *bayan*, on the goals of the revolution. More specifically, this statement demanded "a civil state with a constitution, an independent judiciary, and a peaceful transition of power." It was announced on TV and radio, and sent to international media. Members of the NTC referred to this statement as a "victory statement for the revolution," presumably because it declared their intention to triumph over the old regime.

The next several days saw the first of several public contradictions by the NTC. On February 26, speaking from al-Baida, Chairman Jalil officially announced the creation of the NTC and declared that "it would govern for three months leading up to elections and the selection of a new leader." This was immediately followed by a statement made by Deputy Chairman Ghoga from Benghazi, that the NTC "would administer liberated eastern cities until Colonel Qadhafi's overthrow, and help free other cities in the country."[22] By March 1, the Council had rectified the confusion by stating that it was a unified body of which Jalil was chair and Ghoga was vice chair, and the NTC officially

---

[21] The other two Tripoli representatives were Alamin Bilhaj and Sadiq al-Kabir, both mentioned elsewhere.
[22] Economist Intelligence Unit, *Libya – Country Report*, March 2011, 12.

declared itself on March 5.[23] However, the incident foreshadowed the internal miscommunication and divergences that were to come.

The confusion created by these early conflicting statements was representative of several features of the NTC that would last throughout its tenure. First, it revealed the difficulty of reaching collective decisions, given the physical separation among NTC members, the lack of any precedent for such a council, and the need for secrecy due to Qadhafi's threats. Second, hesitation around calling itself a "government" likely stemmed from the NTC's fear of being seen as a new dictatorship or continuation of the Qadhafi regime.[24] Third, the NTC sought to constantly manage the tension between internal pressures and the need for support and recognition from the international community.[25] Such concerns would continue to color and shape the NTC's activities as time went on.

Moreover, the initial contradictory statements issued by two different members of the NTC immediately following its formation reflect the lack of a clear, central mission for the Council. The absence of a clear purpose was striking: the NTC was more concerned about what it was *not* than what it was. Once the NTC issued a statement declaring itself to be the representative of the opposition movement, it continued to be preoccupied with not being perceived as having seized power.[26] The NTC's meetings would last for days, and decisions over who would fill certain ministerial posts would drag on endlessly in attempts to reach collectively satisfying decisions.[27] As time went on, such concerns would frequently distract members of the NTC from pursuing other aims.

Garnering Legitimacy through Recruitment

Once declared, the NTC continued to bring individuals into its ranks. This effort was coupled with the need to become recognized as representative of the Libyan people and their desires. Targeting individuals

---

[23] See http://ntclibya.org/ (last accessed November 10, 2019).
[24] Cole and McQuinn, eds., *The Libyan Revolution*, 38.
[25] See Rangwala, "The Creation of Governments-in-Waiting," 215–216.
[26] Cole and McQuinn, eds., *The Libyan Revolution*, 38; Rangwala, "The Creation of Governments-in-Waiting," 221; Mundy, *Libya*, 86–87.
[27] Interview with an American diplomat, July 31, 2015. Also see Barfi, "Transitional National What?"

for recruitment or more generally widening its membership thus reflected the NTC's need to secure legitimacy.[28]

A general agreement emerged among the NTC's original members to recruit representatives from all parts of the country and from various oppositional perspectives. However, when it came to decisions about including some individuals, particularly those seen as potentially aligned with the Qadhafi regime, sharp disagreements arose. Ultimately, several individuals who joined the NTC initially would also serve in the post-liberation government that was formed after Qadhafi was killed. Others, however, would break away and become challengers to the NTC.

The original members used strategies of recruitment based on people's background, their constituencies, and sometimes their ability to accommodate all sides. In some cases, original Council members attempted to recruit people from large families or tribes or who could otherwise help form an alliance to counter Qadhafi's tribal and family network.[29] In other instances, however, the NTC recruited members specifically for their lack of affiliation. This reflected two fundamentals of Libyan society and state-society relations: the stark differences between geographical regions – in particular, a distinct, proud identity among those from the east, which had been reinforced through years of marginalization under Qadhafi, and the strong traditional family and tribal structures.[30] Given these sources of tension, it is not surprising that the NTC also had to use some of its energy fending off challengers.

The NTC was composed initially of critics of the regime who emerged to fill certain roles as the legitimacy of Qadhafi's government crumbled. Its chairman, Mustafa Abd al-Jalil, was a soft-spoken lawyer from al-Baida in the east. Born in 1952, Jalil was secretary of the public prosecutor in al-Baida and became a judge in 1978. He was the president of the court of appeals and then of the overall court system in al-Baida from 2002 to 2007 before becoming the minister

---

[28] As is clear in Chapter 2's discussion of how the TPA sourced its legitimacy, the concept is not easily defined. In the case of the NTC, it may be roughly akin to "recognized governing authority." In many cases, legitimacy might also be thought of as *earned* authority, but how much the NTC had earned its authority would, as described below, be disputed.

[29] Lacher, "Families, Tribes, and Cities in the Libyan Revolution"; Pack, ed., *The 2011 Libyan Uprisings*, 155.

[30] See Lacher, "Families, Tribes, and Cities in the Libyan Revolution."

of justice. In that role, Jalil had been openly critical of the regime, famously announcing his intention to resign due to his "inabilities to overcome the difficulties facing the judicial sector."[31] Jalil was considered "fairly apolitical and a "unifying figure," which (along with his history as a regime critic originally from the east who had intervened on behalf of the Abu Salim families) likely explains his nomination as the chairman of the NTC.[32] Deputy Chairman and spokesperson Abdel Hafez Ghoga was a human rights lawyer, former head of the Libyan Bar Association, and son of a senior Libyan diplomat who had served under both the monarchy and Qadhafi.

The man who became NTC's prime minister, sixty-year old Mahmoud Jibril, was educated at the University of Pittsburgh. In 2009 Jibril became chairman of the National Economic Development Board – an instrument of Qadhafi's reformist agenda of the 2000s. During this tenure, he had also become head of the Libyan National Planning Council, another powerful body in introducing liberal economic reforms during that time. In that period, he and other intellectuals were also involved with a project called Libyan Vision, which "sought to establish a democratic state."[33] It is unclear how Jibril became the prime minister (and eventually, foreign affairs representative) of the NTC.[34] However, several sources note that Jibril communicated well

---

[31] Qadhafi rejected his resignation, which was largely motivated by his opposition to the detention of innocent people. This was likely a government effort to retain reformist credentials. According to Human Rights Watch and US diplomatic cables, Jalil's critical views of the Libyan judicial sector were genuine (Gritten, "Key Figures in Libya's Rebel Council").

[32] Quote from an interview with an American diplomat, July 31, 2015. Other interviewees mentioned his network of tribal backings. Also see Chorin, *Exit the Colonel*, 236–269.

[33] Gritten, "Key Figures in Libya's Rebel Council"; Mezran and Alunni, "Libya: Negotiations for Transition," in Zartman, ed., *The Arab Spring*, 252–256.

[34] Various sources address this issue in different ways: Chorin (219) says Jalil selected Jibril (and Issawi) to travel to Paris to meet with Sarkozy in early March, but does not otherwise explain how he became prime minister. Cole and McQuinn (eds., *The Libyan Revolution*, 38) indicate that Jibril took on this title unbeknown to the other members when he was abroad. The International Crisis Group (*Holding Libya Together: Security Challenges after Qadhafi*, 8) wrote that "Jibril himself was never elected, and many rebels, particularly in the west, had little say in his appointment." Feelings that Jibril had "imposed" himself as the prime minister led to hostility toward him from other NTC members (interview with an NTC member, November 8, 2015). One individual from an important Misrata family, Abderrahmane Suweihli, proposed himself as an alternative prime minister; however, this appears to have been more motivated

with Western officials and diplomats; indeed, it was Jibril who met with French president Nicholas Sarkozy and the US Secretary of State Hillary Clinton in Paris in early March and ultimately persuaded them of the NTC's credibility.[35] This would quickly become vital for the work of the NTC.

Fathi al-Baja, a former journalist and academic who had long advocated for reform,[36] became influential in the NTC in several ways. He acted as a political advisor to Chairman Jalil, was close to the French intellectual Bernard-Henri Lévy (who helped orchestrate meetings between the NTC and French officials immediately after the NTC formed and publicly called for international intervention in the conflict), and played an instrumental role in drafting the NTC roadmap documents. Jamal Bennour, who had participated in the initial protests on February 15 and 16, was a lawyer and judge who would serve as a coordinator for justice on the Benghazi local council. Kamel Hodeifah, also a Benghazi judge, was, like Bennour, one of the first protestors in front of the Benghazi courthouse; he later served as the NTC coordinator for the Benghazi military council and the deputy minister of justice. Salah Ghazal, a longtime dissident in Benghazi who had been involved in the 2006 protests, was NTC's mayor of Benghazi until his resignation in January 2012. Ghazal was also one of the drafters of the NTC's original statement of February 22. Finally, there was Fathi Terbil, a well-known lawyer who had defended the families of the Abu Salim massacre victims and whose arrest on February 15 accelerated the planned Day of Rage. Terbil would become the youth minister in the NTC's

---

by local rivalries than by direct resentment of Jibril (Lacher, "Families, Tribes, and Cities in the Libyan Revolution").

[35] In a leaked diplomatic cable from 2009, American ambassador Gene Cretz had described Jibril as "a serious interlocutor who 'gets' the US perspective" (Gritten, "Key Figures in Libya's Rebel Council"). And it is worth quoting Ethan Chorin, who explains that Jibril "emerged at a critical time to articulate Libya's plight in a form that the West (Hillary Clinton, particularly) could understand. Whatever Libyans thought of him at the time, from the West's perspective he had a number of strong pluses: he was articulate; held a PhD from a respected American university, and he did not present as an Al Qaeda sympathizer." Chorin, *Exit the Colonel*, 269.

[36] Chorin describes one of Baja's experiences in publishing an article advocating for the drafting of a new constitution. See Chorin, *Exit the Colonel*, 162–163.

executive council and minster of youth and sport in the postliberation cabinet.[37]

As the coalition became the council and members began to take on
distinct portfolios, other individuals with histories of dissidence began
to join. As with other groups who would become part of the NTC,
these individuals came from different swaths of society. For instance,
Mohamed al-Alaqi, a Benghazi lawyer who had served as a senior
official in the Qadhafi Development Foundation headed by Saif al-
Islam, served as the NTC's minister for justice and human rights and
then as the justice minister after November 2011. Salwa Boughaigis, a
lawyer and activist in the Libyan Bar Association (who would push for
reforms of the legal system) prior to the uprisings, was from a well-
known dissident family in eastern Libya that had been closely associated with the Sanusi monarchy; Boughaigis served as the interim
minister of legal affairs and women's issues. Aref and Rafiq Nayid,
sons of a Benghazi businessman who made his wealth under the
monarchy,[38] became the CEO of the Libyan Investment Authority
(LIA) and a member of the NTC's stabilization team, respectively.

On the military side, NTC's recruitment drew individuals with
similar profiles. Omar al-Hariri had been a general who helped Qadhafi with his coup in 1969 but was imprisoned and sentenced to death
in 1975 when Qadhafi suspected him of plotting an uprising; Qadhafi
unexpectedly commuted his sentence in 1990 and placed him under
house arrest. Considered a hero among the rebels for his attempted
coup against Qadhafi in 1975, Hariri joined the NTC to help coordinate military affairs and "counsel" the young fighters.[39] Hariri, who
was from the Farjan tribe based in western Libya,[40] took the position
of the military affairs representative (or defense minister) when he first

---

[37] Other original members of the coalition eventually played more peripheral roles
in the actual operations of the NTC: these included Hana al-Jalal, who was
appointed to the NTC's executive council but soon resigned; Abdelsalam al-
Mismari, another lawyer who joined the initial protests at the Benghazi
courthouse (Mismari was tragically shot and killed by extremist groups on July
26, 2013); and Zahi Mugharbi. Mismari and Mugharbi both eventually formed
their own groups outside the NTC, each with its own proposals for Libya's
future.
[38] Lacher, "Families, Tribes, and Cities in the Libyan Revolution," 159.
[39] Gritten, "Key Figures in Libya's Rebel Council."
[40] This tribe had a strong presence near Qadhafi's hometown of Sirte, and "his
appointment may have been aimed at wooing influential tribes" (Gritten, "Key
Figures in Libya's Rebel Council").

joined the NTC. This position was later taken over by Osama Juweili, who had initially commanded the Zintan Military Council. Juweili had been a major in the army's electronic support unit, and had left the army in 1992.[41] Similarly, Khalifa Haftar had been living in exile ever since his falling out with Qadhafi following the Libyan invasion of Chad in the 1980s. He, too, was an obvious candidate for the NTC forces owing to his military experience and history of opposition and resistance.[42] Overall, such original NTC members appeared as dissidents or reformers who had been "in waiting."[43]

Several others played key roles as well. Ali al-Awjali, who had been serving as the ambassador in the United States, became the minister of culture and community affairs. Naji Barakat served as the minister for health. Anwar Fituri was the minister for transportation and communication; Hania al-Gumia was NTC's minister for social welfare; and Bilgasim al-Numir was NTC's minister for environment. Issa Abdul-Majjid Mansour, of the Kufra-based Tubu ethnic group, was appointed to supervise Libya's southeast border security.[44] Other members from Libya's south who also belonged to ethnic minorities included the former consul to Mali, Musa al-Kuni (a Touareg).[45] Overall, this mix of historical influences by individual figures and the social groups to whom they were linked, although reflective of the NTC's recruitment strategy, highlights the lack of cohesion or clear characteristics that marked the NTC and often produced fault lines within it.[46]

---

[41] Cole and McQuinn, eds., *The Libyan Revolution*, 269.

[42] Haftar had reportedly led armed opposition groups alleged to have received support from foreign intelligence agencies and been involved in past attempts to overthrow Qadhafi. See Barfi, "Khalifa Haftar: Rebuilding Libya from the Top Down," 4–5; Blanchard, *Libya: Unrest and US Policy*, June 6, 2011, 39–40.

[43] This term is used by various sources specifically in regard to the NTC to suggest an opposition government in exile that is poised to take the helm once a regime has lost sufficient support, especially thanks to international recognition. See, for example, Pargeter, *Libya: The Rise and Fall of Qadhafi*, 239; Rangwala, "The Creation of Governments-in-Waiting."

[44] Pack, ed., *The 2011 Libyan Uprisings*, 178.

[45] Pack, ed., *The 2011 Libyan Uprisings*, 184.

[46] Abdul Ilah Moussa al-Meyhoub, a French-educated law professor who had criticized Qadhafi's political and social theories, became in charge of legal affairs in Quba. Sadiq al-Kabir was the NTC representative from Tripoli along with Abdelrahman al-Kib. Finally, Suleiman al-Fortiya, a representative in Misrata, was a British-educated engineering professor who had been teaching at King Faisal University in Saudi Arabia. In addition, Gritten lists six other NTC

Despite the representation of various social groups, the Council felt it needed to be broadened still further in order to defeat the Qadhafi regime. In particular, the NTC sought to persuade key military leaders to defect to their side. Abdelfatah Yunis, Qadhafi's former interior minister and the minister for public security and special forces commander in the east, thus became the top commander for the opposition. The NTC was initially divided over whether to encourage Yunis to join them because some doubted whether he would truly break with Qadhafi. The NTC negotiated with him through the February 17 coalition members, NTC representatives, or other representatives of the protestors, and Yunis was ultimately persuaded. Another individual, Abdel-monem al-Houni, like Hariri, had been part of Qadhafi's coup in 1969, later had a falling out and become a regime opponent, but reconciled with Qadhafi in 2000. Al-Houni was serving as a Libyan delegate to the Arab League when the uprisings broke out, and apparently polled other members of the delegation on whether or not they would join him.[47] While al-Houni's precise role in the NTC is not clear, it is notable that he was acting as a close advisor to Saif al-Islam, Qadhafi's son, up until the last minute, even helping draft his February 20 speech, before defecting to the NTC side.[48]

Meanwhile, as towns across Libya became liberated, an increasing number sent representatives to serve on the NTC's legislative council, in part to show that the NTC was not dominated by eastern interests. These representatives were selected by local community leaders (such as tribal elders, local notables, and sheikhs), since, due to insecurity and general infrastructure challenges, holding local elections was not

---

members important on local councils but does not give their backgrounds. Their names are Uthman Suleiman al-Megrahi (Batnan); Ashour Hamid Bu Rashid (Derna); Hassan Ali al-Dirwai (Sirte); Mustafa al-Salihin Mohammed al-Huni (Jafra); Hassan Mohammed al-Saghir (al-Shati); and Idris Mohammed Mohammed Bu Fayed (no location given).

[47] Chorin, *Exit the Colonel*, 201.

[48] Cole and McQuinn (eds.) mention a few other military figures, including Major Ali Amlish, a defected army officer who played a central role in developing NTC's military strategy, and Yusuf al-Manqoush, who became the armed forces chief in January 2012 and was therefore closely involved with the security sector reform efforts. Cole and McQuinn, eds., *The Libyan Revolution*, 138–139, 142–143, and 272.

possible.[49] By May, the legislative council had about forty members.[50] While the NTC's consistent reluctance to release the names of all its members led to accusations that it lacked transparency,[51] it nonetheless insisted on the strategy of broadening its geographic representation in order to secure legitimacy.

Several key players in the NTC also came from important aristocratic families from eastern Libya, often with links to the monarchy.[52] Ahmed al-Zubair al-Sanusi, from the important Sanusi family of Cyrenaica and one of Libya's longest held political prisoners,[53] was also a member of the February 17 Coalition. Mansour Saif al-Nasr, who served as NTC's ambassador to France, and Abdelmajid al-Nasr, from Sabha, were both from a tribe of notables who had once been dominant in Fezzan. Others included Mohamed Montasir, NTC's representative from Misrata and also from a historically important family, and Othman Ben Sassi, NTC's representative for Zuwara and son of a businessman who made his wealth under the monarchy.

Like others, this category of individuals (that is, those from prominent eastern families) was not always unified in its stance toward the NTC, contributing to the overall lack of cohesion among NTC actors. Although al-Sanusi had been a member of the February 17 Coalition in Benghazi, other members of the Sanusi family had organized a

[49] Moreover, the actual degree to which the member represented his or her (usually his) town was sometimes unclear. Henry Smith, in his contribution to Pack (ed., *The 2011 Libyan Uprisings*), makes this point about Musa al-Kuni, who ostensibly represented the Libyan Touareg, and one interviewee confirmed this idea (interview with Libyan journalist, September 14, 2019).

[50] Some representatives came to Benghazi by boat, since land travel was too dangerous. Over the month of April, twenty-three Libyan towns from western, central, and southern Libya sent representatives, with most remaining publicly unnamed for security reasons. These new representatives first met in Abu Dhabi and then Doha before returning to Benghazi on May 12 (Cole and McQuinn, eds., *The Libyan Revolution*, 40–41). The total number of NTC members grew as time went on, and by summer had reached fifty-one, including at least one woman. However, the exact final number remains unclear.

[51] Barfi, "Transitional National What?"; Interview with a foreign NGO worker, November 3, 2014.

[52] See Lacher, "Families, Tribes, and Cities in the Libyan Revolution."

[53] Al-Sanusi had been jailed following the failed counter-coup against Qadhafi in 1970. He was released in August 2001. For Zoubir and Rózsa, having Sanusi in the NTC's ranks also provided it with "religious legitimacy," given his connections to the country's religious leaders. Zoubir and Rózsa, "The End of the Libyan Dictatorship," 1271.

"royalist contingent" based in London. This contingent was led by Mohammed Rida al-Sanusi, the son of the former crown prince. As the NTC was taking shape, Mohammed al-Sanusi was reportedly meeting with members of the European Parliament to advocate for reinstating the 1951 constitution.[54]

Following the death and capture of Qadhafi and Jalil's liberation statement of October 23, 2011, the NTC elected a new prime minister, Abderahman al-Kib. Al-Kib had been one of the NTC representatives from Tripoli, and he was to appoint a new interim cabinet (its Constitutional Declaration of August 3 had promised this, as the portfolios and positions of the NTC cabinet members were meant to be temporary).[55] Al-Kib was elected by the members of the NTC's legislative council; he received almost 50 percent of the votes. Like Jalil, al-Kib was seen as an apolitical, unifying choice.[56] The government he appointed reflected a similar attempt to balance eastern and western interests as well as the various ideologies that had come to be present on the Council. Indeed, many cabinet members' deputies – including al-Kib's – came from the Muslim Brotherhood, reflecting the movement's growing influence in the Council.[57] However, this aspect of its recruitment strategy – trying to please all sides – would prove consequential.[58]

In addition to these dissidents, lawyers, military leaders, academics, businessmen, and tribal or monarchy-linked figures, individuals participating in Libyan opposition groups, all of whom had been operating in exile when the uprisings began, also gradually became incorporated, in some fashion, into the council. Historically, Islamist groups are among the most important of these.[59] The National Conference of Libyan Opposition (NCLO) was the most important opposition group in existence prior to

---

[54] Lacher notes one other NTC member, Ahmed al-Abbar, whose family had been closely associated with the Sanusi monarchy, but his actual role with the NTC is unclear. Lacher, "Families, Tribes, and Cities in the Libyan Revolution," 143.
[55] Article 30.
[56] Interview with an American diplomat working in Tripoli, July 31, 2015; Mezran and Alunni, "Libya: Negotiations for Transition," 269. For a discussion of how other cabinet members were selected for their posts, see Mundy, *Libya*, 122.
[57] Interview with an American diplomat, July 31, 2015; interview with Libyan activists, December 4, 2014.
[58] For more on this, see, for example, Pack et al., *Libya's Faustian Bargains*; Pack and Cook, "The July 2012 Libyan Election and the Origin of Post-Qadhafi Appeasement."
[59] For more information, see Pack, ed., *The 2011 Libyan Uprisings*, 194–206; Ashour, *Libyan Islamists Unpacked: Rise, Transformation, and Future*, 1–2.

the formation of the NTC. The NCLO was an umbrella organization that called for protests against the Qadhafi regime. It had brought together several opposition groups based outside of Libya into an alliance in July 2005.[60] During this meeting, which took place in London, participants signed a national accord "calling for the removal of Qadhafi from power and the establishment of a transitional government."[61] A follow-up meeting was held in March 2008. Other than its initial calling for the Day of Rage, however, it does not appear that the NCLO remained a unified group with influence during the period of the NTC.

Also making its way into the array of actors involved with the NTC's work during this period was the Muslim Brotherhood. One of the largest Islamist groups in the country, the Libyan branch of the Muslim Brotherhood had, as the result of severe repression since 1973, been operating clandestinely and outside of Libya. By this point, a nominally Islamist-secularist divide was emerging: several of Libya's longtime opposition activists were Islamists or belonged to Islamist organizations, and they were naturally trying to stake their space in the country's future. The NTC's "secular" profile – composed mostly of lawyers and academics – had worried some Islamists.[62] This competition would intensify and become increasingly violent.[63]

One of the most important figures associated with the Brotherhood was Ali al-Sallabi, who had participated in past dialogues between the Qadhafi government and the Islamists. Sallabi was known to Libyans for his Islamic scholarship;[64] in mid-2011 he was instrumental in

[60] Participants included the National Alliance, the Libyan National Movement (LNM), the Libyan Movement for Change and Reform, the Islamist Rally, the National Libyan Salvation Front (NLSF), and the Republican Rally for Democracy and Justice.

[61] Blanchard, *Libya: Unrest and US Policy*, 40, June 6, 2011. For more background on the NCLO, also see International Crisis Group, *Popular Protests in North Africa: Making Sense of Libya*, 19, and Alunni, "Long-Distance Nationalism and Belonging in the Libyan Diaspora (1969–2011)." According to Alunni, the NCLO and its collaboration with some diaspora groups adhering to an Islamist ideology served as the basis for diaspora mobilization in 2011.

[62] Cole and McQuinn, eds., *The Libyan Revolution*, 183.

[63] It should be noted that the identity of most Libyans is still strongly Islamist, so this labeling "secular" is relative. See, for example, Mezran, "Libya Has Successful Elections but Not Yet Democracy"; Lacher, "Fault Lines of the Revolution."

[64] According to some sources, Sallabi was also "respected enough to be independent from any political group but whose ideas are considered close to the Muslim Brotherhood (and) spent much of the 1980s in Abu Salim Prison before

organizing a "National Gathering" of Islamist groups, partly intended to challenge the NTC. After some internal tension, the Brotherhood left the National Gathering and in March 2012 formed a political party, the Justice and Construction Party, which would go on to be a main competitor in the GNC elections.[65] Prior to this effort to carve out its own space in Libyan politics, many Brotherhood members held positions on the NTC, including Abdallah Shamia, minister of economics, and Alamin Bilhaj, one of the NTC representatives from Tripoli. In addition, Brotherhood members were observed to have been present in emerging groups such as the local councils.[66] In these ways, preexisting Islamist organizations such as the Brotherhood took on an increasingly important role in the Council, even though the NTC had begun with a more "secular" identity.

Libya's second largest Islamist opposition group was originally named the Libyan Islamic Fighting Group (LIFG). Unlike the Brotherhood, this group espoused the use of violence, and had waged a "low-level insurgency" against the regime during the mid-1990s.[67] The LIFG's original leadership had come largely from Libyan university campuses. The next generation of leaders had mostly studied abroad in the 1970s and 1980s; they were influenced by the Muslim Brotherhood ideology.[68] Many members had fought against the Soviets in the 1980s in Afghanistan. By the late 1990s, as a result of its opposition and tactics, hundreds of LIFG members in Libya had been imprisoned or forced into exile.

In 2009, the LIFG's imprisoned leaders renounced violence and entered into dialogue with the Qadhafi Foundation, headed by Saif al-Islam. At the very start of the uprisings, with the release of leading

living in exile in various Gulf countries, most recently Qatar ... During the uprisings he traveled between Qatar and Libya, not only visiting rebel soldiers but also negotiating the Qadhafi family's departure" (International Crisis Group, *Holding Libya Together*, 11). However, as Cole and McQuinn (eds.) explain, his public speeches sometimes ended in controversy. Cole and McQuinn, eds., *The Libyan Revolution*, 193–194.

[65] For more detail on the party's reestablishment in Libya during and after these elections, see Fitzgerald, "Introducing Libya's Muslim Brotherhood."
[66] International Crisis Group, *Holding Libya Together*, 10.
[67] Lacher, "Families, Tribes, and Cities in the Libyan Revolution," 147; Cole and McQuinn, eds., *The Libyan Revolution*, 57.
[68] One way this group overlapped with the Brotherhood was through members' shared experiences as prisoners in Abu Salim. Cole and McQuinn, eds., *The Libyan Revolution*, 179–180.

LIFG figures from prison, the group announced its reorganization and new name, the Libyan Islamic Movement for Change (LIMC). This group now rejected violence as a means of achieving its goals. After the revolution began, several LIFG members were recruited by the various local military councils in the early months following the uprising. One former LIFG leader and one of the organization's founders, Abdelhakim Bilhaj, became increasingly important within the NTC, including by leading one of the Tripoli military groups that liberated the city.[69]

A number of other figures with an Islamist identity were important in the NTC. First, the National Libyan Salvation Front (NLSF) was a member of the NCLO, which also had links with Islamist groups such as the LIFG and joined forces with groups and networks in Tripoli that formed at the start of the uprisings. The NLSF was a central part of the February 17 Coalition of opposition fighting groups in Tripoli (*Itilaf al-sabatash Febriar* – distinct from the February 17 Coalition mentioned above, which formed in Benghazi as a precursor to the NTC), which eventually helped defeat Qadhafi in their city and gained increasing influence with the NTC in the months following.[70]

Finally, Sheikh al-Sadiq al-Gharyani, another religious scholar, had also been the former head of the Supreme Council for Fatwas under Qadhafi.[71] Gharyani, like Sallabi, often preached to Libyans on national television, including on the eve of the battle for Tripoli; the NTC appointed him as head of the Libyan authority for interpreting Islamic law, where he played an initially stabilizing role.[72]

The figure of al-Gharyani represents the way fighting groups, Islamist figures, and former government people all came together in the NTC. The NTC initially emerged as local councils formed to consolidate the uprising and as a coalition of lawyers and activists in Benghazi

---

[69] Another was Sami al-Saadi; differences between Saadi and Bilhaj would later split the movement. See Wehrey, *The Struggle for Security in Eastern Libya*; Pack, ed., *The 2011 Libyan Uprisings*, 215.
[70] Cole and McQuinn, eds., *The Libyan Revolution*, 63–104.
[71] He was also a supervisor and teacher at Al-Fateh University's Department of Islamic Studies in Tripoli, International Crisis Group, *Holding Libya Together*, 11.
[72] In this case, at least, his preaching seemed to have a more positive effect than Sallabi's, whose speech given around the same time, in which he strongly criticized Jibril, was more controversial. Cole and McQuinn, eds., *The Libyan Revolution*, 193–194; Lacher, "Fault Lines of the Revolution," 14–15.

sought to put a "face" to the revolution. A perceived need to recruit representatives from Libya's many societal groups, including Islamist opposition groups, and to strengthen its forces by incorporating former loyalists (especially military), caused NTC membership to widen. Although bringing together this wide array of members seemed necessary at the time, it would contribute to difficulties as time went on.

Establishing New Governing Institutions

The NTC, like many interim governments, was not organized in advance of a *coup d'état* or any other premediated method of taking over from the Qadhafi government.[73] Therefore, it did not necessarily form with responsibilities of governing in mind. Yet it soon found itself tasked with the provisioning of public services, securing financing for the revolutionary effort as well as daily governance, and the managing of foreign relations.[74]

Many analysts have pointed to Libya's "stateless" character during and prior to the Qadhafi period.[75] In contrast to Tunisia and Egypt, Libya did not have a long history of living under a single entity that worked through security, economic, political, and judicial institutions to exert a monopoly on the legitimate use of coercion over the territory.[76] This meant that although the NTC tried to form an institutional structure for these functions, it was far from state-like. By and large,

---

[73] Two comments are in order. First, as noted, there was some speculation that the NTC emerged out of a preplanned coup attempt or some other form of cooperation against Qadhafi that was thwarted when the uprisings on February 15 began (Pack, ed., *The 2011 Libyan Uprisings*, 45–46; Mezran and Alunni, "Libya: Negotiations for Transition," 254). Second, this claim should be qualified, as revolutionary interim governments occasionally *do* have a chance to work and develop as an organization before taking power. Perhaps the most famous case is the Gouvernement Provisoire de la République Algérienne (GPRA) in Algeria (see Shain and Linz, *Between States*; Rangwala, "The Creation of Governments-in-Waiting").

[74] Interview with an NTC member, November 9, 2014. Also see Cole and McQuinn, eds., *The Libyan Revolution*, 57.

[75] E.g. Vandewalle, *A History of Modern Libya*; Anderson, *The State and Social Transformation*.

[76] Weber, "Politics as a Vocation," in Gerth and Mills, eds., *From Max Weber: Essays in Sociology*.

Libyans were carrying out the daily functions of governing without norms, rules, and processes through which to work.

Like the TPA, the NTC lacked a Libyan precedent as well as inherited governing documents to guide it. The NTC therefore sought to survive by relying on the methods it knew. It structured itself on the local congresses and popular committees that had been the local governance structures and a national parliament under the old regime.[77] Meetings (including, presumably, at the level of the local councils) were described as extremely inefficient, in part because decisions were meant to be collective rather than based on an hierarchy. Debates over who would fill certain ministerial posts would drag on endlessly, in attempts to reach collectively satisfying decisions.[78]

The NTC formed central governing institutions whose performance appeared effective at the start but quickly weakened as time went on. As the NTC was forming, around the country local councils continued to fill in for state functions, such as providing basic public goods including security. In theory these local councils were subordinate to the NTC. As time went on, however, the extent of the NTC's control over the local councils and the relationship between them became increasingly murky.[79] The local councils frequently appeared to hold more responsibility for managing day-to-day public affairs than the NTC.[80] Some, such as that of Bani Walid, expressed resentment toward the NTC for its anti-Qadhafi stance and its attempts to centralize authority, and demanded a certain devolution of power.[81] Thus, rather than finding ways to complement one another (with the NTC

---

[77] Interview with an American diplomat, July 31, 2015. Also noted in Pack, ed., *The 2011 Libyan Uprisings,* 73. Roughly speaking, the NTC had local councils (the equivalent of the Basic People's Congresses) that sent delegates to a national congress (akin to the General People's Congress), while something like a ministerial cabinet (the Executive Committee for the NTC; the elected General Popular Committee under the *Jamahirriya*) also existed under both systems.

[78] Interview with an American diplomat, July 31, 2015. Also noted in Barfi, "Transitional National What?"

[79] Blanchard, *Libya: Unrest and US Policy,* June 6, 2011, 38–39.

[80] Interview with a foreign NGO worker, November 3, 2014. An American diplomat working in Tripoli said he believed the NTC *was* effective at coordinating the local delivery of services; however, that same interviewee noted the important role of Libya's "unsung heroes," meaning citizens bravely volunteering to protect and help the people of their towns survive. Interview, July 31, 2015.

[81] Pack and Barfi, *In War's Wake,* 12.

focusing on external support, for instance, and the local councils focusing on internal governance), the NTC and the local councils exhibited a weak structural relationship.

Meanwhile, towns were arming themselves in the fight against the Qadhafi regime. The NTC managed to set up a central command structure in Benghazi, meant to oversee all the local military councils/ fighting groups ("revolutionary brigades"), thereby creating what it called the National Army (also called the "Free Libya Armed Forces)."[82] The main task of the central army leadership was to guide the local brigades in defeating Qadhafi's forces; it also served as the counterpart for the NATO operation that supported the opposition movement in its struggle to take down Qadhafi. However, several local military councils reportedly had independent funding, allowing them to operate outside NTC's control.[83] This challenge, combined with the indiscipline and inexperience of many of the fighters, thwarted the effectiveness of the national army and the international coalition that was assisting it.[84]

The NTC also often lacked control and awareness of the movement of weapons into and across the country. Some groups were armed with weapons they had looted from the former regime's stockpiles or that the regime had distributed; others acquired weapons as foreign powers gave their support to various units. Several arms depots remained unsecured, and the disarray of the state army and police left people feeling vulnerable, leading to hoarding of arms and ammunitions. Minefields laid by loyalist troops in different regions of the country

---

[82] Analysts such as McQuinn distinguish among the groups doing the major fighting from February to October 2011: "post-revolutionary brigades" which formed after the fall of Qadhafi, and other, generally more violent and extremist militias. However, as the International Crisis Group reported at the time, and others subsequently noted, use of the term "revolutionary" became increasingly problematic after the country had been liberated, causing struggles over legitimacy and control. These issues are discussed in more detail in Chapter 5. See McQuinn, "Armed Groups in Libya: Typology and Roles"; International Crisis Group, *Divided We Stand*, 10–11.

[83] E.g. International Crisis Group, *Divided We Stand*, 19.

[84] Suleiman el-Obeidi, after he replaced Yunis as the National Army's chief of staff, often didn't control the local military councils. Those that funded themselves reportedly raised money through local activist groups, pressuring businessmen, or sometimes being suspected of taking foreign money. International Crisis Group, *Divided We Stand*, 19–20.

also needed to be cleared.[85] Though the NTC made some efforts to monitor the weapons coming into the country and to control human rights violations by its fighters,[86] managing armed groups was a challenge that plagued the NTC from beginning to end.

The NTC's central cabinet/executive committee, formed in mid-April, was another example of the NTC's lack of structural capacity. This office began as a Crisis Management Committee led by Prime Minister Jibril, and with the explicit task of interfacing with the international community. By mid-June, it had become an Executive Office (or cabinet), with individuals taking on ministerial portfolios such as health, finance, and foreign affairs.[87] Mahmoud Jibril was the head of the office, and Ali Issawi was his deputy. By June the Executive Council comprised fourteen ministerial portfolios; there were also a few "ministers at large."[88] The executive office was to oversee day-to-day affairs, while the legislative arm drafted and voted on interim laws for the country.[89]

Thus, within a few months, the NTC's Executive Office had grown from something ad hoc, reactive, and loosely modeled on the previous system to a body with a wide range of responsibilities. This new organizational structure helped solidify the functions of key ministries such as the Defense Ministry, which was to be in charge of weapons

---

[85] Bell and Witter, *The Tide Turns*, 25.

[86] Interview with an NTC member, November 8, 2014; also see Cole and McQuinn, eds., *The Libyan Revolution*, 127–176. However, other descriptions of "prison centers" established during the NTC period illustrate the limit to which the NTC could control human rights violations. See Mattes, "Libya Since 2011: Political Transformation and Violence," 67.

[87] The education portfolio was ultimately left unfilled: it was initially given to Hana al-Jalal, who resigned early on.

[88] In addition to these Libya-based ministers, the NTC appointed four diplomatic representatives abroad. This reflects the NTC's prioritization of shoring up international support.

[89] Again, the division of labor between these institutions is a bit murky. According to Cole and McQuinn (eds.), "Over time the Crisis Management Committee became an executive implementation body – the 'Executive Committee', with the NTC like a legislature responsible for devising policy. Perhaps a better division might have been external and internal affairs. However, the precise relationship between the NTC and the Executive Committee was never completely settled and was a source of tension throughout the revolution." Cole and McQuinn, eds., *The Libyan Revolution*, 38.

being supplied to the NTC from Qatar and elsewhere.[90] However, the executive committee was formed in order to create a certain impression (largely for the international community), not to fill any particular structural gap. As Cole and McQuinn explain:

This management overhaul and structural metamorphosis allowed for the impression that the NTC was better able to address the growing list of issues under its purview. This included efforts to help Misrata and communities displaced by fighting in the Nafusa Mountains; deal with the proliferation of security groups in Benghazi; tackle corruption on the Egyptian border, which was impeding imports; manage local councils; receive an increasing number of visiting delegations; and feed an insatiable and growing group of foreign patrons with the story that the NTC had a plan for everything, which it did not.[91]

In short, the NTC was now organized more superficially than effectively.

Meanwhile, the fight between the opposition and the regime for control of the Western Mountains and the western cities of Zintan, Misrata, and Zawiya were long and difficult. Zintan became the center of the Western Military Council (WMC), which coordinated closely with Benghazi to get funds and supplies and was central in the battle for Tripoli. The WMC also claimed to act as an umbrella for some 140 military councils. Finally, the Misrata Military Council (MMC) became the strongest and most independent (vis-à-vis the NTC) of all local military councils, reportedly even going to Paris to meet with international allies unbeknown to or unapproved by the NTC.[92] Generally, these local brigades in the west – as well as those in the east – were known for their loose central command and consensus-oriented decision-making.[93]

The NTC's preliberation military units in Tripoli were representative of its organizational and structural weakness. Tripoli fighting forces

---

[90] See Cole and McQuinn, eds., *The Libyan Revolution*, 72. However, the International Crisis Group reveals that the ability of the Defense Ministry to carry out such functions was not so clear. International Crisis Group, *Divided We Stand*, 21, n. 160.

[91] Cole and McQuinn, eds., *The Libyan Revolution*, 42–43.

[92] Bell and Witter, *Stalemate & Siege*, 28.

[93] McQuinn, "Armed Groups in Libya," 2; International Crisis Group, *Divided We Stand*, 3. For more detail on these brigades and the friction among them, also see Cole and McQuinn, eds., *The Libyan Revolution*, 257–284.

began forming in February, after an initial peaceful uprising was suppressed. Various individuals and groups began to organize themselves in order to battle regime forces, through networks that "cut across neighborhoods"[94] and with help from outside forces and regime defectors. Several of the most prominent of these networks formed the February 17 Coalition (*Itilaf al-sabatash Febriar*), which was critical for the oppositionist victory during the battle for Tripoli.

This arrangement of military groups was unstable throughout the NTC period, especially once Tripoli fell. Abdelhakim Bilhaj, who had become increasingly important in the fight for Tripoli, emerged as the central figure in leading and organizing those forces. On August 25 he announced the formation of the Tripoli Military Council, which oversaw several military brigades in Tripoli. One of these was another important Tripoli brigade, the Tripoli Revolutionaries Battalion, headed by Mehdia al-Hariati, who became the Council's deputy. Although the Tripoli Military Council supposedly had NTC Chairman Jalil's backing, it was frequently criticized and challenged.[95]

The NTC was largely ineffective at managing these disparate fighting groups. With the launch of the NATO mission, outside actors and members of the NTC were all coming under increasing pressure to demonstrate to international governments and reassure constituents that they had a plan for rebuilding Libya once the military struggle had concluded. As part of this effort, members of the NTC's executive committee proposed in early May a Tripoli Taskforce to oversee military efforts to liberate Tripoli and postliberation stabilization, which would also play a role in coordinating the increasing foreign military and technical support arriving in Benghazi.[96] This taskforce was originally intended to include ten thousand to fifteen thousand Libyan troops, supported by foreign forces from the United Arab Emirates.[97]

---

[94] International Crisis Group, *Divided We Stand*, 4.
[95] International Crisis Group, *Divided We Stand*, 21.
[96] Cole and McQuinn, eds., *The Libyan Revolution*, 67.
[97] See Economist Intelligence Unit, *Libya – Country Report*, August 2011, 10. As described below, the UAE was one of the Arab states initially cooperating with the NATO coalition to protect the rebels from regime violence but that would come to provide arms and other forms of support to certain groups, helping fuel Libya's internal conflict.

However, due to power struggles within the NTC and accusations of exclusion by tribal and regional groups, the Tripoli Taskforce would not last. Ultimately, its leader, Aref Nayid, recommended to Jalil that it be reconstituted as a "stabilization committee" to be headed by Jibril. This stabilization committee worked with the United Nations and international community and local councils in the Nafusa Mountains to prepare for the fall of Tripoli. However, it was constrained by a lack of knowledge and skills of its members as well as a division among staff of loyalties to the Tripoli Local Council and the central NTC ministries. Loyalty of fighters was often accorded based on the connections that had brought them into the taskforce.[98] By the time Tripoli fell to the opposition in late August, the NTC's attempt at institutionalizing military and security efforts had been drastically weakened.

Given this chaos, the NTC struggled to keep internal tensions and rivalries from emerging. First, there was much speculation that Chairman Jalil and Prime Minister Jibril did not get along, or at the very least did not communicate well.[99] Several individuals resented the manner in which Jibril joined the council, having not been among the original Benghazi-based members and immediately traveling to Doha in February 2011.[100] Jalil's appointment incited another kind of suspicion, simply because he had been a minister under Qadhafi who suddenly became the lead representative of the opposition. The chaotic conditions and need for outside support, however, meant that even people with reservations about Jalil or Jibril felt forced to accept them for the sake of unity.[101] These authoritative bodies' inability to control the country's mosques was another example of their inability to act as a source of stability.[102] In short, the NTC's executive and legislative bodies consistently stumbled in their efforts to act as central guiding authorities.

An even uglier fault line developed within the NTC around the presence of General Abdelfatah Yunis in the Council, reflecting a lack

---

[98] Cole and McQuinn, eds., *The Libyan Revolution*, 96–98; International Crisis Group, *Divided We Stand*, 7.
[99] Cole and McQuinn, eds., *The Libyan Revolution*, 38–39.
[100] As one NTC member explained: "We were at war, the country was suffering … and he just appointed himself the head and was based outside the country. This was not logical." Interview, November 8, 2014.
[101] Interview with a Libyan civil society activist, July 8, 2015.
[102] Pack and Barfi, *In War's Wake*, 8.

of unity and trust among its members. Some NTC members were worried he would remain loyal to the old regime, while others argued that his defection would be a big boost for opposition forces.[103] Yunis was mysteriously assassinated in July 2011, but divisions around him persisted. Although his assassination may have been linked to double-crossing the NTC, at least one source states that Yunis "remained an outspoken advocate for the opposition movement until his death."[104] Following Yunis's death, Suleiman Mahmoud al-Obeidi replaced him as the military chief. Both men were from the Obeidi tribe, a large tribe from the northeast, which had been favored under the Qadhafi regime.

Regardless of the facts surrounding it, the assassination reflected deeper distrust among members. For instance, many of the judges who were members of the NTC had been political prisoners when Yunis was serving as a top figure in the regime security forces; mutual suspicion about his loyalties may have remained.[105] Moreover, the assassination took place just after certain Benghazi-based members, who were also former judges, had summoned Yunis to Benghazi for questioning. These members, potentially worried about being sidelined or even double-crossed, may have been trying to discredit Yunis in order to weaken Jibril's plan for organizing the security forces once Tripoli had been liberated.[106]

Moreover, the NTC struggled from the start to gain firm military leadership. Tensions between commanders such as Yunis and Haftar emerged quickly, weakening the military effort as different NTC factions scrambled over weapons and failed to present a unified position to their NATO allies. Khalifa Haftar appears to have been combative,

---

[103] Interview with an NTC member, November 8, 2014.

[104] Blanchard, *Libya Unrest and US Policy*, September 9, 2011, 18. Blanchard (28) also reports that "human rights concerns prior to and potentially during the unrest could have involved forces under his command." Some blamed his assassination on extremist Islamist elements who took advantage of a mentally handicapped member of Yunis's tribe to arrange his killing (Interview, November 8, 2014). Two of Yunis's senior aides, Colonel Mohammed Khamis and Lieutenant Nassr al-Mokhtar, were also reportedly abducted and killed. See Economist Intelligence Unit, *Libya – Country Report*, August 2011.

[105] Interview with an NTC member, November 8, 2014.

[106] This included Issawi, Salim al-Shaikhi, Fawzi Bu Katif from the February 17 Battalion, and defense minister Jalal al-Daghaili (Cole and McQuinn, eds., *The Libyan Revolution*, 49–50). These authors also note that Jalil himself opposed Jibril's plan.

frequently in an argument with someone.[107] Some reports suggested that, sometime during the summer, "the NTC may have sought to remove him from a command role, and that Haftar resisted those efforts."[108] Haftar and Yunis also jockeyed for position until Yunis's death;[109] and Haftar was subsequently rebuffed by Jalil and perhaps other NTC leaders when he proposed himself to become the chief commander.[110] Though no major public conflicts around Haftar developed before the end of the NTC's work, he was a figure who would reappear at a moment when the country was becoming much more clearly divided.

Perhaps most importantly, the NTC lacked the leadership skills and political savvy to achieve some of its crucial tasks. Several accounts note the interference of members' personal ambitions with the Council's larger goals, most notably that of Ali Tarhouni and Mahmoud Jibril. For example, while Tarhouni's leadership was critical during the crisis moments of late July and early August, observers also describe his inability to maintain control over competing fighting groups.[111] Jibril was criticized for being outside the country most of the time while the NTC was working.[112]

Part of the problem was that members of the NTC lacked experience governing democratically. Partly as a result, the NTC frequently was accused of opacity. Although several representatives from non-liberated cities and towns joined the NTC's legislative arm, their identities were kept a secret, allegedly for security reasons.[113] The NTC's failure to publish a final list of its members aroused suspicion in many corners.[114] Also for security reasons, the NTC did not hold open meetings, which under different circumstances may have helped

---

[107] One member of the NTC claimed Haftar would refuse to shake Yunis's hand because of Yunis's association with the old regime. Interview with an NTC member, September 18, 2019.

[108] Blanchard, *Libya: Unrest and US Policy*, August 26, 2011, 18–19.

[109] Cole and McQuinn, eds., *The Libyan Revolution*, 192.

[110] See Barfi, "Khalifa Haftar: Rebuilding Libya from the Top Down," for more detail on the problems Haftar would create for NTC leadership. According to one interviewee, Haftar may have also insisted on bringing his sons into the armed ranks, who caused concern by breaching security protocols. Interview with a Libya analyst, September 19, 2019.

[111] Cole and McQuinn, eds., *The Libyan Revolution*, 101–103.

[112] Chorin, *Exit the Colonel*, 260; Vandewalle, "Rebel Rivalries in Libya."

[113] See ntcLibya.org (last accessed November 10, 2019).

[114] Barfi, "Transitional National What?"

it gain trust from the public.[115] Indeed, Libyans lacked an understanding of the NTC and its internal proceedings and were wary of corruption within the Council.[116] Other NTC activities also remained obscure: the details of Yunis's assassination, for example, or relationships between the Council and countries such as Qatar and France.

On top of this, Libyan state administrative functions were weak, and the NTC could not depend on them to provide services and fulfill their mandates. This was partly the reason the Defense Ministry and Interior Ministry struggled to keep the militias and other fighting groups under their command.[117] Other ministries similarly struggled to carry out their responsibilities; the health ministry, for example, was especially burdened with humanitarian demands.[118] And in terms of international assistance, the absence of clear channels for the NTC to articulate its needs (whether in the form of technical, humanitarian, or military assistance) and inability to reach swift decisions often frustrated the international community.[119]

In addition to the challenge of building strong central state institutions, the NTC had lacked a single, unifying figure around which people could rally in order to fight for a common cause. Although Jalil initially represented such a figure, his subsequent actions led many to accuse him of "political stupidity."[120] For example, in his statement following the Yunis affair, he called for the elimination of "fifth columns," or Qadhafi loyalists still active in the east. Such a statement, which, rather than unifying Libyans around the NTC's cause, risked

---

[115] Interview with a Libyan civil society member, July 8, 2015.
[116] Barfi, "Transitional National What?"; Doherty, "Building a New Libya," 12.
[117] No defense ministry even existed under Qadhafi, which meant the NTC defense ministry had no preexisting staff or structure to facilitate its duties.
[118] See International Crisis Group, *Holding Libya Together*, 15–17. Several sources also note the role of ordinary citizens in trying to fulfill tasks such as the delivery of basic supplies and services. Some interviewees commented that the health ministry in particular struggled against corruption/nepotism (interview with Libyan activists, December 4, 2014). These same interviewees noted, however, that the education ministry managed to get new schoolbooks printed during this time. Also see International Crisis Group, *Divided We Stand*.
[119] Interviews with NTC members and Libyan civil society members, November 8, 2014 and July 31, 2015. Chollet and Fishman describe this also, although their focus is more on the period between 2012 and 2014. Chollet and Fishman, "Who Lost Libya?," 156.
[120] Interview with a Libyan civil society activist, July 8, 2011.

provoking retaliations or forcing people to align with one side for fear of being identified as a traitor.[121] Jalil's "Liberation Speech" of October 23 was also criticized by many liberal-leaning figures for focusing on unrelated issues such as polygamy.[122] In general, neither Jalil nor anyone else in the NTC had the requisite political experience to lead it through these challenging tasks.

The important decision of where the interim government should be based was a point of contention that the NTC failed to resolve satisfactorily due to its overall lack of political experience and weak leadership ability. Following the killing of Qadhafi on October 20, the NTC began moving its seat to Tripoli. This decision was made in the name of continuity (as the seat of government had previously been there), or perhaps as an effort to reassure western Libyans that the country would not be dominated by eastern interests. However, the NTC itself was not firm about this move, and Jalil expressed reluctance and proposed to move only the Executive Council, "relenting only when the security disputes in Tripoli ... compelled his presence."[123]

Many would later call this move a mistake, blaming Jalil's lack of political courage and sometimes attributing the decision to the growing influence of figures like Bilhaj over him. These critics argue that moving the NTC's key ministries to Tripoli reopened them to the channels of corruption that had built up under the Qadhafi regime, and gave power to figures from the old regime who did not have the interests of a future democratic Libya in mind.[124] The decision to move the seat of the government from Benghazi to Tripoli was so contentious that it sparked a protest movement, which became known as the

---

[121] Vandewalle, "Rebel Rivalries in Libya."
[122] Two interviewees described the speech as "weird." Because the speech was delivered on October 23, three days after Qadhafi had been called, some even wondered if Jalil was purposely trying to avoid an appearance of celebrating the death of Qadhafi. Others described Jalil as a "pushover" and perhaps "a weak old man who has the Libyan trait of trying to please everyone." (Interview with a Libyan civil society activist, July 8, 2015; interview with a Libya analyst, September 19, 2019.)
[123] Cole and McQuinn, eds., *The Libyan Revolution*, 214.
[124] Interviews with Libyan activists and civil society members, November 8, 2014; July 8, 2015. However, it should also be noted that others such as businesspersons may have been encouraging the NTC/Jalil to make the move (interview with a Libyan civil society activist, July 8, 2015).

"12/12 movement" for the manifestations in Tree Square in Benghazi on December 12, 2011.[125]

A few – admittedly important – NTC institutions were more successful in carrying out their functions. For instance, the Council declared in March 2011 that it had established a National Oil Corporation (NOC) and Central Bank in Benghazi and that these bodies were independent from those in Tripoli. The defection early in the conflict of one of the major NOC-owned oil companies, the Arabian Gulf Oil Company, allowed the NTC to appoint one of the company's former employees to oversee oil production and exports, to negotiate oil procurements with Qatar and other countries, and to establish relationships with foreign oil companies that had previously signed contracts with the Qadhafi government.[126] By August the NTC had also begun diverting oil shipments intended for the regime in Tripoli and had restored enough infrastructure to consider resuming production. In November 2011, the NTC formed an oil ministry, which it said would share responsibility over the oil sector with the NOC.

The NTC's establishment of an independent Central Bank in Benghazi allowed it to circumvent international sanctions. This was important for paying salaries (essential for retaining authority, something that would later complicate its control over armed forces) as well as making electricity and fuel payments. The NTC also set up social programs and reparations to victims of the regime and ran monetary policy through the Central Bank. Nonetheless, financing remained a major issue for the NTC.

In sum, the NTC attempted to institutionalize the revolution by creating centralized, representative institutions for overseeing public service provision and the military effort, for conducting policy making, and for interfacing with the international community and garnering international support. This entailed both setting up institutions with new functions, such as the stabilization committee in charge of post-conflict reconstruction, and taking over responsibilities of existing organizations such as the National Oil Company and the Central

---

[125] Cole and McQuinn (eds.) explain how the move generated resentment among easterners, who felt some propriety over the revolution and also recalled Qadhafi's "relocation of government and symbolic institutions (such as the then national airline carrier and National Oil Company) from Benghazi to Tripoli." Cole and McQuinn, eds., *The Libyan Revolution*, 214.

[126] Economist Intelligence Unit, *Libya – Country Report*, July 2011, 14–15.

Bank. The NTC also tried to create security institutions by consolidating the groups of Libyans around the country who were taking up arms in the fight against the Qadhafi regime. Yet overall, the institutional structure established under the NTC was hampered by its inexperienced and fractured leadership and lack of strong state institutions historically.

Prioritizing International Assistance

Soon after the NTC formed, Jibril led its effort to rally the international community. The first challenge, however, was persuading international interlocutors of the Council's legitimacy. Its declaration of pursing the formation of democracy was partly in pursuit of its goal of recognition by the international community.[127] Because the NTC was operating *alongside* the challenged dictatorship, the international community, in order to justify deployment of its resources, sought to ensure the NTC wouldn't emerge as an equally ruthless dictatorship once Qadhafi was overthrown. It was therefore incumbent upon the NTC to reassure the international community of its democratic intentions.

The international community reacted immediately to the outbreak of violence in Libya. The United States, France, and other members of the European Union responded in two ways, neither of which required – at that point – direct engagement with the NTC. Immediately, the United States reinstated financial sanctions on Qadhafi and regime members and froze certain financial assets from Libya. The United Nations (UN) issued an arms embargo and travel ban for Libya and asset freeze on the Qadhafi family. Second, these governments attempted to coordinate a reaction to the violence. UN Secretary-General Ban Ki-Moon urged the United Nations Security Council (UNSC) to take "decisive action" in response to the crisis, and American president Barack Obama, British prime minister David Cameron, French president Nicholas Sarkozy, German chancellor Angela Merkel, Italian prime

---

[127] See, for example, the *New York Times* exposé discussing US Secretary of State Hillary Clinton's role in the debate over whether and how to intervene at the beginning of the conflict. The article quotes one of her assistant secretaries as saying, "opposition leaders 'said all the right things about supporting democracy and inclusivity and building Libyan institutions ... They gave us what we wanted to hear'" (Becker and Shane, "Hillary Clinton, 'Smart Power,' and a Dictator's Fall").

minister Silvio Berlusconi, and Turkish prime minister Tayyip Erdogan began engaging in "frequent discussions" in an attempt to coordinate their policies toward Libya.[128]

France and Qatar took the lead in offering support to the NTC and lobbying other major Western powers to do the same. Two French figures publicly led this effort: President Nicholas Sarkozy and the journalist/philosopher/activist Bernard-Henri Lévy. Lévy is credited for meeting with Jalil in the early days of March and organizing for Jibril, representing the NTC, to travel to Paris to meet with Sarkozy in order to request his support.[129] As a result, Sarkozy quickly moved to make France the first country to formally recognize the NTC, whom it would steadfastly provide with weapons throughout the war (even conducting airstrikes before the UN-authorized intervention had officially begun, drawing some criticism).[130]

The international community's more profound reaction was the beginning of what would become an international military intervention in Libya. By February 26, a UN Security Council Resolution (UNSCR 1970) had been adopted unanimously, which placed targeted financial and travel sanctions on Qadhafi and other individuals and imposed an arms embargo on Libya. Other multilateral bodies, namely the Gulf Cooperation Council (GCC) and the Arab League, urged the imposition of a no-fly zone over Libya.[131] Meanwhile, officials from certain key countries and regional bodies, including France, the United States, and the GCC, took tentative steps toward recognizing the NTC.[132]

These discussions culminated on March 17 with the adoption of UNSCR 1973, which permitted members to impose a no-fly zone. The debates leading to this resolution had two notable features. First, several permanent members of the UNSC (including China, Russia,

---

[128] Bell and Witter, *Escalation & Intervention*, 15.

[129] Erlanger, "Thinker Led the President to War."

[130] Bell and Witter, *Escalation & Intervention*, 24.

[131] A no-fly zone is the legal prohibition of airplanes flying over a certain territory. Instating a no-fly zone via international law would allow international alliances such as NATO to monitor and shoot down any planes that violated it and take other actions to prevent attacks on civilian targets.

[132] The Gulf Cooperation Council (GCC) on March 10 announced it favored recognizing the NTC, and French President Nicolas Sarkozy and US Secretary of State Hillary Clinton both met with the NTC's external representatives, Jibril and Issawi.

India, Brazil, and Germany), abstained from the vote; this showed that even those countries whose diplomatic agendas might be threatened by supporting the resolution did not have any grounds for blocking (vetoing) it.[133] Second, the resolution prohibited ground forces from occupying Libyan territory, reflecting the shared concern among Security Council members about prolonged military engagement. Although debate over the framing of and NATO allies' adherence to this mandate,[134] as well as conflicted members of the Security Council (namely South Africa) due to their role in other international organizations, continued, the organization nonetheless provided the means for the international community to organize an intervention that would dramatically alter the experience of the NTC.

France, Qatar, and, to an extent, the United Kingdom had spearheaded the international intervention in Libya. The United States was initially more hesitant to recognize and devote resources to aiding the NTC, famously reluctant to engage in another war in the Middle East.[135] Thanks largely to the efforts of Lévy, US Secretary of State Clinton met with Jibril in Paris on March 14 (a few weeks after the NTC had formed, and shortly before UNSCR 1973, the Security Council Resolution authorizing intervention in Libya, would be passed). Meanwhile President Obama met with his national security advisors (March 15) and a few days later voted, as a permanent member of the UNSC, to authorize the use of force, including "all necessary measures," to protect the Libyan civilian population. Naturally, given the strength of its defense forces and its proportional contribution to the alliance, American participation in the NATO mission that was to lead the militarily intervention in Libya was critical.

The other governments credited with facilitating the intervention were regional partners. Involving these partners was important politically because it helped the NTC to avoid accusations of neocolonialism or Western control over an Arab country. Gulf Cooperation Council (GCC) ministers in Abu Dhabi met in March and encouraged the Arab League to "take responsibility for the Arab response to the fighting in

---

[133] Notably, Russia had threatened to veto the resolution and criticized the military campaign after it had begun but was persuaded by the United States to cooperate (Bell and Witter, *Stalemate & Siege*, 29–30).
[134] See Boguslavsky, "The African Union and the Libyan Crisis."
[135] Pack, ed., *The 2011 Libyan Uprisings*, 121; Chorin, *Exit the Colonel*, 210.

Libya." Two days after UNSCR 1973 was passed, NATO convened a summit in Paris to "craft the coalition's political and military agenda."[136] Participants included both Arab and non-Arab partners as well as representatives from the Arab League. In sum, the international community, including Arab partners, had relatively swiftly found common ground for limited action in regard to the Libyan crisis.

By that point, the Qadhafi regime was engaged in full-on warfare with the opposition movement on the ground, referred to broadly in the international media as the Libyan "rebels" and represented politically by the NTC. Fierce battles had led to the downfall of eastern cities like Brega, while other western cities like Misrata and Zawiya had seen major casualties as the opposition and regime engaged in an armed struggle for control. Although most eastern cities had fallen from government control quite quickly, by the time of UNSCR 1973 the regime had managed to hold opposition forces at Ajdabiya and was pushing toward Benghazi.

The international campaign to assist the opposition was called "Odyssey Dawn" and began on March 19 with the launching of missile strikes by French, British, and American warplanes, just as Qadhafi forces were beginning their assault on Benghazi. By about March 27, opposition victories in Ajdabiya and some other eastern cities indicated that the intervention was helping tip the military balance in favor of the opposition. However, despite the widespread support for UNSCR 1973, splits within the international community delayed the transfer of leadership of the campaign from the United States to NATO.[137] Even with the creation on March 29 of an "International Contact Group" designed to coordinate the coalition of international partners that had launched Odyssey Dawn, and even with those opposition victories, the war intensified. The stage was now set for a prolonged struggle between the Qadhafi regime and the Libyan opposition movement, represented by the NTC and supported by a not-always-fully-united international community.

[136] Bell and Witter, *Escalation & Intervention*, 23.
[137] Bell and Witter describe how NATO partners first were able to transfer the part of the resolution authorizing an arms embargo to France and Britain (March 23) but it took another couple of days (until March 31) to get the maintenance of the no-fly zone into NATO hands. The name of the mission then became "Operation Unified Protector." Bell and Witter, *Escalation & Intervention*, 25–26.

On March 29, the NTC brought to an international summit in London a "Vision for a Democratic Libya," in which it stated its intentions to transfer power via free and fair elections and prepare for the drafting of a new constitution that would be put to popular referendum. It also declared its support for principles such as peace, democracy, and freedom.[138] It further entered into negotiations with Qatar, one of the first countries to officially recognize the NTC along with France, over the brokering of a deal that would allow Qatar to buy oil from the NTC, giving it an inflow of funds. Finally, the leader of the NTC military forces, Abdelfatah Yunis, started requesting more weapons at the NATO headquarters in Brussels.[139]

Without the UNSC resolution to support the Libyan opposition and the NATO-led military intervention, the experience of the NTC would likely have been drastically different, as its fighting forces almost certainly would have been defeated.[140] The arrival of this assistance did not provide automatic relief, however: the NTC and especially its military side had to work closely with NATO troops and Operation Unified Protector (the name of the mission), which was often made difficult by constraints such as getting and sharing information.[141] Although the two sides would ultimately form a fruitful partnership, their joint defeat of Qadhafi came at the expense of much frustration and many mistakes.[142] The NATO mission officially ended after seven months of engagement, but the overall value of the intervention remains debated.[143]

---

[138] Economist Intelligence Unit, *Libya – Country Report*, April 2011, 13; Cole and McQuinn, eds., *The Libyan Revolution*, 39.

[139] Cole and McQuinn, eds., *The Libyan Revolution*, 64–65.

[140] Some good sources on the importance of the NATO operation for the NTC's military efforts include Wehrey, *The Burning Shores*, and Bell and Witter, *The Libyan Revolution* (Parts 1–4).

[141] Cole and McQuinn, eds., *The Libyan Revolution*, 113–117. As several sources describe, Operation Unified Protector was also plagued by political and technical challenges. For instance, Bell and Witter (*Escalation & Intervention*, 26) explain that Turkey and France had been at odds over their foreign policies, leading Sarkozy to exclude it from the initial Paris summit. Later, Turkey's cooperation with the NATO mission improved.

[142] See Cole and McQuinn, eds., *The Libyan Revolution*, 105–127; Wehrey, *The Burning Shores*, 44.

[143] E.g. Chivvis, *Toppling Qaddafi*; Chollet and Fishman, "Who Lost Libya?"; Kuperman, "A Model Humanitarian Intervention? Reassessing NATO's Libya Campaign"; Gazzini, "Was the Libya Intervention Necessary?"; Roberts,

In addition, the NTC aimed to persuade international partners to provide material support. Countries such as France and Qatar were forthcoming with weapons; still their transfer and continuing provision required a fair amount of diplomacy. For example, Qatar had to be careful not to violate end-user agreements by supplying the NTC with weapons it had purchased from France. This also complicated the UAE's ability to supply weapons. Moreover, such support was often contingent on the NTC demonstrating that it had plans for restoring stability.[144]

Further, the NTC requested from international partners finances in the form of international aid and the transfer of unfrozen assets or assets seized from the Qadhafi regime. This financing was often difficult for the international community to supply: the transfer of frozen assets, for example, required special funding mechanisms and finding many loopholes. It also partly caused a liquidity crisis for the NTC.[145] Thus, persuading the international community of its worthiness remained a key preoccupation of the NTC until the defeat of Qadhafi.

Two regional countries, Qatar and Sudan, provided superior levels of support to the NTC and its fighters. Qatar worked hard to secure oil contracts that would provide the NTC with much-needed financial support.[146] It was the second country, after France, to recognize the NTC, and it then took a lead role in setting up the Libya Contact Group (LCG, the coordinating mechanism for the NATO mission) and hosted the groups' first meeting in Doha.[147] However, Qatar insisted

---

"Who Said Qadhafi Had to Go?"; St John, "From the 17 February Revolution to Benghazi: Rewriting History for Political Gain."

[144] Cole and McQuinn, eds., *The Libyan Revolution*, 64–66. One international NGO worker who spoke with NTC leaders before the Qadhafi regime had been defeated remarked that they clearly had no plan for the demobilization of fighters, even though they insisted they did (interview, November 3, 2014).

[145] For more on this, see Cole and McQuinn, eds., *The Libyan Revolution*, 45–47.

[146] Qatar reportedly not only established mechanisms to provide the rebels with food, fuel, and medical supplies in exchange for oil in at least one exchange, it also helped the NTC market oil, brokering deals with countries like China (Economist Intelligence Unit, *Libya – Country Report*, April 2011, 15).

[147] As Ulrichsen, in his contribution to Henriksen and Larssen, *Political Rationale and International Consequences of the War in Libya* (124–125), discusses, Qatar was also instrumental in garnering opposition to Qadhafi and support for the rebels via the media, especially the Doha-based channel *Al Jazeera*, which is influential in the Arab world. Also see Pack, ed., *The 2011 Libyan Uprising*, 191–223.

on arming certain militia groups, likely due to personal connections.[148] This fed into the delicate and sometimes explosive divisions of leadership in the struggle against Qadhafi, and especially the battle for Tripoli during August 2011, and exacerbated the already daunting challenge of building a functioning security apparatus.[149]

Sudan, as a result of Qadhafi's support historically for one of the main Darfur rebel movements, the Justice and Equality Movement, provided significant military support to the NTC. This included weapons, ammunitions, and supplies, and even communications equipment, intelligence officers and trainers. Although Sudan subsequently failed to convert this into "political capital,"[150] its aid to the NTC fighters helped unequivocally. By June, Sudan and Qatar were the two main foreign suppliers of the weapons that allowed the opposition to take Tripoli.

The NTC's preoccupation with obtaining foreign support often came at the cost of undertaking more difficult, longer term tasks. Jibril in particular, who was in charge of foreign affairs, made several promises to the international community (such as the Libya Contact Group) that the NTC was not prepared to keep. Key examples of such promises include the overly ambitious timetable it set for the transition and the NTC's assurance that it had a plan for demobilizing the

---

[148] Cole and McQuinn, eds., *The Libyan Revolution*, 71–79; Henriksen and Larssen, *Political Rationale and International Consequences of the War in Libya*, 122–129; International Crisis Group, *Holding Libya Together*, 21. There was particular concern over weapons coming in from Qatar, since much of Qatari support – though not all – came through Islamist networks, with whom Bilhaj was associated. According to Zoubir and Rózsa, Bilhaj's ties to al-Qaeda in the Maghrib (AQIM) made Algeria, which had been working to combat AQIM in its south, reluctant to recognize the NTC. Zoubir and Rózsa, "The End of the Libyan Dictatorship," 1276–1277.

[149] Some Western think-tank reports at the time were calling for international support in helping train police and security forces, support disarmament, demobilization, and reintegration (DDR), and supporting negotiated solutions among armed groups (e.g. Mezran, "Negotiating a Solution to the Security Problem in Libya").

[150] Alexander De Waal explains how Sudan immediately provided the opposition "more than enough" weapons and supplies to liberate Kufra, a town in the southern Libyan desert on the road to Sudan, then continued to help it secure Kufra and establish an overland supply route through the desert to arm the NTC. Even after the liberation of Tripoli, Sudan reportedly continued to help monitor the southern Libyan border. De Waal, "African Roles in the Libyan Conflict of 2011," 376–378.

opposition fighters once the country had been liberated (which it clearly didn't).[151]

Foreign countries' agendas sometimes interfered with the NTC's ability to control events. Sometimes the NTC appeared able to coordinate among different external actors: Sudan, for example, intended to send supplies and troops in southeastern Libya, which it did; a second shipment was then canceled once it became clear that Qatar could get supplies to NTC fighters in time.[152] Other times, however, foreign assistance to the NTC's cause became confusing and sometimes harmful. The UAE and Qatar had their own geostrategic interests in arming certain groups with Islamist ideologies, which contributed to disunity and a sense of competition among fighting groups.[153] It also interfered with elections, as certain parties gained a reputation of being tied to foreign interests or Islamist ideologies.[154] This exacerbated another challenge the NTC already faced in the domain of external support: overcoming or mitigating Libyan's mistrust of foreign influence.[155]

At several points, certain NTC members tried to cooperate with the international community to mediate a compromise solution with Qadhafi.[156] Mediation initiatives led by the African Union (AU), Venezuela, and Russia, as well as the GCC, the Arab League, and the European Union, occurred during May, June, and July 2011, when the military struggle between the opposition and Qadhafi forces were at an impasse.[157] The AU, mainly through its Peace and Security Council (PSC), issued a communiqué that included a "roadmap" for

[151] Interview with a foreign NGO worker, November 3, 2014. Also see Cole and McQuinn, eds., *The Libyan Revolution*, 42–43.
[152] Cole and McQuinn, eds., *The Libyan Revolution*, 74.
[153] For more discussion, see Henriksen and Larssen, eds., *Political Rationale and International Consequences of the War in Libya*; Wehrey, "After Gaddafi: Libya's Path to Collapse," 7.
[154] For example, as Pack and coauthors explain, Abdelhakim Bilhaj and his al-Watan party became perceived as a front for Qatar, possibly even contributing to their poor performance in the 2012 elections. Pack, ed., *The 2011 Libyan Revolution*, 216.
[155] Sawani, "Post-Qadhafi Libya: Interactive Dynamics and the Political Future," 23.
[156] The individuals from the NTC who led this effort were Jibril, Fathi al-Baja, and Abd al-Rahman Shalgham.
[157] Chollet and Fishman even reference a mediation attempt by a Russian chess player. Chollet and Fishman, "Who Lost Libya?," 155.

a diplomatic solution, and set up an ad hoc committee to implement it.[158] Russia offered its full support, "convinced that the position of the African Union should be completely taken into account when further moves toward Libyan settlement and peaceful and democratic realization of the legitimate demands of the Libyan people were contemplated."[159]

African Union and PSC representatives met with both Qadhafi and NTC leaders several times, but these international actors were never able to reach a diplomatic solution. This was in large part due to the disunity or lack of coordination among them.[160] For instance, the African Union in March announced a roadmap for a diplomatic solution, the essence of which was to impose a ceasefire, administer humanitarian assistance to civilians, and begin talks for a negotiated solution. An ad hoc commission from within the AU planned to travel to Benghazi on March 20, but the launching of NATO airstrikes in the second of half of March delayed the trip until April 10. Throughout the summer, the military conflict continued to interfere with the diplomatic processes.[161] The issuing of an ICC warrant for Qadhafi in the spring also jeopardized the option the AU had been preparing at the time, which was for Qadhafi "quietly going into exile."[162]

Additionally, the AU and Russia's efforts were not consistently supported by the Libya Contact Group. The AU's initial communiqué was mentioned in UNSCR 1973, and South Africa and the two other

---

[158] A key concern of the African Union (AU)/ Peace and Security Council (PSC) was the threat of a conflict in Libya spilling into other African countries. Both Libyan and non-Libyan actors were concerned about Qadhafi's potential use of fighters from other countries. Particularly given the difficulty in securing Libya's borders combined with the availability of weapons in Libya, this would represent a serious threat to the region. De Waal, "African Roles in the Libyan Conflict of 2011," 370. Also see Bell and Witter, *Roots of Rebellion*, 30.

[159] Boguslavsky, "The African Union and the Libyan Crisis," 72.

[160] For a good discussion of the complicated role of the AU in this conflict, see Boguslavsky, "The African Union and the Libyan Crisis," and Mundy, *Libya*, 67–79.

[161] Note that the African Union and Russia had objected to some of the provisions of UNSCR 1973. This disagreement between Russia and the AU on one side and Western and regional powers, led by France, Qatar, and the United States, on the other, would continue until the fall of Tripoli in late August. The other country modestly attempting to carve out a role for itself as mediator at this time was Turkey. See De Waal, "African Roles in the Libyan Conflict of 2011," 367–368; Mezran and Alluni, "Libya: Negotiations for Transition," 267.

[162] De Waal, "African Roles in the Libyan Conflict of 2011," 375.

African members of the UN Security Council (Nigeria and Gabon) had voted in favor of the resolution. But the AU remained concerned throughout the intervention that Western powers would implement its provisions selectively in order to pursue regime change.[163] Tensions arose between these two groups of outside actors due to their conflicting approaches, first, when the initial imposition of a no-fly zone interfered with AU/PSC representatives' planned travel to Benghazi and Tripoli to meet with the different parties, and later when, just as the NTC and the Qadhafi government were to meet for negotiation in Addis Ababa, the United States decided to formally recognize the NTC, prompting it to abandon the talks. The United States even successfully intervened in Russia's attempts to support a negotiated solution. At the G8 summit in Deauville in late May, President Obama persuaded Russian president Dimitri Medvedev to leverage its longstanding supportive relationship with Qadhafi to persuade the former leader to step down. Some analysts have even suggested that the LCG or the P3 members (the United States, Britain, and France) were deliberately trying to thwart the AU and Russia's efforts.[164] In sum, the NTC's courting until Qadhafi's death in October 2011 of the international community led to a critical intervention, but this commanded significant time and attention from the NTC and often came at the cost of unity both internally and among its foreign partners.

Developing a Roadmap

The NTC knew it needed to codify its intentions to hand over power to an elected government, which it tried to do initially in a series of statements issued in early 2011. This roadmap strategy was motivated by several factors. First, it would serve to reassure internal and external supporters that the NTC had not seized power. Additionally, the declarations and roadmap, vague as they were, had a utilitarian purpose of helping the NTC move toward its goal of holding elections.

---

[163] Their main concern was over the wording "all necessary measures" and the fact that the main three advocates for the resolution within the UNSC – France, Britain, and the United States, known within the UNSC as the P3 – never presented a plan for a negotiated solution. See De Waal, "African Roles in the Libyan Conflict of 2011"; Gazinni, "Was the Libya Intervention Really Necessary?"; Roberts, "Who Said Qadhafi Had to Go?"

[164] Boguslavsky, "The African Union and the Libyan Crisis."

Thirdly, these statements, though written by the NTC, could act as a sort of interim constitution, or "basis of rule," until the new constitution was ratified.[165] By declaring itself the leader in this way forward, the NTC inevitably had to fend off increasing challenges from all sides as it pursued its roadmap.

The Council issued a *bayan* (or statement) in late February, in which it articulated protestors' demands, including an explicit statement of "hopes and intentions to create a democratic and unified state."[166] However, this document lacked details on how exactly the NTC and its successors would achieve this. The NTC's next official statement of its intentions was on March 29, ahead of a planned summit of foreign powers in London.[167] This was the first statement to lay out the Council's "vision." It promised to build a democratic state based on the rule of law and respect for human rights through the drafting of a new constitution "crafted by the people and endorsed in a referendum." The statement also promised that this state would "[recognize] intellectual and political pluralism and [allow] for the peaceful transfer of power through legal institutions and ballot boxes."[168] Whether this statement was purposely aimed at getting official recognition from foreign powers is unclear, but France, Qatar, Italy, and Kuwait had all recognized the council or announced their support for it by early April.

May 5 was the next public declaration of the NTC's vision and plans, but its effect was much less unifying. The main authors were Fathi Baja and Mahmoud Jibril, both central NTC members. This draft roadmap generated much controversy when it was presented at a Libya Contact Group meeting in Rome; the NTC therefore issued a Constituent Covenant for the Transitional Period, endorsed by the executive committee on June 21.[169] However, this draft failed to resolve key controversial issues, including how the NTC would hand over power.

[165] Mezran and Alunni, "Libya: Negotiations for Transition," 265.
[166] Chorin, *Exit the Colonel*, 196.
[167] *News24.com*, "Libya Opposition Vow Free, Fair Vote."
[168] McGreal, "Libyan Rebel Efforts Frustrated by Internal Disputes over Leadership."
[169] At least four groups issued alternative drafts of the plan (Cole and Mcquinn, eds., *The Libyan Revolution*, 51).

Finally, the NTC issued a Constitutional Declaration on August 3.[170] As described in Chapter 5, the important task of adopting the declaration was meant to help set a roadmap for guiding both the NTC and its successors, but because it was constantly being amended, right up until the eve of its adoption, the document failed to play that guiding role.

Constitution-expert Zaid al-Ali praised the declaration for its progressive aspects, such as guaranteeing the right to social security, but expressed reservation about others. In particular, al-Ali worried that many of the frontline fighters would take issue with the NTC's claim that it derived its legitimacy from the constitution, and that while the text implied that its members would be elected by local councils, not making this explicit "opens the possibility that direct appointments could be made through non-democratic means."[171] In other words, the document's failure to clearly delineate the NTC's mandate, membership, and authority carried implications for the future of the transitional process.

The most controversial article in this document was Article 30. In its initial form, Article 30 stated that the NTC would continue working even after the elections for a constituent committee and parliament had occurred, and included a timeline for organizing elections once the country had been liberated. The biggest critics of this article were members of the NTC representing the Muslim Brotherhood, who felt the NTC should be dissolved with the completion of elections. According to some accounts, the Brotherhood was leery of the secular profile of NTC members, and therefore wanted to limit its power.[172]

Article 30 thus sparked a protracted debate within (and outside) the NTC. An emergency meeting was called on July 27 to finalize the document. In the final version, Article 30 stated that the NTC would dissolve itself once a new national congress, which was to form a new cabinet and constituent committee, had been elected. But, coming just

---

[170] This document is sometimes referred to as the Temporary Constitutional Declaration, or TCD.

[171] Specifically, al-Ali argued that the articles aiming to establish the role of the NTC – Article 17, which stated that the Council "derives its legitimacy from the revolution," and Article 18, which stated that the Council's members would be selected by local councils, but did not specify the selection mechanism – could cause concern. Al-Ali, "Libya's Interim Constitution: An Assessment."

[172] Cole and McQuinn, eds., *The Libyan Revolution*, 183.

at the time of General Yunis's assassination, and thus owing to a renewed sense of urgency within the Council to present a united front, this official roadmap was drafted in haste and without all voices at the table. Some members felt the Muslim Brotherhood had taken advantage of the confusion and chaos created by the assassination to push through what it wanted. In short, the NTC felt pressured to issue *something* rather than to take more time to reach consensus around its content.[173]

Overall, the Constitutional Declaration contained several important elements. First, it was part of the NTC's strategic goal to "keep the many different forces within the opposition together." To that end, the declaration included as its second important feature clear principles for rebuilding a democratic state in Libya, including "dialogue, tolerance, cooperation, national cohesiveness, and political and intellectual pluralism" as well as a peaceful transfer of power through elections. It further recognized the need of the country for a new constitution that included separation of powers and other democratic institutions. Third, the Declaration laid out the steps meant to lead to a new national constitution: (1) elections for a General National Congress (GNC), (2) appointment of a constitutional drafting committee, (3) popular referendum and ratification of a draft constitution, (4) creation of a Supreme National Elections Council to oversee general elections, and (5) elections for a new government.[174] Importantly, the NTC would alter this step-by-step plan in the eleventh hour before the GNC elections nearly a year later.

Organizing Elections

The bulk of the NTC's attention and resources from February through August 2011 were thus devoted to managing the war effort and securing the support of the international community. However, the

---

[173] Importantly, al-Ali notes: "With the proviso that it is close to impossible from outside the country to obtain a full picture of how the text was prepared, it seems at the very least that the draft was released before most of the revolutionaries that had been fighting on the frontlines for months had had a chance to see the text – let alone comment on it." And interviewees who were close to the drafting process claimed that the final form of the article was a surprise to many members of the drafting committee (interview, September 18, 2019).

[174] Mezran and Alunni, "Libya: Negotiations for Transition," 262–265.

NTC performed these tasks under the explicit assumption that their accomplishment would permit the Council to organize elections for a new democratic government to take over. With the fall of the capital in late August, the NTC could finally turn its attention to this task.

In September, following the liberation of Tripoli, the United Nations Security Council unanimously voted to send a support mission to Libya. This mission, the United Nations Support Mission in Libya (UNSMIL), mostly provided technical support in three domains: the GNC elections, security sector reform, and human rights, transitional justice, and the rule of law. Particularly in its early months, UNSMIL served as a critical resource for Libya's transition and post-conflict reconstruction.[175]

In November 2011 the NTC appointed an Elections Committee, which, in January 2012, in collaboration with UNSMIL, created a High National Elections Commission (HNEC). The HNEC granted certain international organizations permission to send observing missions for the elections and worked with UNSMIL advisors to draft legislation for the elections.[176] Under the guidance of these advisors, the HNEC rebuilt the existing electorate database and managed to register 2.87 million (of an estimated 3.5 million eligible) voters in the first three weeks of May.[177] The HNEC also oversaw candidate registration during the same period and credited a special commission to determine candidate eligibility. However, conducting major voter education campaigns as well as registering candidates in time for them to have a significant campaign period proved impossible, and

---

[175] Pack and Barfi, *In War's Wake*; Pack et al., *Libya's Faustian Bargains*; Cole and McQuinn, eds., *The Libyan Revolution*, 150–151. Ian Martin, who led the UN Support Mission in Libya (UNSMIL) describes the challenges the mission faced. While it was able to provide significant guidance to the NTC as it prepared for the GNC elections, particularly in developing a legal framework, making progress in the other two areas was much more challenging. This was largely due to the difficulty of establishing a central authority over the growing number of armed groups, most of whom did not have experience with international human rights standards. See Cole and McQuinn, eds., *The Libyan Revolution*, 127–152.

[176] These were Law #3 and Law #4 respectively. See Cole and McQuinn, eds., *The Libyan Revolution*, 134; Carter Center, *Libya's Constitutional Drafting Assembly Elections: Final Report*.

[177] McCurdy, *Backgrounder: Previewing Libya's Elections*.

the NTC – controversially – was forced, at the recommendation of the HNEC, to delay the elections from June 19 to July 7.[178]

Unfortunately, the organizing of elections was also difficult because of the ever-prominent divisions among those put in charge of the task (reflective of the divisions among the NTC as a whole). The HNEC was originally meant to include seventeen members but by the time of the election had only eleven. Othman Gajiji, who was appointed chair of the HNEC in early 2012 (who had originally been an advisor to the al-Kib government), was ultimately dismissed that April along with four other members, for reasons that are unclear.[179]

Moreover, the NTC often insisted on sticking to its elections' time-table at the cost of obtaining consensus on fundamental issues. The drafting of the electoral law in spring 2012 also became the source of great debate. The first draft law, passed on February 12, was non-committal about the allocation among regions of seats in the GNC. On March 14, however, the HNEC announced the allocation: 102 seats for western Libya, sixty for the east, and thirty-eight for the center and south.[180] This left some eastern members feeling that their region was underrepresented. Several groups organized conferences to discuss the draft, during which they focused their discontent with that article. Aggressive protests began in January and February, reaching a climax when protestors stormed the NTC office. These protests were so disruptive that NTC member Abdel Hafiz Ghoga resigned in frustration. In March 2012, thousands of actors announced the Barqa Council (discussed more in Chapter 5), whose purpose was to advocate for

---

[178] This special commission, called the High Commission on the Application of Standards of Integrity and Patriotism, or National Integrity Commission for short, went through two rounds of disqualifying various candidates. The criteria were mostly related to having served in the former regime. This delayed the registration process, as many disqualified candidates then appealed. The candidate-registration period was open from May 1 to May 17; a final list of candidates was issued by the commission on June 18 (McCurdy, *Backgrounder: Previewing Libya's Elections*).

[179] See McCurdy, *Backgrounder: Previewing Libya's Elections*, 4. Also, according to some sources, Islamist groups, in an effort to gain an upper hand in the elections, were asserting their influence indirectly by pressuring certain high-ranking individuals in the al-Kib government, such as Alamin Bilhaj, to remove HNEC members with opposing views, including technical details that could diminish the group's likelihood of electoral success. Interview with an HNEC member, September 14, 2019.

[180] Cole and McQuinn, eds., *The Libyan Revolution*, 215–216.

more autonomy for the east and create a federal region. Two months before the elections, the Barqa Council, which had originally been planning to field candidates, called for a boycott by eastern residents. It also threatened that violence would ensue if the elections went forward.[181]

These threats put the NTC, and particularly Chairman Jalil, under pressure from two directions. First, Jalil was concerned that any delay of the elections would undermine the entire process, opening the NTC to accusations of clinging to power. On the other hand, and more importantly, the NTC needed to find a way to appease the Barqa Council's demands for changes to the electoral law that would further its goals of creating a federal region in the east. For this reason, the NTC announced in March 2012 that the General National Council (GNC) would appoint a sixty-member committee to draft the new constitution rather than drafting it themselves. The appointed committee was to have an equal number of representatives from each region. More dramatically, on July 5 – two days before the elections – the NTC announced that the sixty-member committee would be directly elected, through an electoral process that the GNC would set up, and its decisions would be taken with two-third plus one majority. In short, the NTC struggled until its last days to settle the controversy of allocation of members and to stick to its declared roadmap.[182]

Conclusion

Throughout its life, the NTC continued to evolve and shape its own functions in response to events rather than according to a clearly defined mission or purpose.[183] Initially focusing solely on basic services and coordinating the military effort, it soon turned to another vital task: getting outside help. It also codified the basic demands of its members and, as time went on, its own roadmap and goals. As the summer of 2011 wore on, while the NTC retained its democratic goals, its primary aim became restoring peace and stability. Once the country

---

[181] Cole and McQuinn, eds., *The Libyan Revolution*, 220.
[182] See Pack et al., *Libya's Faustian Bargains* and Pack and Cook, "The July 2012 Libyan Election and the Origin of Post-Qadhafi Appeasement," for further discussion of this incident and the consequences it would bring.
[183] Cole and McQuinn also describe the NTC as lacking a cohesive strategy. Cole and McQuinn, eds., *The Libyan Revolution*.

had been liberated from Qadhafi, it could focus more on getting to elections.

None of these efforts, however, quite amounted to an articulation of a cohesive strategy or larger vision. The NTC's primary function remained filling a void – and therefore shifting its aims/changing its goals – rather than laying the groundwork for a future Libya. This was partly due to the heavy weight of past legacies, including operating through "leaderless" structures, as well as a perceived need to be representative and to weaken the loyalist movement by recruiting from certain societal groups. The NTC's recruitment and organization efforts as well as its chosen agenda all reflected the difficult circumstances in which the Council found itself as well as its own handling of the situation.

Moreover, over the course of its tenure, the NTC was forced to take many actions that placed it between a rock and hard place. Knowing, for example, that delaying the GNC elections would cause further unrest, Jalil and the NTC were constantly forced into tradeoffs between sticking to the timeline and making sure all issues were resolved. Moving the capital to Tripoli, similarly, was not subject to extensive debate within the Council, yet it served to further upset those whose agenda was carving out more autonomy for the east. Finally, the NTC took many decisions, such as prioritizing assistance from the international community and deprioritizing the economy, that would help fuel the instability that was to come.

5 | *Impacts of the National Transition Council*

In the first half of the period in which it operated, from February to October 2011, the National Transition Council (NTC) faced constraints mainly stemming from the military engagement between its supporters and the Qadhafi army. These included the urgency of securing international assistance, the need for financing, and the difficulty of communication. The NTC was also pressured by time and an inability to control events. Furthermore, the military conflict with the Qadhafi regime, the instability in neighboring countries such as Egypt, Tunisia, and Mali, as well as the agendas of foreign partners on whom the NTC depended for survival were all factors outside its control and raised uncertainties that severely constrained its ability to plan. Finally, as described in the Chapter 4, the NTC was marked by a lack of cohesion and shared vision.

Despite these challenges, the NTC managed to see the country through the democratic elections of July 7, 2012. This achievement should not be understated. Nonetheless, this achievement did not mean that the NTC had resolved key issues or established a unified vision for Libya's future. The failure to resolve many of these issues led to increasing instability over the years following those elections.

This chapter presents the ways in which the NTC, through its situation as both an influencer and a body heavily constrained by the legacies of the past and the need to not overstep its authority, created the conditions for the subsequent phase. This phase was delineated by the peaceful transfer of power from the NTC to a successor congress – which became increasingly beholden to the demands of armed militias thanks in part to the decisions of the NTC – and an attack on the new government's headquarters by a renegade general, Khalifa Haftar, who had fought on the side of the NTC. With this, the unity that had been superficially sustained under the NTC fully broke down.

Forming a New Government

Elections for a new General National Congress, Libya's second interim government that was meant to – according to the decisions taken by the NTC – oversee governing and organize elections for a Constitution Drafting Assembly (CDA), took place on July 7, 2012. The occasion was viewed as momentous in that free and fair elections had never happened in Libya, and many Libyans felt the country was entering a new era. The elections also took place in an atmosphere of minimal violence. Nonetheless, the many challenges the NTC had faced in the process of organizing these elections did not disappear.

The results of these elections were surprising to many. The Islamists fared poorly, despite expectations that the Muslim Brotherhood's Justice and Construction Party enjoyed widespread support, especially in the east, and because of recent Islamist electoral victories in post-revolutionary Tunisia and Egypt.[1] The party that won the plurality of seats, Mahmoud Jibril's National Forces Alliance (NFA), was a broad coalition of groups adhering to various ideologies, and was considered by some a referendum for national unity.[2]

The GNC was sworn in on August 8, 2012. With the NFA holding the most seats, members decided that the positions of prime minister and chairman/speaker of the GNC should be split between the east and the southwest. In early August, the GNC selected Muhammad el-Magariaf, a longtime oppositionist from Ajdabiya and the head of the National Libyan Salvation Front (an Islamist opposition group), as chairman. The selection of Magariaf "was greeted with applause in the east – both as a signal of provincial inclusion and as a clean break from the Qaddafi era."[3]

Unfortunately, the selection of a prime minister, who would then name a new interim cabinet, did not proceed as smoothly. This was achieved on September 12, when Mustafa Abushagur – an independent who had been serving as the deputy prime minister since the previous November – narrowly defeated Mahmoud Jibril for the position. However, one month later the GNC removed Abushagur in a vote of no-confidence after his proposed new cabinet drew heavy

[1] Daragahi, "Libya: From Euphoria to Breakdown," 44–45; Wehrey, *The Struggle for Security in Eastern Libya.*
[2] E.g. Wehrey, *The Struggle for Security in Eastern Libya.*
[3] Wehrey, *The Struggle for Security in Eastern Libya.*

criticism from both inside and outside the GNC (supporters of the NFA even stormed the assembly in protest of the presence of Justice and Construction members and the absence of the NFA among the nominees). On October 18 the GNC voted for Ali Zeidan, a former regime defector and critic and member of the National Alliance Front, to replace Abushagur. Under Zeidan's premiership, it soon became clear that elected officials were at the mercy of armed groups operating largely outside the framework of the state. This enormous challenge manifested itself most severely with his kidnapping in October 2013.[4]

Restoring (In)stability

The political instability of the second interim phase, launched by the absence of a clear leadership within the NTC and its inability to develop strong institutions, was mirrored in the security realm. Unfortunately, the weaknesses that had characterized the NTC, despite its ability to organize elections and define a transitional roadmap, made it difficult for a peaceful transition to be restored following this series of events. In addition to the increasing weakness of the political process vis-à-vis armed militia, the NTC's overall inability to rally Libyans around a shared identity or vision for the future left a legacy (not entirely unlike that of earlier times in Libyan history) of a weak or absent central authority.

When the fight for the capital city began in August 2011, NTC military forces had lacked a clear leadership structure. It soon divided into two camps over the question of how to bring the fighters together. Mustafa Abd-al Jalil was forced to mediate between Jibril and Aref Nayid (the head of the Tripoli Taskforce) on the one hand and key militia figures associated with the Muslim Brotherhood, notably Abdelhakim Bilhaj, head of the Tripoli Military Council, on the other.[5] Though the dispute was temporarily resolved when the Tripoli Taskforce was taken away from the Executive Committee (and thus from Jibril), the inability of the NTC to build up unified security forces reflected these divisions among its top leadership.

Throughout the spring and summer of 2011, and even after Tripoli had been liberated, the number of armed groups around the country

---

[4] Interview with a Zeidan government member, October 20, 2019.
[5] Cole and McQuinn, eds., *The Libyan Revolution*, 64–71.

had proliferated. Despite NTC's declarations and promises to create a police force and an army that would protect the Libyan people, these groups continued to act on their own initiative. After the fall of Tripoli, the NTC's first attempt at Demobilization, Disarmament, and Reintegration (DDR) was a December 2011 initiative called the Warriors Affairs Commission, set up as an interministerial body under the authority of the prime minister. With the goal of "register(ing) all fighters still mobilized, channel(ing) them into training programs and, eventually, toward employment in the labor, interior and defense ministries," as well as simply gaining information about the various brigades, the commission worked through local civilian and military councils to distribute registration forms to fighters. However, it quickly became overwhelmed with the paperwork and abandoned its task. Other parts of the NTC would thus pursue other initiatives to bring the fighters under their control.[6]

Moreover, although the NTC had early on established a Defense Ministry under the leadership of Osama Juweili, in September 2011 it established a Supreme Security Council (SSC) to bring the fighters around the country under a central command and to fill the gap left by the breakdown of the state police function. The SSC was originally meant to be under NTC's executive committee control but later became part of the interior ministry and operated as more of a "parallel, hybrid institution" alongside the existing armed forces and police.[7] The SSC, with UN and bilateral support, immediately rolled out a program for young armed Libyans to be given basic police training in Jordan.

The SSC tried to establish its authority over the plethora of armed groups in Libya by paying them salaries. As a result, between February and April 2012, the number of armed fighters registered with the SSC grew quickly. This decision would also have later implications for the NTC's successor, as armed groups refused to cooperate without substantial salaries. The SSC was also given, in December 2011, certain

---

[6] In exasperation with this process and out of mistrust for the man put in charge of the Warriors Affairs Commission, the interior and defense ministers at the time tried to start their own registration processes. The numbers were so great that both ministers "tried to register and authorize entire brigades at once," leading to disastrous consequences (International Crisis Group, *Divided We Stand*, 12). Also see Pack et al., *Libya's Faustian Bargains*, 44.

[7] Cole and McQuinn, eds., *The Libyan Revolution*, 103.

investigative responsibilities. For several reasons, it would come into clashes with many other security institutions set up by the NTC.

Finally, several revolutionary brigades formed a national force called the Libyan Shield Force (LSF) in early 2012. This was partly in response to the communal conflicts that were occurring with increasing frequency, and partly because many of the most powerful armed groups did not trust the existing state army.[8] As the NTC's defense ministry struggled to incorporate the various militias and brigades through ad hoc processes, Minister Juweili – who was becoming increasingly at odds with other members of the NTC – in April 2012 gave official sanction to the LSF.[9] The LSF operated as a parallel security force, like an "auxiliary army," which, although meant to be neutral, was sometimes accused of taking sides.[10]

Within this context, the NTC's transfer of power to the GNC took place amid a growing number of security incidents. The most high profile of these was the assassination of US Ambassador J. Christopher Stephens and three other American embassy officials outside the US consulate and CIA outposts in Benghazi on September 12. Other incidents included attacks on and release of prisoners and a series of attacks on Sufi shrines around the country. These incidents reflected the glaring inability of Libyan authorities to control the armed groups around the country, which were becoming increasingly involved with local conflicts and tribal feuds.

The NTC had taken some steps toward controlling the armed clashes and preventing insecurity from unravelling, and the GNC was trying to follow suit. For instance, in April 2013 it passed a law criminalizing torture, kidnapping, and illegal detention. But the ineffectiveness of its attempts had already become clear. In late September 2012, following the killing of Ambassador Stephens, more than thirty thousand protesters demonstrated in front of the Ansar al-Sharia camp (the group that had claimed responsibility for the attack), coming into a head-on confrontation with three thousand Ansar al-Sharia supporters.

The inability of NTC and its successors to bring the fighting groups under their control ultimately led to a Libya in which the armed groups

---

[8] See International Crisis Group, *Divided We Stand*, 16–17; Cole and McQuinn, eds., *The Libyan Revolution*, 254 and 139–140.
[9] International Crisis Group, *Divided We Stand*, 14–16.
[10] Cole and McQuinn, eds., *The Libyan Revolution*, 140.

controlled them, rather than the other way around. Many cite the decision to pay salaries to the various fighting groups as the moment when governing authorities fully lost control of them, and one of the NTC's great mistakes.[11] Others trace it back to the granting of immunity to revolutionary fighters in May 2012.[12] In either case, the result was that none of the NTC's successor cabinets or parliaments would be able to insulate itself from the influence of these armed groups. This meant that compromise politics was no longer possible.

As time went on, the strength of the fighting groups undermined other state security institutions as well. Fighting groups attacked state police, leading to decline in public trust of police capability, and increasingly took on "policing" duties themselves. The police lacked the necessary arms (since many of them had been seized by the various fighting groups) and personnel to arrest those brigades, which were known to have committed crimes.[13] The Libyan General Prosecutor's office struggled to carry out its duties, including the promised investigation into the September 2012 attack on the American consulate and the November 2012 attack on a Sufi shrine in Tripoli, because judges assigned to the investigation resigned due to fear of retaliation.

In addition to dominating state security and judicial functions, militia groups gradually managed to prevent state legislative functions from being carried out. In March 2013 there were reported attacks on the GNC's office, as well as the prime minister's office and the Justice Ministry. Laws such as the highly controversial May 2013 Political Isolation Law were therefore not negotiated and voted as a democratic legislature would intend; rather they were adopted "at gunpoint."[14] More generally, this growing instability made governance more difficult. For example, attacks on hydrocarbon

---

[11] Several NTC observers blamed Jalil for this problem. These individuals claimed that they, as close comrades/colleagues, warned him that such a move would lead the government to lose control over the fighters. Interviews with NTC members, November 13, 2014 and November 8, 2014.

[12] International Crisis Group, *Trial by Error*, 28–29.

[13] International Crisis Group, *Trial by Error*, 27.

[14] Interview with a foreign NGO worker, November 3, 2014. Mezran and Lamen ("Security Challenges for Libya's Quest for Democracy"). Analysts describe the involvement of militias as the law was being pushed through, noting that revolutionaries occupied or surrounded the ministries of foreign affairs and justice in May 2013 as a means of putting pressure on lawmakers. See Cole and McQuinn, eds., *The Libyan Revolution*, 160; Daragahi, "Libya: From Euphoria to Breakdown," 45. Members of government at the time lamented that these

infrastructure prevented the necessary production and export of Libya's most lucrative resource.

This situation exploded in May 2014 when General Khalifa Haftar, who had been one of the top commanders under the NTC, led a successful military campaign that suspended the GNC.[15] During this multi-week campaign, Haftar led an attack on the parliament building in Benghazi which unraveled into prolonged fighting with militias identified as Islamist. In Tripoli and other cities, thousands demonstrated in support of Haftar and in opposition to the parliament; meanwhile, a coalition of mostly western-based militia began to form in Tripoli in an effort to take control of the airport and other strategic resources. According to some analyses, the ultimate goal of Haftar's campaign was to force negotiations for an amendment to the Political Isolation Law, but this did not occur. Armed groups affiliated with the town of Zintan tried to block a Congressional vote to confirm a new government, but the vote went ahead.

This conflict also prevented the newly elected House of Representatives (HOR), meant to act as the next interim legislative body until permanent elections under a new constitution could be held, from taking its seat in Tripoli. The HOR's move to Tobruk prompted the GNC to refuse to recognize it; however, militias from Zintan aligned with General Haftar's forces then began attacking the GNC offices. These myriad divisions, which had begun under the NTC, had now come fully into the open, as possession of weapons became far more important than rule of law.

After June 2014, conditions in Libya were effectively those of a civil war. The GNC in Tripoli became closely associated with an extremist coalition with Islamist affiliations calling itself Libya Dawn, made up of Islamist and other militia from revolutionary towns in the country's west.[16] The HOR was controlled by a loosely coordinated set of

---

occupations would set back government work by weeks (interview, October 27, 2019).

[15] That February, Haftar had also led a "pseudo-coup" attempt against the GNC, which failed due to inadequate support and poor coordination among the backers.

[16] It is important to note this was not necessarily a battle between Islamist and anti-Islamist forces. The attacks by Haftar were partly in response to a series of assassinations against former security officials from Qadhafi's regime, which were supposedly carried out by jihadi-type groups (with connections to Zintan). However, Wolfram Lacher explains that disparate groups with varying agendas

eastern groups, including eastern tribes, federalists, and disaffected military units, known as Operation Dignity and led by General Haftar. Several observers note that despite the dominant influence of armed militia and the continuing clashes among groups of sometimes conflicting tribal or local loyalties, the period immediately following the NTC and the elections of the GNC felt distinctly different from the period that began in mid-2014.[17] This period, described in Chapter 6, nonetheless was partly born from the inability to restore unity and security and stability in the earlier revolutionary and postrevolutionary days.

Establishing Authority

Although the international community would come to recognize the NTC as the sole legitimate representative of the Libyan people, its actions were contested by several Libyan actors.[18] This stemmed in part from the lack of unity that characterized the movement from the outset (see Chapter 4). In addition, a growing divide was emerging among Libyans between those claiming "revolutionary legitimacy," either because they had fought on the frontlines against Qadhafi in early 2011 or had been victims during his rule, and those perceived as somehow tied to the former regime.[19] Such factors would ultimately subject the NTC's successors to similar challenges.

One of the most vocal movements against the NTC was the federalist movement, which took the shape of the Barqa Council in March 2012. The Barqa Council called for a reinstatement of the old 1951 Libyan Constitution, which granted significant powers to provincial and regional governments. The council, which named Ahmed al-Zubair al-Sanusi – an original NTC member turned critic – as its head, was thus calling for an alternative to the NTC's Constitutional Declaration. Although its influence subsided, for several critical

were aligned with both Haftar's forces and the Zintani militias, and that these attacks led certain forces – including more radical Islamist groups such as Ansar al-Sharia, as well as more moderate Islamist groups and groups defined by their local communities – to align with those who were attacked. Lacher, "Libya's Transition: Towards Collapse."

[17] Interview with a Zeidan government member, October 27, 2019. See also, for example, Lacher, "Libya's Transition: Towards Collapse."
[18] Even the African Union (AU) reluctantly recognized the NTC after the fall of Tripoli and eventually Qadhafi's defeat.
[19] See, for example, International Crisis Group, *Trial by Error.*

months it succeeded in garnering significant support as a challenger to the NTC.

Although the Barqa Council's calls for federalism met significant opposition,[20] they were reflective of long-standing national issues that the NTC, despite having originally unified opposition movements around it, could not suppress. The internationally guided establishment of a constitutional monarchy in Libya had originally set up a federal system of government for the country, but the king eventually abandoned it in favor of a more centralized form of government, especially after the discovery of oil. However, as several sources on the post-Qadhafi period note, numerous subnational dynamics reemerged and continued to shape conflicts and debates as the country tried to rebuild itself.[21]

After the July 2012 elections, even with Jibril's National Forces Alliance (which had won a plurality of seats in the GNC elections) calling for unity, debates over federalism continued to rage.[22] Even with the relative decline of the Barqa Council, other groups, such as the Libyan Unionist Party, began to emerge, calling for local control over budgets and municipal services. Demands for revenue-sharing from oil would make the GNC increasingly susceptible to challenges,[23] ultimately erupting in 2013 with the seizure of several important oil fields by a commander of the Petroleum Facilities Guard (the security apparatus's oil protection wing, discussed in Chapter 6).

In addition, some of the intellectuals who had been part of the February 17 Coalition, notably Abdelsalam al-Mismari and Zahi Mugharbi, were critical of many of the NTC's actions. Mugharbi, along with other lawyers, writers, intellectuals, and political activists left the NTC to join the "think-tank styled" Consultative Support Group, based at the Libyan International Medical University. The

---

[20] Mezran and Alunni, "Libya: Negotiations for Transition," 274; Blanchard, *Libya: Unrest and US Policy*, August 26, 2012. For more detail on this movement and how it eventually lost support, see Ahram, *Break All the Borders*, 69–94; Wehrey, *The Struggle for Security in Eastern Libya*.

[21] E.g. Cole and McQuinn, eds., *The Libyan Revolution*; Pack, ed., *The 2011 Libyan Uprisings*; Lacher, "Families, Tribes, and Cities in the Libyan Revolution."

[22] See Mezran and Alluni, "Libya: Negotiations for Transition," 273, and Blanchard, *Libya: Unrest and US Policy*, September 14, 2012, 15, for more detail on the NFA's platform.

[23] Wehrey, *The Struggle for Security in Eastern Libya*.

group appears to have focused on political transition in Libya; for example, Mismari contributed to drafts of alternative roadmaps following the NTC's original Constitutional Declaration draft.[24]

Finally, Islamist actors such as Ali al-Sallabi frequently expressed their own opinions on what was to happen with Libyan governance. For example, after the opposition's siege of Tripoli in late August, Sallabi appeared on television to denounce Jibril's Executive Council, which was beginning to come under pressure to organize the various fighting groups.[25] Like Mismari and Mugharbi, Sallabi drafted an alternative to the NTC's May 5 roadmap (which came to influence the final Constitutional Declaration). Islamist challengers, more so than other challengers, would grow in number and became increasingly important, especially in later phases.

A frequently cited mistake committed by the NTC, and especially by Jalil, was the inability to respond to Islamist demands in a manner acceptable to all. This was evidenced by the chairman's focusing on topics important to conservative Muslims, such as the presence of polygamy in the country, during the "liberation speech" of October 23. Such perceptions of the NTC leaders exacerbated their existing inexperience and weak leadership skills.[26]

Several analysts have also traced back the growing presence of groups with a Salafi identity to decisions taken around security-sector reform during this time, chiefly the decisions to transform the armed *thuwwar* (or "revolutionaries" making up many of the armed militia) into official soldiers by registering, training, and employing them. The brigades the NTC incorporated into the SSC and Libyan Shield Force, due to their mixed character, "invariably ... contain[ed] a number of Salafi militias."[27] The increasing involvement of the members of Libya's Salafi movement in the country's affairs became most

---

[24] Cole and McQuinn, eds., *The Libyan Revolution*, 38.

[25] This incident was in the context of increasing Islamist-secular tension, and Sallabi was criticized for his "highly personalized" remarks. Cole and McQuinn, eds., *The Libyan Revolution*, 193–195.

[26] Pack et al., *Libya's Faustian Bargains*; Pack and Cook, *The July 2012 Libyan Election*, more generally label these types of decisions as the Libyan authorities' "policies of appeasement." Several interviewees described how Jalil later publicly acknowledged his mistakes.

[27] Wehrey, *The Wrath of Libya's Salafis*.

worrisome as attacks claimed by the extremist group Ansar al-Sharia grew.[28] In 2012 and 2013, the group demonstrated its control over the cities of Derna (which has been noted for its disproportionate number of residents with ties to jihadism[29]) and Benghazi by staging parades, which were met with "fierce opposition."[30] In short, the divisions and clashes beginning to profoundly mark Libya were tied to what had happened under the NTC, particularly its inability to make Islamist groups feel sufficiently included or to control the armed militia that were sprouting up around the country.[31]

The rise in security incidents – including the attack on the American consulate in September 2012, shortly after the appointment of the new interim cabinet – also stymied the GNC's work, and suspicion of foreign agendas continued to fuel mistrust.[32] Hostilities among various factions became so tense that, in December 2012, former NTC chairman Mustafa Abd-al Jalil was brought to trial for having orchestrated the assassination of General Yunis. In short, when the NTC left power, it left many divisions and unresolved issues behind it.

Thus, the NTC's experience fending off challengers was transferred to the GNC. As with eastern demands for autonomy, the struggle for control over natural resources – which under Qadhafi had been completely centralized – interfered with the central government's control in the south. In Kufra, for instance, a conflict between the Tebu and Zway ethnic groups began in February 2012 and evolved into significant fighting, causing more than one hundred deaths. The conflict had historical roots and came to be seen by some as driven by a Tebu desire to avenge the marginalization it had experienced under Qadhafi, as well as a longstanding competition over resources, including oil. The NTC – still in place at the time – deployed a coalition of brigades

---

[28] These include attacks on Sufi shrines.

[29] Pack, ed., *The 2011 Libyan Uprisings*, 210.

[30] Wehrey, *The Wrath of Libya's Salafis*; interview with a Libyan interim government member, October 27, 2019.

[31] For more information on Salafis across the Maghreb during this period, see Wehrey and Boukhars, *Salafism in the Maghreb*.

[32] See the Economist Intelligence Unit, *Libya – Country Report*, April 2012, 4; Sawani, "Post-Qadhafi Libya: Interactive Dynamics and the Political Future," 23. Several sources note that such suspicion caused problems. Lacher also observes that any external backing for security-sector reform had the potential to be perceived as backing one faction against another (since armed groups were characterized by rivalries). Lacher, "Families, Cities, and Tribes in Libya's Revolution," 150.

known as the Eastern Libyan Shield, which, by playing into longstanding hostilities toward the non-Arab Tebu, only served to aggravate the conflict.[33] These types of tensions, therefore, continued long after the NTC handed over power.

Importantly, Libyan civil society often filled in for the NTC's and its successors' lack of clear authority and control. In the wake of the uprising, associations and ad hoc volunteer groups sprung up in every location.[34] Local councils became critical in ensuring the continued provision of public services. And as threats to security and the number of attacks from jihadist and other anti-state movements grew, civil society activism worked tirelessly to counterbalance them.[35]

Impacts of International Assistance

The NTC, unlike the Tunisian Provisional Administration (TPA), was formed in the wake of an uprising against a dictatorship that had not completely fallen. Without full international recognition as the replacement for the outgoing regime, it lacked the access to the external financial resources often necessary for governance. Since defeating the former regime required sustained military engagement, the NTC had to seek assistance from outside. This, in turn, made it more vulnerable to the interests of other governments as well as multilateral entities that challenged its autonomy.

The NTC's plea for foreign funds was criticized from many angles. Conspiracy theories arose about the eagerness of certain international partners, especially France, the UK, and Qatar, to assist the NTC. Some pointed to French and British desires to secure oil contracts (noting that both governments had had personal ties with the Qadhafi family that quickly transformed into relationships with leading NTC members).[36] Others pointed to Qatar's links to Islamists, arousing suspicion among the wider population about its long-term objectives.[37]

---

[33] Pack, ed., *The 2011 Libyan Uprisings*, 178–181; Wehrey, *The Struggle for Security in Eastern Libya*.

[34] Interview with a Libyan activist, September 16, 2019; Also see Tempelhof and Omar, *Stakeholders of Libya's February 17 Revolution*.

[35] Wehrey, *The Wrath of Libya's Salafis*.

[36] *Canal +*, "Special Investigation: Gaz et Pétrole – guerres secrètes."

[37] Pack, ed., *The 2011 Libyan Uprisings*, 125.

Furthermore, the NTC often lacked the capacity to absorb the military and technical assistance offered by the United States, Qatar, and other countries. Even in the domains of development, humanitarian, and reconstruction assistance, the NTC was unable to secure what was needed.[38] Although the UN did help the NTC and the al-Kib government to carry out peaceful GNC elections, it was unable to provide all the technical assistance and capacity building it had to offer during its tenure in Libya, especially in the security sector.[39] It also struggled to support the implementation of a system for preventing the human rights abuses and impunity by opposition fighters.[40]

At some points, the NTC faced an acute shortage of funds, forcing it to make desperate pleas to the international community.[41] The NTC was so reliant on foreign assistance that sometimes the mere prospect of ending assistance caused a crisis. During a meeting between French president Nicholas Sarkozy and Jibril in mid-May, for example, Sarkozy warned Jibril that France could not support the NTC forever, implying that Jibril needed to find a way to overcome the impasse.[42] Soon after, US Secretary of State Hillary Clinton also expressed concern about the opposition's ability to take Tripoli. As a result of demands from international funders, the NTC was compelled to establish communication networks and plans that helped it ultimately in taking Tripoli. The NTC did manage to secure more funds from countries such as Turkey. Nonetheless, the country clearly could have benefited from more sustained assistance, given the political, security, and humanitarian crises that would develop.

Despite its involvement, the international community's eagerness to withdraw from Libya once the country had been liberated appeared to many Libyans to outweigh its willingness to intervene at the start of the

---

[38] Chollet and Fishman, "Who Lost Libya?," 156; Chorin, *Exit the Colonel*, 300–301.

[39] Cole and McQuinn, eds., *The Libyan Revolution*, 150. The United Nations Support Mission in Libya (UNSMIL) would end up having its mandate extended by three months.

[40] In fact, according to Human Rights Watch, the United Nations never even had human rights on its agenda (see Saleh, "Militias and the Quest for Libyan Unity"). Ian Martin, the head of UNSMIL, tells how the UN tried to work with the NTC to transfer detainees from prisons set up by the fighting battalions into state custody but was "disappointed" by interim government's lack of action (Cole and McQuinn, eds., *The Libyan Revolution*, 145–146).

[41] Bell and Witter, *Escalation & Intervention*; Cole and McQuinn, eds., *The Libyan Revolution*, 43–48.

[42] Cole and McQuinn, eds., *The Libyan Revolution*, 65.

conflict.[43] Given the other wars ramping up in the region (namely in Syria, soon to be followed by Yemen) and the international community's desire to be efficient and leave only a "light footprint," this was unsurprising. However, in hindsight it would appear a mistake: many people close to the NTC at the time realized that Libya's new government(s) and its society still desperately needed help.[44]

Like the NTC, international partners whose (presumably) true intention was to protect Libyans from violence and instability, even if they also sought to advance other foreign policy, suffered from severe constraints, not the least of which included the GNC's unwillingness to accept their offers for assistance. Participants in or close observers of the international community's involvement in Libya during the NTC period and its withdrawal following the death of Qadhafi have reflected on ways these foreign partners could have otherwise handled the challenge. Noting that their Libyan interlocutors were adamant on preventing foreign meddling and preserving Libyan independence, Obama administration advisors Derek Chollet and Benjamin Fishman subsequently wondered if international partners should have been more insistent on providing post-conflict assistance, in order to prevent conflict.[45] Others have similarly speculated that more attention to mediation efforts might have helped build a political atmosphere in which competing viewpoints understood the need to compromise and deal with (rather than use violence against) their opponents.[46] In any case, the reduction of international support following the death of Qadhafi would only open the space for further problems and eventually a reentanglement of the international community (described in Chapter 6).

Drafting a Constitution

As discussed in Chapter 4, the NTC had prioritized laying out a roadmap for transition, which was codified in the Constitutional

---

[43] Interview with a Libyan civil society activist, July 8, 2015.
[44] Interview with a Libyan civil society activist, July 8, 2015. Also see Pack, ed., *The 2011 Libyan Uprisings*, 139–141; Pack and Barfi, *In War's Wake*.
[45] Chollet and Fishman, "Who Lost Libya?," 156–157.
[46] Interviews with Libya experts, September 15 and 19, 2019. The first of these interviewees lamented that the international community neglected questions of genuine economic reform, which could have also helped prevent the resource struggle that later emerged.

Declaration of August 3, 2011. What this foresaw, of course, was a process in which Libyans could discuss and work together to define their collective identity. The reality of the way things unfolded, however, reflected the many ways in which the NTC had failed to maintain a larger or shared vision, fend off extremist or individualist elements, and thus prevent future conflict.

The internal conflicts and pressures from various sides shaped the NTC's work, and this had an impact on later transition phases. The eleventh-hour change to the electoral law guiding the elections for the GNC that specified the election, rather than the selection, of a sixty-member constituent committee with one-third of the seats allocated to each of Libya's three regions was a response to pressure from those within and outside the GNC promoting a federalist agenda, and was not a unanimously favored decision among the drafters of the NTC's Constitutional Declaration.[47] As a result of the last-minute change, the GNC was elected without a mandate to draft a new constitution. Rather, it was to organize popular elections for a constitutional committee. This hasty decision obscured what Libyans were actually voting for, undermining the credibility of the elections in addition to stalling the constitution-writing process.[48]

Given its new mandate, the GNC passed an electoral law in July 2013. Despite the turmoil that had ensued, the GNC had managed to organize elections for a constituent assembly, thus following the procedures established under the NTC. The elections for the constituent committee were originally to have been held within one year of the GNC elections, but were later postponed until February 2014. When they finally did take place, the elections were marred by relatively low turnout and violence. Moreover, the committee, the CDA, was stymied by lack of experience, continuing insecurity, and political chaos. In short, as the deepening polarization that preceded these steps shows, the chance for establishing general consensus on the transition process had been lost.[49]

---

[47] See Pack and Cook, *The July 2012 Libyan Election*, 186–187; Mundy, *Libya*, 145. Pack and Cook analyze the decision in light of the fact that the main alternative was to delay the elections again, which would have been risky.

[48] Mezran, "Libya Has Successful Elections but Not Yet Democracy." One expert said Libyans were essentially participating in "elections for new elections" (interview, November 3, 2014).

[49] See Pack et al. for a discussion of the flaws in this law and the overall process. Pack et al., *Libya's Faustian Bargains*, 54.

In June, elections with a very low turnout (given the poor security conditions) brought into the position of national congress a new House of Representatives (HOR). The HOR became increasingly challenged by armed groups, which continued to back the GNC based in Tripoli and to reportedly have ties to Islamist groups like Ansar al-Sharia and the western town of Misrata. The struggle had begun between pro- and anti-Islamist forces (Haftar had partly rallied his supporters by blaming Islamist groups for a recent string of assassinations and killings in Benghazi[50]), between former regime members and revolutionary fighters (*thuwwar*), and between east and west, yet there were no clear lines among the fighting factions. Haftar's group was not comprised only of anti-Islamists or fighters from the west. Nor were his opponents all Islamists; they included representatives of disparate forces.[51] Thus, by summer 2014, any semblance of national unity that had existed under the NTC was fully dissolved.

The GNC that had been elected to replace the NTC was thus barely able to function as an interim national congress throughout the two years following the 2012 elections. Ali Zeidan, the first prime minister who had managed to appoint a cabinet, was eventually removed by a vote of no confidence after he was kidnapped by armed militia in October 2013. By then the GNC's legitimacy was already in serious jeopardy. Zeidan was replaced by Abdullah al-Thinni, who was then removed in a vote of no confidence and replaced by Ahmed Maiteg in the divisive vote of May 2014 following Haftar's campaign.

Addressing Human Rights and Transitional Justice

Like the TPA, the NTC struggled with questions of human rights and transitional justice. This required taking on the weighty tasks of investigating and prosecuting former regime members for their crimes, controlling abuses by militia and local military groups, establishing a legal framework for protection of human rights, and allowing former regime officials to participate in politics. Additionally, international human rights groups such as Amnesty International and Human

---

[50] In addition, several security officers were killed in Benghazi, armed groups kidnapped Prime Minister Zeidan, and militias killed protesting civilians in Tripoli and Benghazi. See Blanchard, *Libya: Transition and US Policy*, August 3, 2015, 4.

[51] See Lacher, "Libya's Transition."

Rights Watch were, from the moment the uprisings had turned violent, working with Libyans and the NTC to document violations and advocate with the international community.[52] And the International Criminal Court (ICC) had begun investigations into violations of international law committed by the former regime. Although the NTC did not ignore these issues, its handling of them was inadequate, with implications for subsequent transition phases.

For instance, the first arrest warrants issued by the ICC on June 27 were for Colonel Qadhafi, his son Saif al-Islam Qadhafi, and the head of military intelligence, Abdullah al-Sanusi. The Libyan opposition resisted the idea that these individuals be tried in the ICC, preferring to try them in Libya. Thus when Saif al-Islam was captured in late 2011, Zintani militia decided to transfer him to his hometown of Sirte rather than surrender him to the ICC. This insistence on trying former regime officials in Libya led to slow, difficult prosecutions of many officials and prevented Libya from benefitting from the experience of other post-conflict war-crime prosecutions.[53]

The belief among some opposition fighters that former Qadhafi regime members should be prosecuted through the Libyan system led to an episode that demonstrated the NTC's failure to address the issue of transitional justice. In June 2012, two female advisors from the ICC who had been meeting with the imprisoned Saif al-Islam were detained and held in a prison in Zintan. The advisors' two male colleagues elected to stay in the prison with them, prompting Libyan authorities to accuse the advisors of "attempting to pass messages and communications equipment" to Saif al-Islam.[54] After being held for approximately a month, the four prisoners were released, following an agreement between the ICC and the NTC. Despite the agreement, suspicion between the ICC and the Libyans remained.

In addition to managing international involvement with transitional justice processes, the NTC had to address violations of human rights

[52] Libyan human rights activists worked closely with these international groups to document the human rights abuses that were occurring (interview with a Zeidan government member, October 20, 2019).

[53] Cole and McQuinn, eds., *The Libyan Revolution*, 166. For more detail on the treatment of former regime officials in Libya, see Lacher, "Fault Lines of the Revolution," 30–31; Boduszynski and Wierda, "Political Exclusion and Transitional Justice: A Case Study of Libya."

[54] See Economist Intelligence Unit, *Libya – Country Report*, July 2012, 17.

by opposition fighters. International organizations documented numerous instances of torture and ill-treatment against detainees whom "rebel" militias were holding, usually for alleged loyalty to the Qadhafi regime.[55] It documented cases in places like Tripoli, Zawiya, and Zintan, especially against dark-skinned Africans living in Libya – mainly legal and illegal migrant workers whom the opposition fighters accused of being "mercenaries." Some of the most notorious cases were against Touareg, members of a dark-skinned community south of Misrata whom the Misratans accused of committing atrocities against them and whom they attacked, hunted, and abducted, and the Tebu in Kufra, who were attacked by the Zway and Ouled Suleiman tribes.[56]

Legally, the NTC did little to hold these "revolutionary fighters" accountable for their crimes. This was due to its shrinking capacity to control armed groups, combined with its ongoing struggle to ensure fair judicial processes and erect transitional justice mechanisms. The NTC organized several conferences on the issue of national reconciliation, for example, but with few results. In response, fighters who had helped defeat the former regime began accusing the NTC of trying to "reconcile" with those former regime officials who had committed crimes, and used this as a basis for taking matters into their own hands.[57] For instance, some militia refused to obey prison guards, whom they accused of working for the old regime.[58] Meanwhile, killings and abuses of prisoners were rampant.

The NTC at times facilitated the use of "traditional" reconciliation or mediation mechanisms, many of which involved principles of Islamic sharia law, such as compensation and other community conflict-resolution mechanisms. Sometimes the NTC (as would the GNC) sent reconciliation committees to mediate local conflicts, which were occurring with increasing frequency. These were of limited effectiveness, however, because they largely amounted to mediation of local

---

[55] See, for example, Human Rights Watch, *Suspend Deaths against Qadhafi Loyalists.*

[56] International Crisis Group, *Holding Libya Together*, 6–7; Harchaoui, "La Libye depuis 2015." Addressing minority rights – never guaranteed and often manipulated by Qahdafi – was, sadly, an issue that got lost as the country struggled to adopt a constitution. See, for example, Toaldo, "A Constitutional Panacea for Libya?"

[57] Cole and McQuinn, eds., *The Libyan Revolution*, 163.

[58] Interview with an NTC member, November 8, 2014.

disputes rather than addressing the roots of conflict. The NTC was meanwhile falling short in its promises to develop a roadmap for national reconciliation, leaving many feeling frustrated.[59]

In addition, the NTC issued texts in three relevant legal areas: judicial reform, treatment of former regime members, and treatment of counterrevolutionaries. It also gave brief consideration to reparations for victims of Qadhafi-era abuses. Having defined standards for judicial independence in its Constitutional Declaration,[60] the NTC established a Judicial Reform Commission to help clean the court system of its corruption and lack of independence. The NTC worked closely with the United Nations on this matter.[61] It also took steps like passing Law #4 in November 2011, which was intended to make the Supreme Judicial Council more independent by altering its composition.[62] However, the process was slow, because even as courts reopened and judges returned to work, several were accused by NTC fighters of working for the former regime. This led to calls for "cleansing" the system of anyone who might have such associations.[63]

The NTC also struggled with decisions over how to legally handle former regime members. According to some, this question became marred for the NTC at its creation, when several regime members took prominent positions on the Council.[64] No laws addressing such questions were formulated until the NTC established a High Commission for Integrity and Patriotism (or Integrity Commission) to review the eligibility of candidates wishing to run in the elections. Even then, processes for distinguishing between types of former regime officials were murky.[65] On May 2, the NTC's legislative council passed Law

---

[59] Cole and McQuinn, eds., *The Libyan Revolution*, 162–163.
[60] The declaration (Article 32) stated that "The Judicial Authority shall be independent ... Judges shall be independent, subject to no other authority but the law and conscience."
[61] Cole and McQuinn, eds., *The Libyan Revolution*, 146.
[62] Under Qadhafi it had been headed by the justice minister; Law #4 changed it to be headed by the Supreme Court chief. The law was criticized because the council remained financially dependent on the Justice Ministry and because both the Supreme Court chief and prosecutor general would be appointed by the legislature (International Crisis Group, *Trial by Error*, 16, n. 63).
[63] International Crisis Group, *Trial by Error*, 20; Cole and McQuinn, eds., *The Libyan Revolution*, 163.
[64] Interview with an NTC civil society activist, July 8, 2015.
[65] This commission, established through Law #26 in April 2012, vetted candidates according to their involvement with the former regime and whether they had

#38, which was supposed to grant amnesty for militia, security forces, or civilian acts "made necessary by the February 17 revolution."[66] Such moves to elevate those who had fought against the regime and excuse their human rights violations without clarity on how to handle former regime members, all during the run-up to elections, would have later implications for stability.

An important step in transitional justice is collecting facts, but in this area too, the NTC made little progress. The NTC established a Fact-Finding and Reconciliation Commission in February 2012, but by April 2013 it had not yet commenced its work, partly due to difficulty in reaching an agreement over its composition.[67] The commission was also overwhelmed by the high number of alleged human rights abuses it was charged with investigating.

During this time, the NTC also passed Law #37, which prescribed prison punishment for any insults against Libya or its people, insults against Islam, attempts to impede the February 17 revolution, and glorification of Moammar Qadhafi and his sons.[68] This law was heavily criticized by international human rights groups[69] as well as by the National Council for Civil Liberties and Human Rights, which had been established by the NTC. Eventually, the law was repealed, but it was indicative of the NTC's difficulty in passing acceptable laws aimed at reconciling with the past.

Another issue in need of urgent addressing was reparations for victims of past abuses. The NTC tried with little success to resolve

been committed to the revolution. Specifically, certain former regime members would be eligible if they "unequivocally established" their allegiance to the revolution prior to mid-March; other regime members were "forbidden from holding office regardless of when they pledged allegiance to the revolution." As observers noted, however, "the process for establishing whether one pledged allegiance to the revolution by a certain date [was] unclear, and the extent to which one must have 'joined' the revolution has not been established. Some criteria for disqualification, such as 'those known to glorify the former regime,' do not require concrete evidence in order to disqualify the candidate" (McCurdy, *Previewing Libya's Elections*, 7; Law #26; http://itcadel.gov.ly/wp-content/uploads/pdfs2013/law26-2012.pdf).

[66] Quoted in Economist Intelligence Unit, *Libya – Country Report*, May 2012, 10. According to the International Crisis Group (*Trial by Error*, which was published shortly before the law was amended), the law said that even revolutionary fighters guilty of rape, torture, and murder would be granted immunity.

[67] Cole and McQuinn, eds., *The Libyan Revolution*, 145.

[68] Law #37.

[69] See Human Rights Watch, "Libya: Revoke Draconian New Law."

the issue of reparations. The NTC tried to use reparations to garner loyalty among various groups without any comprehensive truth-seeking process to accompany it. It first passed a law issuing reparations for former political prisoners and then one for the opposition fighters, leading war-wounded fighters to occupy the GNC offices until they were also promised financial support. The NTC also never figured out how to deal with harms caused by land tenure laws passed under Qadhafi.[70]

Altogether, these efforts fell far short of restoring justice and of eradicating the existing, biased judicial system in order to lay the foundations for a robust and independent one. The Supreme Judicial Council, for instance, became marred in political debate before it could create such a committee.[71] Some analysts note that the NTC's proposals "never came close to proposing a total overhaul of the judicial system."[72] In short, justice and judicial reform were a central task of the NTC, but these institutions played a marginal role in its activities.

After the NTC stepped down and the GNC took office, it became clear that such controversies had not disappeared. Early on (October 2012), reportedly driven by suspicions that Qadhafi sympathizers were being harbored in Bani Walid, the GNC issued Resolution 7, authorizing "'allied forces' – including armed groups from Misrata – to take all necessary measures to apprehend" the suspected individuals. Targeting Bani Walid was not coincidental – the town was famous for being "one of the last pro-Qaddafi strongholds to surrender during the 2011 uprising."[73] This move fueled fears that the newly empowered Qadhafi opponents were using their recent victory to "settle scores."

Such contests over legitimacy were reflected in the Political Isolation Law of May 2013. This law was an amendment to the NTC's Law #38 granting immunity to revolutionary fighters. The Political Isolation

---

[70] In fact, laws attempting to revise the rules from the Qadhafi era that stripped thousands of their property rights, and to provide reparations for the victims, were drafted but never adopted by the GNC. See Ibrahim and Otto, *Resolving Real Property Disputes in Post-Qadhafi Libya, in the Context of Transitional Justice.*

[71] Lacher, "Fault Lines of the Revolution," 30–32.

[72] International Crisis Group, *Trial by Error*, 16.

[73] Democracy Reporting International, *At a Glance: Libya's Transformation 2011–2018*, 40. The incident was also cited as highly problematic by several interviewees (interview with a Libyan journalist, September 14, 2019; interview with a member of the Zeidan government, October 20, 2019).

Law categorically excluded individuals involved with the former regime from politics, making it appear an attempt by newly formed parties and alliances to exclude their rivals from participation in politics.[74] It was revoked again after the HOR was elected, but by then Haftar had launched his attack on the GNC, and the country was soon faced with two legislatures that refused to recognize one another. In sum, the years following the period of the NTC saw, as part of a larger struggle for control, an ongoing contest over how to deal with the former regime.

Further reflective of the NTC's failure to promote a culture of respect for human rights and further the rule of law through judicial reform was the assassination of the prominent human rights activist Salwa Boughaigis in June 2014. Boughaigis, who had been a member of the NTC, was killed by gunmen outside her Benghazi home the day Libyans were called to vote for the new HOR to replace the GNC. Her husband, Issam, was also abducted in the incident. Like with other such crimes, the flailing legal system meant that the attackers would never be brought to justice.[75]

Thus, in human rights, transitional justice, and judicial reform, the NTC's shortcomings had several consequences. The GNC continued the NTC's efforts to carry out judicial reform. However, due to the increasing strength of the armed groups and the depth of corruption in the judicial system under Qadhafi, these efforts were limited.[76] The more obvious legacy left by the NTC's efforts in this area was the growing issue of "revolutionary legitimacy" and the violent fights between groups who believed themselves defenders of the revolution and those they believed had remained loyal to the old regime. These conflicts escalated as arms spread and reconciliation processes stalled.

[74] See Cole and McQuinn, eds., *The Libyan Revolution*, 160–161. Lamont ("Contested Governance: Understanding Justice Interventions in Post-Qadhafi Libya"); Lacher ("Libya's Transition: Towards Collapse"); Mezran and Alluni, ("Libya: Negotiations for Transition"), and Boduszynski and Wierda ("Political Exclusion and Transitional Justice") also discuss how this law played a central role in the political polarization and paralysis that followed. Several observers remarked that the law was problematic simply because of the length of Qadhafi's rule, which meant it was nearly impossible to identify people who were *not* implicated in some way (e.g. Daragahi, "Libya: From Euphoria to Breakdown," 45).
[75] Wehrey, *The Burning Shores*, 178–179.
[76] For more detail, see Bertelsmann Stiftung, *BTI 2018 Country Report – Libya*, 12–13.

Conclusion

The phase following the transfer of power to the GNC, which lasted from July 2012 to roughly June 2014, saw the deepening of many conflicts and issues that had roots in the work of the NTC. Prime examples include the NTC's inability to establish its authority over challenging groups, notably Islamists and so-called federalists; its decision to legitimize rather than try to disarm and demobilize militias; its welcoming of followed by resistance to international assistance; its failure to garner consensus on the documents meant to guide the drafting of a new constitution; and its difficulty in managing a process of transitional justice or dealing with human rights abuses. In the roughly two years between the closure of the NTC and the outbreak of full-scale civil conflict, the Council's successor interim government could not contain the rising resource struggles, incidents of armed attacks (including on the government), or collapse of the judiciary and transitional justice process. Although the individual acting as prime minister during this time, Ali Zeidan, attempted to respond to various interests, these armed groups ultimately demonstrated their total control over him and his government.

As Chapter 6 will show, the tenuous legitimacy of the newly elected HOR in summer 2014 ultimately allowed the GNC to unilaterally reinstate itself, effectively creating a situation in which two competing governments – both controlled by armed groups – vied for control. The fact that the international community had for several years already been channeling arms and funds to various Libyan actors allowed for, with the collapse of all central authority, a proxy war to emerge. Finally, earlier efforts of "revolutionary" fighters or other groups who had been excluded in some way under Qadhafi to contest any legitimacy of former regime members would evolve into a full-fledged struggle over resources.

6 | Impacts of the Tunisian Provisional Administration and National Transition Council in Later Years

In this chapter, I show how the decisions and actions taken by the Tunisian Provisional Administration (TPA) in Tunisia between January and October 2011 and by the National Transition Council (NTC) in Libya between February 2011 and July 2012, which were the first interim governments in each country, influenced events between 2014 and 2019. In Tunisia, where the TPA had insisted on abiding by a "spirit of consensus" that helped its successor government, the National Constituent Assembly (NCA)/Troika, overcome its crisis of 2013, a second republic had been inaugurated under a constitution that was written in this spirit. However, governing in this spirit – implementing and operating through consensual institutions – proved much more difficult and caused many challenges in later years. By the end of 2019, elections for a second (permanent) post-uprising government were complete, and the country was shakily moving ahead with the development of a new democratic republic. In Libya, the NTC had been unable to assert a moderate, unifying narrative and governing presence; it was instead drowned out by extremist forces as the NTC gave way to its successor, the General National Congress (GNC). The GNC became so plagued by the features and decisions of the NTC – among others, its inability to control armed groups or assert a shared Libyan vision – that the next several years were defined by spiraling conflict among groups of varying goals and identities. Although many actors involved with the attempted transition in Libya were hoping at the end of 2019 that elections for a permanent government could soon be held, the continued violence among rival factions indicated that the country was far from the installation of a shared democratic vision.

Tunisia

The most important achievements after 2014 in Tunisia's political transition and adoption of a new constitution were the election of the first non-interim government, the creation of new institutions called for by the constitution, and the completion of municipal council elections. Alongside these achievements, however, several concerning events took place. Attacks along Tunisia's borders and in its major cities led to an increase in repressive security measures by the state, while transitional justice processes and other democratic reform measures consistently met with resistance. Meanwhile, elite bickering perpetuated an economic crisis. Finally, repeated impasses in other processes called for by the constitution – sometimes overcome through a last-minute scramble – along with general deterioration in economic conditions contributed to growing voter apathy and fears of renewed instability.

This section begins with an overview of the events that occurred in Tunisia's transition following the adoption of the new constitution. Many of these events were grounded in decisions made by the TPA. The next section describes the issues that characterized the Tunisian experience during this period, in order to highlight the continuation of the principles and practices set forth by the TPA within a larger, halting transitional process.

Chronological Narrative

With the adoption of a new constitution in January 2014, Tunisians were ready to elect a new president and parliament. The focus of 2014 was thus electing a new electoral commission (ISIE), writing a new electoral law, and then monitoring campaigns for the legislative and presidential contests. In the fall of 2014, Tunisia first held elections for the new single-chamber parliament, the People's Representative Assembly (ARP), in which Nida Tounis (the party of TPA prime minister Béji Caïd Essebsi, created in 2012) took a plurality of seats, followed by the main Islamist party Enahda (which had led the Troika). Presidential elections then took place in two rounds, with Caïd Essebsi defeating former Troika president Moncef Marzouki in a runoff that December. In January, Nida Tounis nominated Habib Essid, former interior minister under the TPA, as the new prime minister.

Essid first tried to form a cabinet comprising mainly nonpolitical technocrats. His first proposal was rejected in parliamentary votes because it was not sufficiently representative of the largest parties.

It also did not include any Enahda ministers, even though the party had been urging him to form a government of national unity.[1] Despite having the option of forming a secularist coalition that could have theoretically garnered sufficient votes to hold a majority, Essid ultimately won approval for a national unity government that included Enahda and ministers from four other secular parties.[2] Leaders from both major parties claimed that the time had come to put aside Islamist-secular differences in order to pursue much-needed political and economic reforms.[3] This cabinet therefore reflected the compromise and consensus politics that had marked the work of the TPA and permitted the transition from authoritarian rule to advance.

Nonetheless, most of those reforms did not occur. Security-sector reform – which had already been stalled under the TPA and NCA – was further stalled in the new government. As a result, the country witnessed three high-profile attacks in 2015, the year in which the new coalition government took office. In January of that year, an attack by Islamist-identifying gunmen on the Paris offices of the satirical magazine *Charlie Hebdo*, which had published cartoons of the prophet Mohammed in Paris, revived in full vigor the fierce identity wars that had dominated political discourse in Tunisia.[4] In March, two gunmen killed twenty-one people and injured approximately fifty, including twenty foreign tourists, in an attack on the Bardo National Museum in downtown Tunis. Tunisia was still reeling from this attack, which was later claimed by armed Islamist groups, when in June a lone gunman killed thirty-nine people, mostly British tourists, on a beach resort in Sousse. Throughout the year regular clashes occurred between security forces and armed extremist groups at the Tunisian borders. In November, twelve members of the presidential guard were killed by an exploding bomb in the capital.

---

[1] Economist Intelligence Unit, *Tunisia – Country Report*, February 2015, 3. National unity governments are a form of powersharing among former opponents, often introduced in transitional democracies as a means of putting aside political differences in the name of broader national interest (Kubinec and Grewal, "When National Unity Governments Are Neither National, United, nor Governments," 2).

[2] These were the Union Patriotique Libre (UPL); Afek Tounis; the Front Populaire; and the Congrès pour la République (CPR).

[3] Kubinec and Grewal, "When National Unity Governments Are Neither National, United, nor Governments," 2–3, 7.

[4] Henneberg, "Understanding Charlie Hebdo: Lessons from Tunisia."

Later that year, conflict and turmoil within the Nida Tounis party began to become evident, when thirty-two parliamentarians resigned from the party, accusing President Caïd Essebsi of grooming his son Hafedh to take over as the party leader. Several more defected the following March to join the newly formed party of Mohsen Marzouk, who had until then been the Nida Tounis secretary general. This split within Nida Tounis (which had formed in 2012 mostly in opposition to the powerholders at the time, rather than around a unifying ideology or goal) and defection by several of its representatives meant that Enahda was now the party with the largest number of seats in the ARP.

The following June, Caïd Essebsi called together the parties in the governing coalition (that is, the national unity government formed under Essid) as well as four additional parties and three civil society organizations, including the General Tunisian Workers' Union (UGTT). At this meeting, participating parties declared their intent to "double-down on power-sharing."[5] Analysts observed that growing concerns over the deteriorating security situation and persistent economic woes also prompted the move, along with Caïd Essebsi's concern about the fate of his party.[6] The signatories to the agreement, called the Carthage Declaration, laid out a six-point agenda for governing, setting as priorities combatting terrorism, increasing economic growth with a focus on job creation, fighting corruption, improving the country's fiscal and social policies, implementing targeted regional and local development initiatives, and increasing government efficiency.

But the Carthage Declaration did not mend the divisions within the government. In late July, the ARP dismissed Prime Minister Essid in a no-confidence vote, and replaced him with forty-year-old Yousef Chahed, who had been nominated by Caïd Essebsi. Chahed was notable for his relatively young age; like Essid, he brought a technocratic profile.[7] He soon announced a new cabinet, which was also approved.

By the following summer, Chahed had come into conflict with President Caïd Essebsi, mainly due to his moves to weaken the role

---

[5] Kubinec and Grewal, "When National Unity Governments Are Neither National, United, nor Governments," 7.
[6] Feuer, *A National Unity Government for Tunisia.*
[7] Unlike Essid, Chahed was relatively unknown.

of the major parties, including Nida Tounis.[8] Chahed's "war on corruption," launched in 2017 – a move ostensibly in line with the agreement signed at Carthage but which was met with hostility by Caïd Essebsi because it implied an attack on many of his own allies and possibly the president himself – caused further tension.[9] Caïd Essebsi renewed his tactic of operating outside formal political institutions, for example, by calling meetings like the one that led to the Carthage Agreement.[10] With the prime minister and the president no longer allied, and the second National Unity Government blocked from legislating, causing a crisis among Tunisia's political elites, including within secular parties, reforms appeared even more distant.[11]

In spite of the ongoing power struggles, the attempted transition in Tunisia saw some noteworthy accomplishments during this period. In late 2016, the *Conseil Supérieure de la Magistrature* (CSM, or High Judicial Council) held its first meeting.[12] Reaching this step had been an arduous process, and was important for the implementation of the constitution's guarantees of judicial independence.[13] In summer 2017, in a move that received praise from international human rights groups, Parliament passed a law outlawing violence against women, raising the consent age for marriage to sixteen, and tightening restrictions that allowed men who had sex with underage girls to avoid prosecution. Even certain economic reforms, such as the "startup act" passed in April 2018, which supported entrepreneurship, were considered progress toward Tunisia's liberalization more generally.

The Truth and Dignity Commission (TDC), whose existence was owed to the work and recommendations of the Bouderbala and Amor

---

[8] See International Crisis Group, *Stemming Tunisia's Authoritarian Drift*.
[9] International Crisis Group, *Restoring Public Confidence in Tunisia's Political System*.
[10] Indeed, such a meeting had led to the agreement between Caïd Essebsi and Enahda head Rachid Ghannouchi in August 2013 that had, alongside the National Dialogue, ended Tunisia's constitution-drafting crisis.
[11] See Kubinec and Grewal, "When National Unity Governments Are Neither National, United, nor Governments," 21–22; Yerkes and Ben Yehmed, *Tunisia's Revolutionary Goals Remain Unfulfilled*. Amel Boubekeur's general argument is similar to that of Grewal and Kubinec, namely that political elites' compromises for the sake of "national unity" came at the expense of legislating and undertaking important reforms. (See Boubekeur, "Islamists, Secularists, and Old Regime Elites in Tunisia.")
[12] Dermech, "Magistrature – le conseil supérieure désormais opérationnel."
[13] Pickard, *Tunisia's New Constitutional Court*.

Commissions (two key institutions within the TPA), was launched, as per the constitution, following the passing of a new transitional justice law in December 2013. The TDC soon began accepting and reviewing complaint files from victims of state-led abuse since 1955 (which totaled 63,000), and a year later began holding public hearings broadcast on prime-time television. Despite the commission's eventual completion of its work, it received little support from the government, even including from Enahda, whose members "constituted the largest group of state-led human rights violations before 2011."[14]

Two events in the spring of 2018 most dramatically illustrated the new Tunisian political system's conflicted character and frequent impasses, which it would often overcome at the last minute.[15] The first was a parliamentary vote in March that prohibited the TDC from working until the end of the year. This caused an outcry among civil society organizations, which argued that the decision would deny justice for thousands of victims.[16] Some legal experts also criticized the decisions and procedures around the vote itself.[17] Ultimately, through a confusing sequence of events, the government was able to reverse this parliamentary ruling in late May, and the TDC completed its constitutional mandate. The event was reflective of the continuous battles the TDC had been fighting since its creation,[18] and of the ways

[14] For a good summary of the experience of the Truth and Dignity Commission (TDC) and how it was perceived by the Tunisian public, see Chomiak, "What Tunisia's Historic Truth Commission Accomplished – And What Went Wrong."

[15] In this sense, the new government, several years on, was not a replica of the TPA, which, as described in the previous chapters, operated by strictly circumscribing its own mandate and trying to be as noncontroversial as possible. This character of the new Tunisian political system was nonetheless a reflection of the TPA's insistence of finding a way to include everyone – even if that had the potential to lead to blockages.

[16] See "Joint Open Letter: Appeal to the Government to Put an End to the Widespread Impunity."

[17] Ben Aissa, "La décision relative au refus de prorogation du mandat de l'Instance Vérité et Dignité (IVD) adoptée par l'Assemblée des représentants du peuple (ARP) le 26 mars 2018." As Ben Aissa explains, this happened through a statement by the minister of human rights (also signed by the TDC) that contradicted the parliamentary ruling by proclaiming the government's commitment to respecting the constitution, including the articles regarding the TDC and its responsibility to "understand the past and achieve national reconciliation." Importantly, his article also makes clear that this chaos around the TDC was the result of inexperience among governing officials.

[18] As discussed in Chapter 3, the appointments to the commission quickly became politicized, but even once the commission was in place, it struggled to conduct its

the TPA, with its recognition of both the importance and the delicate and political nature of transitional justice, handled the issue.

The other event of May 2018 was the local (or municipal) council elections. As with many issues throughout the policy arena over the previous years, the parliament had repeatedly reached an impasse when trying to advance this process. These continuous conflicts had delayed the elections for more than one year. Yet these elections were important both for "transitional" and political reasons.[19] In terms of the former, the elections were part of a decentralization process called for in the constitution, intended to enhance Tunisia's democratic system through more direct participation and representation. Their successful completion would therefore represent both progress in the implementation of the constitution itself and the realization of democratic practices. The political stakes, however, lay largely in the struggle within each of the two main parties, Nida Tounis and Enahda, to retain support by gaining seats at the local level. Other parties also stood a chance of increasing their voice in the government.

Although they were deemed free and fair and, indeed, represented a milestone in the transition process, only 36 percent of citizens voted in Tunisia's 2017 municipal elections, as compared to 64 percent in the 2014 legislative elections. This suggested widespread disillusionment with the overall democratization process (as well as a lack of awareness of the municipal councils' importance[20]). The high number of independent candidates who ran and gained municipal council seats also reflected the low trust in political parties generally.[21] Like the TDC and the near accomplishment of its mandate, therefore, the local/municipal council elections were, simultaneously, achievements in the overall democratization process and evidence of the TPA's inability to guide the behavior of future governing elites.

---

investigations due to a lack of cooperation by certain government agencies, especially the Ministry of Defense and the Ministry of Interior (Amnesty International, *Tunisia: Attempts to Obstruct Work of Truth and Dignity Commission Undermine Victims' Rights and Threaten Transitional Justice*).

[19] Nouira, "Tunisia's Local Elections"; POMED, "Q&A: Tunisia's Municipal Elections."

[20] Nouira, "Tunisia's Local Elections." The preceding statistics are also taken from this piece.

[21] See POMED, "Tunisia's Municipal Elections – The View from Tunis," 2.

In September 2018, Caïd Essebsi formally announced the end of his party's alliance with Enahda.[22] The conflict between Prime Minister Chahed and President Caïd Essebsi (which had intertwined with the conflict within Nida Tounis itself[23]) had ultimately caused Enahda to side with Chahed. The growing rift between the two parties had become increasingly clear, through Caïd Essebsi's endorsement of legislation that removed the influence of Islamic law on women's inheritance rights and his investigation into allegations that Enahda was tied to terrorism.[24] The split between the parties fueled doubts about the future of Tunisia's political transition, given that the consensus between these former enemies had come to be seen as one of the key reasons for the progress in Tunisia's attempted transition, especially compared to neighboring countries like Egypt.

The ninety-two-year-old Caïd Essebsi died in office on July 25, 2019, shortly before the end of his term. According to the constitution, new elections were to be held within forty-five days, resulting in a revised (and more compressed) electoral timetable for the fall. This meant that the first round of presidential elections would occur before legislative elections, potentially influencing decisions for the latter. In early September, twenty-six presidential candidates launched their campaigns. Given the strong disillusionment with political parties that had developed among the Tunisian public, many candidates for both president and parliamentary representatives ran as independents. The two presidential finalists, Nabil Karoui of the newly created Qelb Tounis and independent constitutional law professor Kais Saed, entered into a runoff on October 6. Although Saed defeated Karoui, who was in prison for charges of money laundering, Qelb Tounis fared better than all other parties except Enahda in the parliamentary vote, taking thirty-eight seats.[25]

Entering into the electoral cycle of 2019, with political parties divided and mistrusted and the economy in shambles, Tunisia was still lacking one of the most important institutions called for in the

---

[22] Al-Hilali, "Tunisia in Limbo after Essebsi Ends Enahda Alliance."
[23] The last straw for Caïd Essebsi was when Chahed suggested publicly following the 2018 municipal elections that Nida Tounis's poor performance was due to the party leadership of Caïd Essebsi's son Hafedh.
[24] Cherif, "Can Tunisia's Democracy Survive?"
[25] In fact, this constitutes only 17.5 percent of the assembly's 217 seats, reflecting the wide distribution of votes across many parties. Enahda won fifty-two seats.

constitution – the Constitutional Court.[26] The constitution described the court as "the sole body competent to oversee" the constitutionality of various legal questions and to resolve disputes between the president and the prime minister. Certain appointments within the High Judicial Council (CSM) had not been filled by mid-2019, which in turn prevented it from making its appointments (one-third of the membership) to the Constitutional Court. Parliament, which was also meant to agree on one-third of the appointments to the court, was similarly stymied for political reasons.[27] As the next section explains, this key gap in the transitional process contributed to blockages elsewhere.

Issues

Constitutional Issues

Tunisia's new constitution, hailed by many as an exceptionally liberal constitution among Arab countries and a milestone in the process of transitioning from authoritarian rule, strongly reflected the "consensual" ideas thought of as part of the Tunisian political tradition and emphatically invoked under the TPA. The constitution also reflected the context in which it was written – an understanding of the need to reach consensus but with explicit references to the main civil society and political groups asserting their interests during the period. These included the UGTT, the Bar Association, and of course, the Islamists.[28] Because the new constitution and the process of its development continued to influence events and issues through the next five years, this section begins with a brief summary of the issues with which the NCA wrestled in 2012–2013 when it was drafting the constitution.

---

[26] One interviewee (January 21, 2019) called the Constitutional Court "primordial" for democracy.

[27] Brumberg, "Confronting Gridlock and Fragmentation."

[28] On the role of the General Tunisian Workers' Union (UGTT) during the constitution-drafting period, see Baccouche, "Les Droits Economiques et Sociaux et la Constitution." The Bar Association's role was reflected in provisions like Article 105, which reads, "The legal profession is a free and independent profession that contributes to the establishment of justice and defense of rights and liberties. Lawyers are entitled to the legal guarantees that ensure their protection and the fulfillment of their tasks." This type of provision has been interpreted as a reaction to the authoritarian ways of the past and an unusual specification for a constitution (interview with a constitutional expert, January 17, 2019).

The emphasis on consensus that characterized the work of the TPA in 2011 became extremely important within its successor, the NCA. Even before the launching of the National Dialogue in mid-summer 2013, NCA delegates had recognized the profound risk it faced from the secular-Islamist polarization within the assembly. In drafting the constitution, the NCA formed a Consensus Committee to lead negotiations through the most contentious issues. The consensual nature of the text that was the ultimate fruit of this process heavily shaped Tunisian governance going forward.

For example, one of the key issues the Consensus Committee helped resolve was around the mechanisms for guaranteeing judicial independence. Enahda (and its allies) argued that appointment of senior judges should be the prerogative of the Ministry of Justice, but secular parties argued that the role of appointing senior judges should be reserved for the High Judicial Council (CSM). The creation of this council, which is defined in a separate article of the constitution, thus became another point of contention. The Consensus Committee, after several days of negotiation, helped broker a compromise according to which the president would make judicial appointments, but on the exclusive recommendation of the CSM, and following consultations with the prime minister.[29]

In this example, the importance of reaching a consensus is reflected in the complicated nature of both the appointment of the CSM and the role of the various judicial bodies in guaranteeing independence from the executive. Yet the consensual resolution of the issue of judicial independence – like other contentious issues that throughout 2012 and 2013 threatened to kill the process – failed to surmount future blockages. Because the constitution authorized the CSM to appoint judges to the Constitutional Court, the CSM, like the Constitutional Court, plays a critical role in the justice system. Given this important role, it is little surprise that the creation of both the CSM and the Constitutional Court became contentious and protracted issues.

---

[29] A separate article stipulates that two-thirds of the High Judicial Council (CSM) members are to be judges, and the majority of these elected (with a minority appointed); the remaining third "shall be comprised of specialized independent individuals." For more detail, see Ben Abdesselem, "The Making of a Constitution" and Mersch, *Tunisia's Compromise Constitution*.

Equally contentious was the debate over executive powers. Avoiding an over-concentration of authority in the executive was a priority for the NCA, given the experiences of Bourguiba and Ben Ali. As with the judicial branch, however, NCA delegates ultimately agreed on a very complicated division of powers within the executive. The semi-presidential system was the result of insistence by secularists to preserve some executive authority by the direct election of a president (rather than having him or her selected by the legislature).[30] The prime minister – who is appointed by the governing coalition in the parliament – appoints all cabinet members except for a few reserved for the president.[31] The president can, however, call a state of emergency, veto legislation, and dissolve the parliament under certain circumstances. Therefore, this system, while significantly reducing the powers of the president, left the potential for impasse "in the case of political rivalry or personal animosity between" the two heads of the executive.[32] Overall, then, the constitution was strong because it reflected a consensus of all parties (a legacy of the TPA), but weak because it was complicated and posed severe risk of creating institutional blockages (as indeed, it would).

Security, Human Rights, and Transitional Justice

As described in Chapter 3, members of the TPA's Ben Achour Commission had overcome great hurdles in reaching the compromise of Article 15 of the 2011 electoral code. This article treated the issue of how to deal with members of the former ruling party, the RCD. Rather than categorically excluding all RCD party members from running in the elections, the TPA had prohibited candidacies of only the most senior ministers or party officials as well as "*munachidines*," or individuals who had supported Ben Ali's reelection in 2014.[33] This did not, however, prevent former RCD members who had held ministerial

---

[30] Arieff and Humud, *Political Transition in Tunisia*.
[31] The ministerial appointments reserved for the president are foreign affairs and defense, and the president must consult with the prime minister over these appointments.
[32] Bertlesmann Stiftung, *BTI 2016 – Tunisia Country Report*.
[33] Lamont, "The Scope and Boundaries of Transitional Justice in the Arab Spring," 92–93. Also see DL 2011-35.

posts under Ben Ali from creating political parties; several of these parties were authorized by the TPA and competed in the elections.[34]

In fact, the first prime minister, Habib Essid, who was selected by Nida Tounis after its victory in the parliamentary elections of 2014, recalled these somewhat contradictory determinations by the TPA. Essid – who had held ostensibly influential ministerial posts under Ben Ali[35] – had been appointed as TPA's interior minister in May 2011 following the removal of his predecessor (see Chapter 3). Although at the time this sparked protests and fears that RCD's influence had not been fully extracted from the post-uprising political process,[36] by the time of Essid's appointment in 2014 – after, it should be remembered, years of fierce criticism against Enahda, including accusations that it was responsible for the rise in attacks claimed by extremist Islamist groups – Essid was accepted as "an independent and generally well-respected figure."[37]

Essid would also, it was hoped, lead a government that was strict on internal security.[38] Security conditions –already shaky – had grown worse under the NCA/Troika. But the string of high-profile attacks under the new government (led by President Caïd Essebsi, Prime Minister Essid, and the cross-ideological coalition between secular parties and Enahda) was not universally accepted. Shortly following the June 2015 attack in Sousse, Caïd Essebsi announced a state of emergency, declaring it a necessity to protect the country from further attacks and boost the tourism industry, the damage to which was especially painful given its important in Tunisia's already suffering economy. Human rights groups criticized this move, fearing it as a pretext for limiting certain rights, such as through arbitrary arrests.[39] Another concern was that declarations of states of emergency were supposed to be reviewed by the Constitutional

---

[34] Boubekeur, "Islamists, Secularists, and Political Elites," 113.

[35] See *Leaders*, "Pourquoi Habib Essid est pressenti au chef du gouvernement" and Boubekeur, "Islamists, Secularists, and Old Regime Elites in Tunisia,"115.

[36] Murphy, "The Tunisian Elections of October 23, 2011," 234.

[37] Economist Intelligence Unit, *Tunisia – Country Report*, February 2015, 3. Boubekeur ("Islamists, Secularists, and Old Regime Elites in Tunisia") discusses other such figures who reflected a failure/unwillingness on the part of the TPA to fully disempower former RCD ministers, etc.

[38] *Leaders*, "Pourquoi Habib Essid est pressenti au chef du gouvernement."

[39] United States Department of State, *Annual Human Rights Report 2018: Tunisia*, 19.

Court, but Parliament had not yet taken the steps to allow that court to become legally established.

During 2015, Parliament also began considering several controversial laws, some of which it adopted. Under an anti-terrorism law introduced in March following the Bardo attacks, and passed in July, the death penalty would be extended to those convicted of terrorism. Security forces would receive "broad and vague monitoring and surveillance powers"[40] and be allowed to detain suspects without charge or permission to contact a lawyer for fifteen days. In 2013, the government began implementing a measure known as S17, which human rights groups contended was arbitrarily restricting freedom of movement and due process in the name of counterterrorism.[41] These draconian security measures again raised concerns among human rights groups, which claimed that they restricted individual liberties guaranteed by the constitution. Additionally, under the Economic Reconciliation law adopted by the government and sent to Parliament in July, corrupt elites from the Ben Ali era would be granted amnesty in exchange for handing over the funds they were accused of embezzling or obtaining through questionable loans. The law was criticized for threatening to grant impunity for corrupt officials and undermining the process the TPA had put in place of prosecuting individuals for those "economic" crimes.[42]

Overall, these enhanced executive and state powers at the expense of individual liberties emerged, at least in part, from the "space" left by the TPA for former regime elites to assert their influence. The same was true in regards to former "old guard" members' ongoing fierce resistance to the transitional justice process.[43] The difficult experience of reforming the transitional justice process more generally was not merely a product of the continued influence of old regime elites – it was also due to the constraints the TPA, and specifically the Bouderbala and Amor Commissions, had faced when trying to collect

---

[40] Human Rights Watch, *Tunisia: Counterterror Law Endangers Rights.*
[41] Amnesty International, *They Never Tell Me Why.*
[42] Human Rights Watch, *Tunisia: Amnesty Bill Would Set Back Transition.*
[43] Despite the fact that the TDC managed to finish its work and transfer 173 cases of past abuses to be heard in the special chambers created under the 2013 transitional justice law – another product of the TPA's work – in 2019, leading up to new parliamentary elections, a new draft bill was leaked that would have nearly closed down the process.

evidence and draft recommendations (which they had no power to see through), and the politicized nature of transitional justice more generally.

Economic Crisis

The grave economic problems that built up during the years following the TPA stemmed both from structural economic deficiencies the TPA inherited and from distinct decisions it made. The uprising that had brought the TPA into existence was itself the outcome of major problems, namely the inequalities and unemployment as well as a burgeoning informal sector that had been generated through failed or absent development strategies.[44] Starting under the TPA, however, and continuing under the Troika, the interim governments added thousands of public sector jobs. Under Enahda in particular, many posts were filled by highly unqualified party affiliates.[45] This created a bloated public sector that, combined with persistent high unemployment, especially among the youth, contributed to growing external and public debt, high levels of inflation, and a slowdown in growth.[46]

Given the mounting debt crisis – exacerbated by a massive informal sector, which restricted government revenue – Tunisia in 2016 signed an agreement with the International Monetary Fund (IMF) for a $2.8 billion loan package. The loan stipulated numerous difficult reforms, including significant cuts to public sector spending as well as tight monetary policy and other austerity measures meant to rein in inflation and address the economy's numerous imbalances. Prime Minister Chahed's initial embrace of the reforms (in contrast to those of his predecessor Essid)[47] led to significant protests around the country, and general strikes staged in late 2018 and early 2019 led to temporary

---

[44] Ghilès, "Tunisia Has Made Strides in Democratic Transition: Can It Get the Economy Right?"; Cammett et al., *A Political Economy of the Middle East*, 300–301; Alexander, *From Stability to Revolution*, 106–123.

[45] Ben Rhomdane, *Tunisie: La Democratie en Quete d'Etat*, 63–65.

[46] From 2014 to 2018 at least. Essentially, growth levels were higher under Ben Ali, fell dramatically right after the uprising, and then continued to decline until about 2018, when they began to rise marginally. See International Monetary Fund, "Statement Following Assessment Mission to Tunisia" and "Tunisia at a Glance."

[47] The TPA of course included the UGTT as a participant, whose history as a highly engaged political participant had also contributed to the "legacy" of Tunisia's socialist economic model.

shutdowns in transportation and other industries/sectors and forced the government into negotiations.[48]

Ultimately, under the leadership of Chahed, economic reforms were stymied due to the influential UGTT's refusal to accept cuts to public sector wages or jobs.[49] Concessions to the union over preservation of jobs and wages continuously threatened scheduled disbursements of the IMF loan package.[50] As the crisis mounted and politicians began to think about their viability as presidential or parliamentary candidates in the fall of 2019, the prospect of undertaking painful reforms or devising new long-term economic development strategies became even more distant.

Institutional Blockages

The emphasis on consensus that characterized the new constitution and Tunisia's politics after the TPA led to institutional blockages in a variety of sectors. For instance, the delegates of the NCA in 2014 retained several of the provisions taken by the Ben Achour Commission when it had debated the electoral law of 2011 that governed NCA elections. In particular, three important elections-related decisions by the TPA would shape Tunisia's future institutions and the nature of its politics: the electoral system, provisions around gender parity, and decisions around allowing the participation of former regime members.

The Ben Achour Commission had, according to several of its members, agreed on the electoral system for the NCA elections based on recommendations by the commission's expert core.[51] As discussed in Chapter 2, the commission's choice of a closed-list proportional representation (PR) system was, at least in part, a reaction to the majoritarian system used under Ben Ali, which had permitted RCD domination in the Parliament. However, designers of electoral systems face other, more nuanced, choices, including choices about precise

---

[48] A good source on Tunisia's struggle to reform the economy since 2011 is Alexander, *From Stability to Revolution in the Maghreb*, 124–125.

[49] As discussed in Chapter 1, the UGTT had long been very influential in Tunisia's politics and was one of the organizations credited with helping "host" the revolution.

[50] The loan did come through, along with other loans from the European Union and World Bank.

[51] Interviews with TPA members (December 2014–January 2015).

formulas for calculating how votes are converted to seats. In Tunisia, the TPA chose a formula that would give smaller parties opportunities to gain seats.[52] This, combined with the preservation of the moderate-sized electoral districts used under Ben Ali, the relatively low threshold for competing in elections,[53] and the slight bias in district size favoring the historically underrepresented regions,[54] allowed even tiny parties to win seats by forming alliances. Such a system tends to make the elected body as inclusive as possible, and in the NCA elections of 2011, the outcome was that Enahda, the largest party competing, was forced to compromise with coalitions of smaller parties because the system made it difficult for the largest party to win a majority of seats.[55]

However, this choice to maximize inclusiveness in the NCA would have consequences when the time came to vote on a new electoral formula. Unlike for constituent assemblies, experts and experience show that such a system is risky when electing permanent governments

[52] Under proportional-representation electoral systems, parties win seats in proportion to their vote share. Depending on how this is calculated, districts may have "remainder" seats, which are awarded according to the remaining parties' performance. Under the system used in Tunisia, the Hare quotient/largest remainder system, parties that did not gain proportionately enough votes in the initial tally to hold a seat had a better chance of being awarded seats according to "remainder" calculations. See Carey, "Why Tunisia Remains the Arab Spring's Best Bet," 2–3 and appendix; Carey, "Electoral Formula and the Tunisian Constituent Assembly," 2–7, and Murphy, "The Tunisian Elections of October 23, 2011," 235.

[53] The electoral law of 2014 set a low legal threshold (or "minimum vote share") lists must win to be eligible to win seats (Carey, "Electoral Formula and the Tunisian Constituent Assembly," 4). This was based on the precedent set by the TPA/Ben Achour Commission in 2011, where no minimum eligibility threshold was set (see DL 2011-35). A low threshold means smaller parties and alliances are more encouraged to participate because they have more of a chance of getting any seats at all. This provision of the electoral law came up for debate in the run-up to the 2019 elections, when the parliamentary commission for internal rules/bylaws, immunity, parliamentary laws and electoral laws, despite some criticism from civil society, voted in November 2018 to raise the threshold from 3 to 5 percent (Attia, "Tunisie – Seuil de Représentativité Electorale à 5%"). District magnitudes and thresholds matter in these situations because they figure into the calculations for how many seats will remain after "quotas" are awarded and thus the likelihood of small parties winning any seats at all (Carey, "Electoral Formula and the Tunisian Constituent Assembly").

[54] Murphy, "The Tunisian Elections of October 23, 2011," 235.

[55] See Carey, "Electoral Formula and the Tunisian Constituent Assembly"; Carey, "Why Tunisia Remains the Arab Spring's Best Bet"; and Carey and Reynolds, "The Impact of Election Systems."

because too many small parties and shifting alliances can make legislating difficult. Yet due to the high number of small parties represented in the NCA, who favored this system because it gave them a better chance of winning seats, the assembly voted to preserve the same system in the 2014 elections.[56] Unfortunately, the "fragmentation" this produced in the new legislature would make it extremely difficult to reach decisions in Tunisia's new republic.

Thirdly, the final text of the constitution, which read "the state seeks parity between men and women in elected assemblies," left open to the NCA in designing the 2014 electoral law the question of how to ensure female representation. This question had been hotly debated under the TPA (primarily within the Ben Achour Commission), with the agreement finally requiring party lists to alternate between men and women (called a "vertical zipper"). This requirement resulted in women receiving about a quarter of the seats in the assembly. However, the law did not require that parties alternate the gender of the head of their lists across constituencies (called a "horizontal zipper"), which would have achieved near parity.[57] Although for some experts, this result in 2011 suggested a strong argument that could be made in favor of both a vertical and horizontal zipper requirement, the electoral law passed under the NCA used "language nearly identical to 2011's electoral law."[58] Although several proposed versions of the article included a horizontal parity requirement, the voting record shows that there was no agreement on how to impose this rule.[59] As a result of this choice, the proportion of women elected to the ARP was only slightly higher than in the NCA.[60] Again, the TPA had set precedents without knowledge of the exact

---

[56] Interview with an Independent High Electoral Authority 2 (ISIE 2) member (January 24, 2019).

[57] Pickard, *Identity, Islam, and Women in the Tunisian Constitution*.

[58] Tavana and Russell, "Previewing Tunisia's Parliamentary and Presidential Elections," 27.

[59] See the voting record for May 1, 2014: https://majles.marsad.tn/fr/votes . This shows that Article 23 bis of the electoral code, which required eligible lists to be developed on the basis of horizontal and vertical parity, was voted down.

[60] Just over 30 percent (see Bertelsmann Stiftung, *BTI 2016 Country Report – Tunisia*). It should be noted that the ARP *did* adopt the horizontal zipper requirement in the 2017 municipal elections law. It also set requirements intended to raise the proportion of youth (under thirty-five) representation in the government.

consequences; these in turn had implications for the nuances of the new system the interim authorities were creating for their country.

The TPA had thus left its mark in the shaping of the new parliament that was elected in late 2014 in several ways. The continuous strife that characterized the ARP led to delays in important transitional steps like the scheduling of municipal elections. These elections were also beset by other delays caused by similar institutional impasses. The head of the electoral commission, the ISIE, Chafik Sarsar, resigned in May 2017, ostensibly because of the refusal of the other commissioners to cooperate.[61] The need to replace him, along with two other members who had resigned, helped further the delay of the municipal elections (which at the time had been scheduled for December of that year). Even once the vacancies in the ISIE were filled and the electoral law for these elections was finally passed, the Parliament had still not passed an accompanying code on local authorities, which would, among other things, clarify the role of the municipal councils to be elected, thereby enhancing the transparency and effectiveness of the process.[62] This it did barely a week before the voting took place.

Such political squabbling – along with a failure to improve economic conditions – produced severe voter apathy and general disillusionment among the public with the government. Tunisians began to express disillusionment with the "revolution"; some even expressed a wish to return to the days of Ben Ali.[63] The misinformation, confusion, and disinterest of the public was compounded by the irresponsibility among the Tunisian media, which tended to inflame political disputes.[64] As described in Chapter 3, media reform had plagued the TPA and NCA, thanks largely to a lack of cooperation by government officials. Ultimately, INRIC, the commission that had been meant to guide the development of the media into a sector that operated independently from politics, had given up in frustration. In media development too, therefore, legacies of the TPA were visible and posed challenges to the country's progress in transitioning from authoritarian rule.

---

[61] *Leaders*, "Chafik Sarsar – ISIE: Les vrais raisons d'une démission et ses enjeux."
[62] See Nouira, "Tunisia's Local Elections."
[63] Interview with a Tunisian political scientist, January 18, 2019; Hawthorne, *POMED Backgrounder: A Trip Report from Tunisia's 'Dark Regions.'*
[64] Interviews with Tunisian legal experts (January 24, 2019 and January 21, 2019).

Summary

Between 2014 and 2019, Tunisia saw halting progress in its attempted transition from authoritarian rule. Progress on implementation of the new constitution moved forward slowly in some areas but stalled in others, and many began to fear or even welcome an apparent reassertion of old-guard forces as security conditions deteriorated. These trends reflected in many ways the work of the TPA, primarily the emphasis on consensus politics (often at the expense of needed reforms) and the difficulties in advancing a transitional justice process.

Libya

In contrast to Tunisia, where the TPA's emphasis on national consensus led eventually to the establishment of a constitution and new government, in Libya the first interim government, the National Transition Council (NTC), could never garner popular support for the notion of national unity. As described in Chapter 5, this failure manifested itself in numerous events over the years following the closure of the NTC in mid-2012. Any semblance of national unity disappeared entirely after the spring of 2014, when two rival legislatures, each with its own militia, declared themselves the legitimate government.

The next section presents the unfolding of events in Libya following the armed assault on the second transitional government, the General National Congress (GNC), in May 2014 and the election of the House of Representatives (HOR) the following month (which marked the onset of the two rival governments). The subsequent section describes the issues plaguing the country as it became increasingly mired in a conflict widely characterized as a civil war. These issues all harkened back to the challenges the NTC had faced and how they were handled.

Chronological Narrative

Tensions within the GNC had begun to appear long before the election of the HOR in spring 2014. In August 2013, the GNC had endorsed an independent commission to lead a National Dialogue process meant to convene the "collective Libyan polity" in an attempt to articulate a shared identity and vision for the future. Despite significant support from the UN, however, lack of clear parameters and the deteriorating security situation had made it difficult for this process to get off the ground.[65] In December 2013 the Congress had voted to extend its own mandate, provoking protests, following which the GNC (particularly Islamist-affiliated members) reluctantly agreed to hold new parliamentary elections. The following April, the fourth prime minister since September 2012 took office.[66]

In February 2014, a Constitution Drafting Assembly (CDA) was elected.[67] Although this was interpreted as a milestone in Libya's attempted transition process from authoritarian rule, given that no constitution even existed under Qadhafi, the electoral law that guided the process included several provisions that for some undermined the representativeness of the assembly.[68] The legitimacy of the assembly was also questionable because the elections were effectively boycotted by certain groups, notably the Amazigh (who had seats reserved for

---

[65] Pack et al., *Libya's Faustian Bargains*, 59.

[66] The first prime minister, Mustafa Abushagar, was quickly removed in a no-confidence vote following objections and threats of force by the GNC as he tried to appoint a cabinet (Mundy, *Libya*, 126). He was replaced by Ali Zeidan in late 2012. Zeidan, who was kidnapped in October 2013 allegedly by Islamist militia, angry over a US Special Forces abduction of longtime al-Qaeda activist Anas al-Libi, was then removed in a no-confidence vote in March 2014 in a context of generally deteriorating security conditions. Zeidan was replaced by Abdullah al-Thinni, who resigned within weeks after a militia attack on his family. The first attack on the HOR in late April came ahead of a vote for al-Thinni's replacement; ultimately, Ahmed Maitag became the new prime minister of the GNC-backed government (he was eventually replaced by Omar al-Hassi), while al-Thinni's government fled to the east where the HOR ended up being based (Mundy, *Libya*, 159; Lacher, "Was Libya's Collapse Predictable?"; *Middle East Journal*, "Chronology," 68, no. 3 and 4). Overall, then, this instability was linked to the predominance of militias over the political process and eventually the struggle for control over Libya's resources.

[67] This was noted in Chapter 5.

[68] The elections were grounded in an electoral law passed by the GNC in July 2013, which stipulated (also following the NTC's Constitutional Declaration) that the CDA have twenty members each from the east (Cyrenaica), west (Tripolitania), and south (Fezzan), despite the fact that this distribution did not reflect the population distribution. The law also required that a certain number of seats were reserved for women and ethnic groups including the Touareg, Tebu, and Amazigh. Finally, the law included certain provisions for guaranteed representations of ethnic groups which had, in other contexts, sparked electoral violence and "could set a troubling precedent in Libya as well" (Mezran and Pickard, "Negotiating Libya's Constitution," 1–3).

them but refused to present any candidates), and because turnout was only 45 percent of registered voters.[69]

In August the HOR held its first meeting in Tobruk. At this point, the HOR believed it could claim legitimacy as the country's legislative arm because it was internationally recognized, having been elected according to the roadmap laid out by the NTC. The GNC, however, argued that this body could scarcely claim electoral legitimacy, as barely 14 percent of registered voters participated in its election. In November, the Supreme Court also ruled the HOR unconstitutional on procedural grounds.[70] Both the GNC and the HOR soon became dominated by armed groups, with the GNC becoming the "political instrument" of Libya Dawn (*Fajr Libya*), an umbrella group of Islamist-affiliated militias that seized control of Tripoli in late August in response to the poor performance of Islamist candidates in the HOR elections.[71] The HOR, meanwhile, was closely affiliated with Operation Dignity, the shifting coalition of forces led by General Haftar.

By 2015 other political institutions also began suffering from polarization and the dueling legislatures in Tripoli and Tobruk. The Supreme Court in Tripoli "failed to issue judgments on all cases that were heard before it." The Basic Freedoms and Human Rights Council (BFHRC), whose mission was to investigate human rights complaints, was recognized only by the HOR, not the GNC, rendering the completion of its mandate impossible. Even university branches began to announce separate universities due to the political divisions in the country.[72]

As Libya's internal conflicts raged, the international community sought to broker a political solution. French president Emmanuel Macron in particular felt obligated to find a political solution to Libya's conflict. In early 2015, under the leadership of the special representative to the UN secretary general, Bernadino León, representatives from the GNC and HOR flew to Geneva to discuss ways to end

---

[69] Pack et al., *Libya's Faustian Bargains*, 54–55; Carter Center, *Libya's Constitutional Drafting Assembly Elections*. Disorder in certain electoral districts on election day also made it impossible to elect representatives from those districts, leaving thirteen seats of the sixty-member assembly vacant.

[70] See Maghur, *A Legal Look into the Libyan Supreme Court Ruling*. On the ambiguity of the ruling, see International Crisis Group, *Getting Geneva Right*, 3.

[71] Economist Intelligence Unit, *Libya – Country Report*, May 2015, 3.

[72] Bertelsmann Stiftung, *BTI 2018 Country Report – Libya*, 12–15, 26.

the conflict. The goal of the UN was to get both sides to agree on the formation of a national unity government as a "stepping stone" toward a more comprehensive peace agreement.[73]

The international community's efforts led to the signing in Skhirat, Morocco, in December 2015 of the Libya Political Agreement (LPA). The agreement called for the establishment of a national unity government, the Government of National Accord (GNA), which consisted of a Presidency Council made up of a council chair (prime minister), five deputy prime ministers, and three state ministers "each representing a different political and geographical constituency." The agreement also created a consultative High State Council, which was involved in assigning top ministerial posts, and which included most members of the Tripoli-based GNC.[74] It named as chair of the Presidency Council and prime minister Fayez al-Serraj, a relatively unknown HOR member from Tripoli,[75] and affirmed the HOR as the legitimate parliament. Under the agreement, Serraj had thirty days to present a cabinet (the eight other council members) to the HOR for approval. This new government was meant to govern for a minimum of one and maximum of two years, after which elections were to be held in accordance with the provisions of the (still nonexistent) constitution.

However, a lack of commitment by several parties weakened the LPA. From the beginning, both the GNC and HOR were internally divided about the talks and at times suspended their participation. Once the talks were concluded, several key actors who did not agree with its central objectives of forming a unity government and creating a security roadmap simply did not sign the agreement. These included the leaders of the GNC, Nuri Abu Sahmein, and of the HOR, Agileh Saleh. Analysts note that participants felt rushed to reach an agreement, fearing that any deceleration or delay would lead to a breakdown in the entire process.[76]

---

[73] International Crisis Group, *Getting Geneva Right*.
[74] See International Crisis Group, *The Libyan Political Agreement*.
[75] International Crisis Group, *The Libyan Political Agreement*, 3; Mundy, *Libya*, 181.
[76] International Crisis Group, *The Libyan Political Agreement*, 5; Harchaoui, "La Libye depuis 2015," 135. The Skhirat process and the final agreement were also challenged by a competing "Libya-Libya Initiative," launched by some members of the HOR and GNC in November 2015 aimed at reaching a consensus on the Presidency Council's appointments.

Thus, when the agreement began to be implemented, it did not have the intended effect. The GNA took effect in early March, when Serraj arrived in Tripoli. The new government intended to take control of Libya's central ministries and government facilities based in Tripoli, which had previously been under the (albeit tenuous) control of the GNC.[77] However, the HOR refused to recognize Serraj's proposed Presidency Council, causing the head of the new High State Council (HSC) to declare in September that his council would assume all executive and legislative powers. That October, the self-declared prime minister affiliated with the GNC, Khalifa Ghwell, attempted to seize the premises of the HSC, renewing armed clashes between pro-GNA and pro-GNC militias.[78]

In April 2016, the Constitution Drafting Assembly (CDA), which had been elected two years earlier, competed the draft constitution and submitted it to the HOR in Tobruk, as per the roadmap laid out by the NTC. The roadmap had called for the HOR to vote on the document, followed by a popular referendum. However, due to the competing claims for legitimacy between the HOR, the GNC, and now the GNA, such a process was, at least for the time being, impossible.

During the years following the signing of the LPA and the formation of the GNA, the use of force to replace political negotiations – a pattern launched much earlier, with its origins in decisions by the NTC – became even more serious. In September 2016, the armed coalition of militia from Zintan and elsewhere led by General Haftar retook the country's major oil ports from Ibrahim Jadran, a member of the Petroleum Facilities Guard (PFG) who had been blockading several critical facilities since 2013. Jadran had managed to wield sufficient control over the armed forces from Cyrenaica (and supported by some groups from Misrata) by promoting federalism. In order to further weaken Jadran, Haftar agreed to have revenues from those ports go to the Tripoli Central Bank via the Tripoli-based National Oil Corporation (NOC) (even though Haftar was otherwise opposed to the government in Tripoli). By 2017, Haftar, who had taken advantage of his backing from foreign patrons, including Russia, Egypt, and the UAE, managed to retake Benghazi, declaring the city liberated (ostensibly

---

[77] And its associated government, the Government of National Salvation.

[78] See Bertelsmann Stiftung, *BTI 2018 Country Report – Libya*, 6–10. The report tells how all this struggle for control over institutions, had dramatic negative effects on public services and basic goods provision around the country.

from Islamist control) in July.[79] However, by that point, Haftar retained very little support from the elites or locals living there. Thanks in part to the growing antagonism he had stirred up among tribes and emerging Salafi groups supposedly backing him, he even appeared to have lost control of his own forces, sparking the impatience of his foreign backers.[80]

In mid-2017, the CDA voted internally on a final draft of a new constitution. French president Emmanuel Macron also hosted General Haftar, who had become a major contender to the LPA, and Prime Minister Serraj together at a summit in Paris, where they agreed to hold parliamentary and presidential elections "as soon as possible." But the accelerated timeline proved unrealistic, due to the weak legitimacy of the CDA, the strong possibility that the constitution would not be approved when put to referendum, and the opposition to the CDA by a key figure in the roadmap process, Agileh Saleh, head of the HOR.[81]

The second half of 2017 saw ongoing instability as international actors, led by the new special representative to the UN secretary general, Ghassan Salamé, tried to advance the tenuously agreed upon political process. As holding elections appeared increasingly difficult, and the two-year limit for the GNA set by the LPA neared expiration, international and Libyan leaders began discussing an amendment to the LPA. The Italian government, in the context of "intense Italian rivalry with France over Libya," unilaterally decided to hold its own talks among the Libyan groups in Palermo, Sicily. These efforts, too, produced weak results.[82]

Moreover, in June 2018, Jadran had tried to assert a comeback and managed to briefly reassert control over the major oil fields. Although General Haftar regained control in about six days, he also determined that he would no longer cooperate with the Tripoli-based National Oil Corporation (NOC) in funneling those oil revenues. Instead, as part of the battle for controlling these institutions and the resources *they* controlled, Haftar declared that the eastern NOC should administer the ports – shattering the one remaining point of unity among Libya's

---

[79] See Harchaoui, "La Libye depuis 2015," 140; Mundy, *Libya*, 199. Harchaoui says this declaration was "premature by at least six months."
[80] Harchaoui, "La Libye depuis 2015," 140.
[81] Toaldo, "A Constitutional Panacea for Libya?"
[82] Wehrey and Harchaoui, "Is Libya Finally Ready for Peace?"

state institutions.[83] These events were followed by heavy renewed fighting in Tripoli, mainly between militias based in the outskirts of Tripoli, which lasted until a ceasefire was declared in late September.[84]

Libya's intergovernmental conflict and resulting vacuum also permitted illegal activities such as kidnapping, trafficking, and smuggling to thrive. It was in that context that a group known as the Rada militia emerged, garnering support via a rhetoric of "anti-crime" and aligning itself with the GNA.[85] It also claimed to be anti-Islamist, along with several other militia that emerged during roughly the next year. Groups such as Rada, however, had no more intention than any others of providing state services simply to meet the needs of the Libyan people. Instead, such militia contributed to the corruption and illegality that was already running rampant, furthering the rapid deterioration of the economy. In late summer 2018, with the country in shambles, such militia ended their affiliation with the GNA in order to make a further resource grab by launching attacks on Tripoli.

In early 2019, General Haftar took control of the southern cities of Ubari and Sabha and seized the oil field of Shahara, one of Libya's biggest. He used this strategic position to attack Tripoli in early April, triggering what was "probably the largest mobilization of forces in Libya since 2011, with a wide variety of civilian militias, gangs, and other forces from across Western Libya."[86] The international community was divided over how to respond in order to minimize the damage. In September of that year, the United Nations launched a new initiative to host competing sides in the conflict in Berlin. By October, SRSG Salamé had announced a delay of the conference by at least six months, apparently due in part to competing international programs.[87] Meanwhile on the ground, a military stalemate ensued, killing thousands of

[83] For more detail, see Pack, "Fight Over Oil Offers Opportunity to Protect Libya's Wealth"; International Crisis Group, *After the Showdown in Libya's Oil Crescent.*

[84] This fighting produced heavy casualties, reportedly leaving 115 people dead (*Middle East Journal*, "Chronology," 73, no. 1).

[85] Aligning themselves with the internationally recognized GNA allowed these militia to receive payments from the GNA as part of a broader effort to fold them into a national security apparatus (Bodusyznski and Lamont, "Who Controls Libya's Airports Controls Libya").

[86] Megerisi, *Adapting to the New Libya.*

[87] See, for example, Irish, "Egypt, Qatar Trade Barbs at UN on Libya Conflict Interference"; Megerisi, "Can Germany Stop Libya Becoming the New Syria?"

civilians and displacing tens of thousands, and generating incidents such as the abduction from her home of HOR member Sihem Sergiwa in July.[88] In sum, over the course of the years following the NTC and its transfer of power to the GNC, Libya's internal conflict and the inconsistent involvement by the international community that had begun in 2011 and 2012 had only deepened.

Issues

This section briefly reviews how the rivalries and divisions that fueled the conflict after 2014 were handled while the NTC was still in place, before discussing how its actions influenced what came later.

It should be recalled that under Qadhafi, security forces were constantly subject to manipulation, in order to ensure Qadhafi's absolute control.[89] The NTC therefore recognized the need to build a new state security apparatus, creating a professional cadre from a mélange of individuals with particular loyalties. However, this proved extraordinarily difficult from the outset. For one thing, during its armed overthrow of the *ancien régime*, the NTC had selected top commanders for political purposes, not necessarily for national unity. General Abdelfatah Yunis was recruited because he belonged to a significant tribal coalition traditionally favored by Qadhafi. Other top commanders, including Khalifa Haftar, had been longtime opponents of Qadhafi, but brought their own political ambitions and did not necessarily view a unified state security force as favorable.

Moreover, several decisions made by the NTC exacerbated longstanding conflicts between localities, such as the two western cities of Misrata and Zintan. The NTC's selected defense minister, Osama Juweili (who was from Zintan), for instance, gave preferential treatment to Zintani brigades.[90] This sharpened rivalries with high-level military officials from Misrata, who sought to strengthen Misratan and Islamist militias that then aligned themselves with Islamist-identifying

---

[88] Lister and Bashir, "She's One of the Most Prominent Female Politicians in Her Country. A Few Days Ago She Was Abducted from Her House"; Amnesty International, *Libya: Civilians Caught in the Crossfire As Militias Battle for Tripoli.*

[89] For a good discussion of this phenomenon, see Gaub, "The Libyan Armed Forces between Coup-Proofing and Repression."

[90] Pack et al., *Libya's Faustian Bargains*, 41.

politicians in the GNC. The GNC opposed "nationalist" politicians, including former NTC prime minister Mahmoud Jibril.[91] Political groups tightened ties to their own militias, and rivalries became militarized.

Armed Groups and the Fight for Control of Resources

This lack of cohesion and unity among Libya's political and military actors and structures ultimately produced an intense conflict over the country's resources. Beginning in summer 2013, parochial or subnational interests began to overtly compete for control over Libya's primary source of wealth – oil. In July, employees at several oil ports began to strike, demanding more jobs, and later that month strikes and protests shut down Sidre, Libya's largest export terminal, and nearby Ras Lanuf, the biggest refinery. Shortly thereafter, Ibrahim Jadran of the Petroleum Facilities Guard (PFG)[92] seized these important oil terminals in the east and rallied behind him the groups demanding the creation of a Libyan federation. Jadran's timing was not incidental. A federation would strengthen provincial and local control over "Cyrenaican resources," and Jadran wanted to assert autonomy for the eastern region before the Constitution Drafting Assembly (CDA) was seated, forcing the CDA to recognize this arrangement.[93] Jadran and his forces managed to keep these oil ports blockaded until September 2016.

The drastic reduction in oil revenue – the main source of foreign reserves – caused by the blockades at refineries and export ports led to the rapid dwindling of foreign exchange reserves. This contributed to the competition for control over the Central Bank of Libya (CBL), which controlled Libya's foreign exchange reserves. In March 2011, the NTC had declared the Central Bank of Benghazi the official Libyan Central Bank.[94] Following the liberation declaration and the new

---

[91] Many of the militia supporting the "nationalists" were from Zintan, such as the well-known Qaaqaa brigade.

[92] At the time, Jadran was the head of the central division of the Petroleum Facilities Guard (PFG).

[93] See Pack and Cook, "The July 2012 Libyan Election and the Origin of Post-Qadhafi Appeasement," 185; Pack and Cook, "Libya's Happy New Year?"

[94] Cole and McQuinn, eds., *The Libyan Revolution*, 43–47. According to these authors, the NTC would "designate the Central Bank of Benghazi as a monetary authority" and external entities such as the British government could recognize it as "the 'legal central bank.'"

cabinet of ministers appointed under Abderrahim al-Kib in November 2011, the CBL was moved to Tripoli, and Sadiq al-Kabir became its governor. However, starting in the second half of 2014, forces aligned with both Haftar and some of his opponents began pressuring al-Kabir to resign.[95] The first major confrontation came in early April 2015, when HOR prime minister Abdullah al-Thinni ordered the National Oil Corporation (NOC) to stop transferring oil revenues to the Tripoli Central Bank and to transfer them instead to the HOR's bank account in the United Arab Emirates. This happened as al-Thinni's government was facing "an acute shortage of funds."[96] The HOR continued to contest al-Kabir's authority until early 2018, when it appointed its own CBL governor, Mohammed Shokri. The appointment carried some weight because of Shokri's "seasoned experience"; the international community nervously maintained its support for Kabir.[97]

Observers note that such attempts to assert regional control over national resources had been lent momentum by earlier decisions, including those made under the NTC. Some such decisions included those meant to "appease" federalist demands.[98] Admittedly, the historical feelings in eastern regions of neglect and inequality had existed long before the NTC. But hindsight raises the question of whether the NTC should not have been more aware of this sensitive context, for example, when it moved the NOC headquarters from Benghazi to Tripoli following liberation in late summer 2011. This move echoed an earlier one made under Qadhafi in 1970[99] and more generally reflected the NTC's legacy of failing to assuage local grievances, even when trying to call for attention to the national interest.[100] Despite its attempts to preserve the functioning of those key institutions (the NOC

---

[95] For more detail, see International Crisis Group, *After the Showdown in Libya's Oil Crescent*, 8.

[96] Kirkpatrick, "One of Libya's Rival Governments Moves to Control Oil Revenue."

[97] See Harchaoui, "Libya's Monetary Crisis"; and Harchaoui, "La Libye depuis 2015" for comments on the reaction by the international community.

[98] Pack and Cook, "The July 2012 Libyan Election and the Origin of Post-Qadhafi Appeasement"; Pack et al., *Libya's Faustian Bargains*.

[99] See Cole and McQuinn, eds., *The Libyan Revolution*, 210–214.

[100] Armed attacks for control over the oil sector during these years were not limited to the blockades of the oil ports. For example, on January 5, 2015, a warplane aligned with Haftar's Operation Dignity bombed a Greek-operated oil tanker off the eastern port of Derna. Similarly, in 2016, Haftar's LNA threatened to bomb oil tankers using the major ports unless they were authorized by the

and the CBL above all else), the functionally and structurally weak institutions that had characterized it left their mark on the periods that followed.

The conflict over control of the CBL also created a monetary crisis. As a result of Libya's diminishing foreign reserves, the value of the dinar – which was officially maintained at a rate of approximately $1.4 – began to weaken, fueling a parallel black market.[101] Dollars could be purchased at the official exchange rate by obtaining so-called letters of credit, "a form of state subsidy meant to let legitimate commercial-bank customers convert dinars into dollars at the official exchange rate … in order to purchase goods abroad."[102] Thanks to corruption and the prevalence of arms, bank officials could either be bribed or forced to award such letters to traffickers (at least one source suggests that central bank governor Sadiq al-Kabir was able to keep his position despite the growing antagonism against him by turning a "blind eye" to the issuance of these letters).[103] The letters would then permit traffickers to obtain the dollars in cash, which they could then sell for much more than the official rate of $1.4. The strength of armed groups and the weakness of politicians, combined with the deep conflict between forces trying to access Libya's oil revenue and foreign reserves, produced this criminal activity. This, in turn, because it further weakened the currency and general confidence in governance, perpetuated the conflict between the GNC and HOR governments.[104]

In short, over the years following the NTC's work, the central institutions that it had tried to either create or preserve as *national* institutions working for all Libyans became increasingly subject to division, competition, and conflict. Although many of those rivalries and grievances had been produced before the NTC came into being, the NTC's

---

HOR. See Bertelsmann Stiftung, *BTI 2018 Country Report – Libya*, 20; Stephen, "The Libya Paradox."

[101] Harchaoui also notes that the monetary authorities were constrained in their ability to raise interest rates due to "Law Number One," which had been passed by the GNC in 2013 and which forbid usury in accordance with sharia banking (Harchaoui, "Libya's Monetary Crisis").

[102] Harchaoui, "Libya's Monetary Crisis."

[103] International Crisis Group, *After the Showdown in Libya's Oil Crescent*, 15. However, sources generally give the impression that Kabir was trying to maintain neutrality.

[104] See Harchaoui, "Libya's Monetary Crisis"; Mundy, *Libya*, 187; Lacher, *Tripoli's Militia Cartel*.

failure to instate and develop a consensus around the management of the country's resources only created an opportunity for further division and strife.

Internal Divisions and Overlapping Conflicts

The rivalries that plagued the GNC and the various militia and other social groups that became entangled in the growing conflict were more complicated than a simple "Islamist" versus non-Islamist binary. Loyalties to region, cities, family, ethnicity, and tribe (which sometimes closely overlapped) also intersected with ideological formations among the militia, which backed or opposed various leaders of elected bodies (and/or the bodies themselves).[105] This web of conflicts – which the NTC had failed to nip in the bud – helped pave the way for the divisions that emerged with General Haftar's organization of Operation Dignity and the election of the HOR.

The NTC's failure to build legitimate central state institutions also created a vacuum in the management of justice. In addition to the difficulties facing the Supreme Court, the BFHRC, and other national judicial institutions, local judicial institutions were subject to threat and intimidation.[106] The Political Isolation Law, which had been intended to harshly exclude or punish anyone thought to have ties to the former regime, further prompted armed militia to take justice into their own hands, demonstrating the weakness of the NTC and GNC to resist armed groups.[107]

The absence of a shared national vision also fueled conflicts among tribes[108] and ethnic groups in Libya's south. The Tebu and the Touareg, for example, were both non-Arab groups with roots in

[105] For example, one of the most intense rivalries was between two cities of the same region, Misrata and Zintan (Mezran and Pickard, "Negotiating Libya's Constitution"). Misratan militia tended to support Islamist-leaning politicians, but were sometimes divided, particularly as competition over support from southern communities – where an ethnic (i.e. Arab or non-Arab) component was also at play – increased. Other analysts who stress these complicated divisions include Lacher, *Libya's Conflict Enters a Dangerous New Phase*; Lacher, "Was Libya's Collapse Predictable?"; Blanchard, *Libya: Transition and US Policy*, August 3, 2015, 6; and Lemarchand (in El Houssi et al., eds.), "Non-State Politics in Post-Qadhafi Libya," 188.
[106] Mundy, *Libya*, 147–148.
[107] Also see International Crisis Group, *Divided We Stand*.
[108] Lacher in Pack (ed., *The 2011 Libyan Uprising*, 152–154) discusses the question of "What is a Libyan tribe?"

neighboring states (including Algeria, Chad, Niger, and Mali). Unlike the Touareg, the Tebu had never allowed themselves to be coopted by Qadhafi's call for fighting forces. Yet the post-Qadhafi security apparatus was unable to assert control over conflicts between the Tebu and "Arab" tribes like the Zawia of Kufra,[109] which were interlinked with conflicts among militia of the north over accusations of past loyalties to the regime. Although for several years many Tebu gave tacit support to Haftar in his attempts to control territory, as the General's rhetoric became increasingly ethno-nationalist, he gradually dropped the Tebu from his coalition. This in turn opened up the possibility of an alliance between the Tebu and the Misratan militia, which were almost uniformly opposed to Haftar.[110]

This overlap of competition between Haftar and the Tripoli-based GNA with other local and regional grievances manifested itself in other ways. For instance, competition for control over the CBL had become complicated by the fact that Haftar, despite his opposition to the Tripoli-based GNC, had largely cooperated with the CBL and NOC in Tripoli, "allow[ing] oil exports to be shipped from eastern ports under his control even though the revenues would be accrued to the Tripoli Central Bank."[111] This was a strategic move by which Haftar (after storming the major ports of Sidre and Ras Lanuf) secured the support of local tribes who had otherwise been backing Jadran; in exchange for this, the NOC in Tripoli declared both ports open.[112] Although the HOR and Haftar were similarly challenging the NOC chair, Mustafa Sanalla, at this time, Sanalla, like Central Bank Governor Sadiq al-Kabir, insisted on preserving the institution's neutrality. In short, the inability of the NTC to impose a common vision, plan, or goal overran the few remaining voices calling for prioritization of the

---

[109] Technically the Zawia are part of Cyrenaica (Harchaoui, "La Libye depuis 2015," 143; Pack and Cook, "The July 2012 Libyan Election and the Origin of Post-Qadhafi Appeasement," 188. Also see Lemarchand, "Non-State Politics in Post-Qadhafi Libya."

[110] Recruiting instead support from the Awlad-Suleiman tribe, with which the Tebu since 2012 had come increasingly into conflict (see Harchaoui, "La Libye depuis 2015," 144; Lacher, *Libya's Conflict Enters Dangerous New Phase*, 203).

[111] Lacher, *Libya's Conflict Enters Dangerous New Phase*, 1–2.

[112] Stephen, "The Libya Paradox."

national interest, with longstanding or newly emerging local rivalries compounding the challenge.[113]

Entanglements of the International Community

Although from 2015 onward the international community was attempting to mediate between Haftar and his opponents, it was far from united in its views of a favorable outcome to the Libyan conflict. This was a legacy from the NTC period, during which, despite the NATO-led intervention that ended the armed fight against Qadhafi, differing views and initiatives among international actors sometimes interfered with the NTC's goal. Moreover, the disperse initiatives at the time of the NTC by local communities to organize themselves militarily, frequently taking advantage of foreign support and the availability of weapons from Qadhafi's cache, was compounded by the NTC's and GNC's successors' inability to assert centralized authority. The growing entanglement of the international community between 2014 and 2019 was thus, in part, a product of what had begun under the NTC.[114]

Governments in the region were divided about how to support Libya's post-2014 internal conflict. Egypt, Saudi Arabia, and the UAE, fearing retaliation by Islamists, increasingly supported Haftar, while Qatar and Turkey maintained relations with Islamist factions and provided financial support to militias that were aligning themselves against him.[115] On both sides, this included the transfer of weapons, including helicopters, jets, and armored vehicles as well as light weapons and ammunition. Meanwhile, Algeria and Tunisia were hoping to find a more neutral role.[116]

Movement of people also became a growing concern among Libya's neighbors. The smuggling activity that flourished during Libya's conflict meant that the growing numbers of migrants from sub-Saharan Africa and elsewhere who were moving through Libya were subject to

[113] Also see Lacher, "Was Libya's Collapse Predictable?"

[114] For a good source on the ways this reflected patterns of international involvement in Libya prior to 2011, see Anderson, "'They Defeated Us All.'"

[115] See Harchaoui, "La Libye depuis 2015"; Bertelsmann Stiftung, *Libya Country Report 2018*, 29. These international rivalries also affected Libya's oil production (Sanallah, "How to Save Libya from Itself? Protect Its Oil from Its Politics").

[116] For more detail, see Mundy, *Libya*, 189; International Crisis Group, *Getting Geneva Right*, 9–10.

abuses, including slave trading, and threatening to destabilize Libya's northern Mediterranean neighbors.[117] Moreover, in the absence of a single government authority, combined with the high prevalence of weapons and porous borders across which high volumes of people and goods were being smuggled, extremist groups quickly took root.

The increasing entanglement of communities in the south, among others, with conflicts driven in part by Islamist-leaning militia permitted even more freedom of movement for outside groups such as al-Qaeda and the Islamic State. Most famously, in Sirte (a former Qadhafi stronghold ravaged during the 2011 conflict), the Islamic State built on local militia with Islamist affiliations who were asserting themselves in the security vacuum (these militia included some from Misrata who had been partly responsible for Sirte's devastation[118]). These entanglements, in addition to the growing threat of extremist groups, generated concern in Western capitals, especially Paris, Rome, Washington, and London.

As had been true during the NTC period,[119] each foreign government had its own motivation for intervening in Libya.[120] In this phase, the impact of the intervention, however, was rarely positive. The presence of al-Qaeda and ISIS in Sirte, for example, prompted an international campaign that further devastated the city. The campaign eradicated ISIS but in its wake left space for other extremist ideologies,[121] thus deepening the insecurity created by the torn state security apparatus that was the legacy.

France and Italy were the most affected by the incessant flow of migrants departing from Libya's shores across the Mediterranean. In

---

[117] This was famously reported by CNN in November 2017.

[118] Wehrey and Badi, "A Place of Distinctive Despair."

[119] The 2013 overthrow of President Mohammed Morsi of the Muslim Brotherhood by army general Abdelfatah al-Sisi in Egypt created new divisions among regional powers, mostly those favoring "restoration of order" – which Haftar also claimed to bring – and those seeking to preserve an Islamist role in politics (see Anderson, "'They Defeated Us All,'" 242). I am grateful to Mietek Boduszynski for reminding me of this.

[120] On competing European agendas during this phase, see, for example, Megerisi, "The Promise of Palermo."

[121] The main ideology appearing to have gradually gained influence in Libyan politics and society is known as the Madkhali variant of Salafism. See for, example, International Crisis Group, *Addressing the Rise of Libya's Madkhali-Salafis.*

an attempt to control these flows, Italy in 2017 signed an agreement with the GNA to equip Libya's poorly trained and managed coastguard to detain migrants trying to cross the sea, in addition to forming deals with various armed groups to increase border controls. This agreement led to a sharp drop in the numbers of migrants reaching Italy but was a disaster for the migrants themselves, who became subject to increased abuses by militia-aligned security forces operating largely with impunity.[122] The agreement also reinforced the instability in Libya by allowing militias to profit from the reported direct cash gifts and financial incentives paid through the GNA by the European Union to act as migrant deterrent forces.[123] This overwhelming of the Libyan government by outside and local forces thus echoed events under the NTC (and GNC), such as the moment when armed groups forced then prime minister al-Kib's government to pay their salaries. Moreover, the drop in the numbers of migrants, like the eradication of ISIS and al-Qaeda, caused a distinct slowdown in the urgency for Western countries to deal with the Libyan crisis.[124]

This mixed and inconsistent involvement of the international community had a decided effect on the political process. For example, their pressure on Libyans to reach an accord led to the rushed signing of the LPA and, in turn, its ineffectiveness. The hasty signing of the LPA recalled the rushed roadmap put forth by the NTC in August 2011, which, while not an agreement between warring parties, was signed under pressure from the international community to realize a certain vision. The effect of the LPA was a new government that had been hastily stood up by the international community and was not fully endorsed by the political leaders of Libya and thus not likely to lead to reconstruction of state institutions.[125]

In addition, Egypt, France, and increasingly Russia were heavily suspected of transferring weapons to Haftar in support of his claim to be eradicating Islamists.[126] But Haftar could not get support from all Western governments, especially given the human rights violations that had

---

[122] Amnesty International, "Libya's Dark Web of Collusion."
[123] Harchaoui and Herbert, "Italy Claims It's Found a Solution to Libya's Migrant Problem. Here's Why Italy's Wrong."
[124] Harchaoui, "La Libye depuis 2015"; Mundy, *Libya*, 218.
[125] Harchaoui, "La Libye depuis 2015," 135.
[126] Lacher, *Libya's Conflict Enters a Dangerous New Phase*; Mundy, *Libya*, 189–201.

occurred ostensibly under his command.[127] The effect of this discord in the international community was to undermine the negotiation process in Libya and perpetuate the conflict between the two governments.

With Haftar's growing strength in 2017 and 2018 and the prospect of elections dimming, several outside powers (especially France, Egypt, and the UAE) began searching for ways to include Haftar and the forces loyal to him in some kind of political agreement. Strengthening Haftar, however, had unintended consequences; for instance, his advances into Libya's south, which ultimately permitted an assault in April 2019 on Tripoli, only served to compromise the internationally backed Government of National Accord.[128] This experience, then, recalled the days of the NTC when the international community chose to back certain sides and by doing so complicated the dynamics of Libya's internal battles. In short, the international community's lop-sided and inconsistent involvement – a precedent set by the NTC – only exacerbated Libya's conflict after 2014.

Summary

In Libya, the years following the elections meant to replace the GNC were marked by intense conflict over Libya's state resources. This fighting at the national level often played into other local divisions. Meanwhile the international community's involvement seemed only to delay a solution.

Conclusion

The years between 2014 and 2019 in Tunisia and Libya carried the "fingerprints" of the first and second interim governments in both countries. Overall, in Tunisia, the years between 2014 and 2019 reflected in many ways a continuation of the principles and practices the TPA had introduced. Critically, the post-uprising constitution,

---

[127] For example, in 2017 the International Criminal Court issued an arrest warrant for Major Mahmoud Warfalli, commanding a batallion of Haftar's Libyan National Army, following evidence of extrajudicial killings carried out under his command. In 2018 Warfalli reportedly continued to conduct such extrajudicial killings (United States Department of State, "Libya Human Rights Report 2018," 11–12).

[128] Lacher, *Libya's Conflict Enters a Dangerous New Phase*.

which was written in a spirit of consensus following the dire conflict within the NCA – itself a result of the TPA's work – inaugurated a new republic based on liberal democratic principles, which would work through institutions where power was heavily diffused. While laudable, this made consensus and compromise within the new political system very difficult to reach. The text of the constitution itself also reflected in many other ways the context in which it was written, creating (among other problems) ambiguities that could only be resolved by the very institutions that, largely due to their emphasis on consensual decision-making, became frequently blocked. As intractability in governance grew, Tunisia's problems on the ground – security, economics, and transitional justice – became more severe. As the country enters a new election cycle in mid-2019, many analysts fear that low levels of political participation and stalled reforms like the constitutional court will only deepen the crisis.

In Libya, General Khalifa Haftar's advance on Tripoli in spring 2019 represented the complete failure since late 2014 of the attempted political processes facilitated or imposed by the international community. Although the absence of a weak central state by this point was not the product of the NTC but a historical legacy the NTC inherited, several legacies of the NTC also appeared during these years. These included the problems caused by subnational or individual interests, such as calls for federalism or regional control of resources; conflicts among local groups and tribes; or the efforts by General Haftar to claim the "spoils" of war. The involvement of the international community also reflected a pattern set during the NTC period of outside actors supporting some Libyan groups against others but without itself being unified in its stance. Finally, the ability of armed groups to dominate political processes reflected key decisions made by the NTC that rapidly spiraled out of control.

This chapter has illustrated the impacts of the first interim governments in Tunisia and Libya that formed in the immediate wake of the authoritarian regime on the events of the years that followed. Each one's decisions during its short tenure not only heavily influenced the work of their immediate successor, the elected interim governments of the National Constituent Assembly/Troika (Tunisia) and General National Congress (Libya) but also set in motion processes of both cooperation and conflict that would last into the years beyond.

7 | Conclusions

The preceding chapters described the events leading to the formation of the Tunisian Provisional Administration (TPA) in Tunisia and the National Transition Council (NTC) in Libya. They analyzed the actors, institutions, and strategies of each first interim government and the challenges each one faced. The book also highlighted the many ways these first interim governments left their mark on the phases of transition that followed, despite their limited influence.

This two-country case study has provided several insights and lessons about first interim governments more generally. For one thing, it has demonstrated their many contradictory features. First interim governments face enormous burdens of trying to maintain stability in a society amid great upheaval, and of organizing democratic elections in a place where no tradition of genuinely free and fair elections exist – two tasks that are also key to a "successful" transition from authoritarian rule. However, they must also accomplish these tasks while trying to get out of the way as quickly as possible. Moreover, first interim governments must perform these monumental tasks while limiting their own power and authority, and while knowing that any decisions they take may be undone.

The factors shaping this delicate role can thus have critical implications for transition processes as a whole. The cases of the NTC and TPA showed that agents' choices in a situation of authoritarian collapse are not predetermined, and they *will* matter for what happens later. Yet such agents are also not free from the constraints and legacies of the past. In this chapter, I begin by reviewing how that played out in the two cases. I then discuss lessons from these two case studies and offer a framework for future scholarship to build on these lessons in the study of transitions.

Review of the Questions and Arguments

Much of the literature on attempted transitions from authoritarian rule, and particularly on the attempts during and following the uprisings of 2011 in the Middle East and North Africa, focuses on transitions' origins or their outcomes.[1] This book has instead examined what happens *during* that critical moment after an authoritarian regime begins to crumble, but before elections take place, and how much this experience of temporary governing influences events as attempted transitions from authoritarian rule continue. How key decisions are made, the constraints actors face when taking these decisions, and how much these decisions shape future ones are all questions that have been posed by established scholars of democratic transition.[2] This work builds on that scholarship by looking at a particular transitional moment.

Taken individually, each of the two cases examined here sheds light on how transitions happen. In addition, the question of why the processes played out differently in Tunisia and Libya, both during the initial transition phase and in the phases that followed, offers insight into why transitions happen as they do. Comparing and contrasting the two cases provides leverage for understanding how much each interim government was constrained by the structures it inherited, and how much it was able to take advantage of the governance vacuum created by the sudden departure of the dictatorship to shape a new political system. In some ways this simultaneous vacuum in Tunisia and Libya appeared to present tremendous opportunities. For example, the TPA inherited a highly functional state administration, and it built upon this to organize elections for a National Constituent Assembly (NCA) and to maintain stability in the wake of the regime's collapse. Yet in Libya, despite a history of highly personalized forms of governance, the NTC was also able to organize relatively free

---

[1] For example, much of the literature on the Libyan uprising and its aftermath focuses on ties to the politics and structures of the Qadhafi era to the post-2011 events, or else ties the ongoing conflict to the involvement of the international community. Studies of Tunisia tend to focus on factors such as the lack of cohesion among the opposition before 2011, or else on decisions made by actors such as Rachid Ghannouchi beginning in 2012. Thus, while these studies are all helpful, their focus is more on the "before" and "after" rather than the "during."

[2] E.g. Collier and Collier, *Shaping the Political Arena*.

and fair elections for a new legislative assembly – and this after fighting a war that eventually toppled the old regime. The NTC's ability to overcome these odds might tempt us to conclude that first interim governments carry very little "baggage" from their rulers and experiences of the past.

In other ways, however, the study suggests that the TPA and NTC's contrasting decisions and actions were a direct result of their different "starting conditions." Although the TPA was not flush with resources, for instance, it did not face the same resource hurdles as the NTC – frozen assets by the international community that could only be accessed by lobbying for other governments' cooperation. Similarly, the fact that the Tunisian military had supported that country's "revolution" while the Qadhafi regime in Libya had chosen to use force against protestors was the result of contrasting legacies of authoritarian rule that produced very different challenges and constraints for the two interim governments that formed. Finally, different social structures in the two countries help explain some of the differences in character between the TPA and the NTC – for example, while both first interim governments strove for inclusivity, the Libyan NTC faced more challenges, in part, due to the fragmented nature of its society historically. A closer look at how each interim government's "starting conditions," as well as its formation, structure, and actions, affected later phases of transition shows where the countries could overcome their past legacies and where they were unable to do so.

Tunisia and Libya's Different "Starting Conditions"

When both countries broke out into uprising in early 2011, Tunisia and Libya were coming from very different historical experiences. Tunisians brought a long history of constitutionalism (having introduced the first constitution in the Arab world in the late nineteenth century under the Ottoman bey, Muhammed Sadiq Bey) and a "historical sense of state." With the end of the French protectorate in 1956, the first postindependence president, Habib Bourguiba, introduced progressive reforms such as a Personal Status Code specifying certain rights for women, making Tunisia distinct among its Arab neighbors.[3] He also made sure Tunisians had access to free and relatively high-

---

[3] For more on this, see Masri, *Tunisia: An Arab Anomaly*.

quality education, creating an educated middle class. However, the neoliberal reforms introduced under Ben Ali (a necessity following decades of state-led development) helped deepen socioeconomic equalities that fell largely along regional lines. Both leaders' cultivation of a "modern" Tunisian national identity that incorporated the French notion of *laicité*, or strict separation of church and state (again, relatively uncommon among Arab countries), encouraged an Islamist opposition to foment, alongside a secular one that objected to political and other forms of repression.

Libya's modern history, on the other hand, was characterized by an absence of a strong central state. Three Ottoman provinces, each with its own historical experiences and character, were subject to Italian invasion and brief colonization in the early twentieth century, followed by a monarchical system created by the World War II victors and headed by King Idris of the traditional Sanusi order based in the east. However, the discovery of oil in 1959, the relative political cohesion of the military, and the influence of Arab nationalist movements in the region, especially Gamal Abdel Nasser's triumph in Egypt, produced the 1969 coup led by then Captain Moammar Qadhafi and his Revolutionary Command Council. This in turn triggered forty-two years of highly personalized and repressive rule, sending most opposition into exile. Thus, Qadhafi's Libya saw much more blatant, brutal, and unpredictable efforts to squash opposition movements, as compared to Tunisia, producing a highly fractured[4] and frightened population.

In 2011 both countries witnessed a rapid and unexpected overturning of their respective dictatorships. In Tunisia, Ben Ali's flight in the face of nationwide mass protests left a governance opening quickly filled by the Tunisian Provisional Administration (TPA), an amalgamation of commissions and governing structures working together to lay the groundwork for the country's first free and fair elections in history and ultimately lead to the adoption of a new constitution. In Libya, the protest movement that displaced the Qadhafi regime created the space for a National Transition Council (NTC) to form. The NTC soon declared itself the sole representative of the Libyan people (also via recognition and support from the international community) and the

---

[4] As Chapters 2 and 3 mention, this is not to ignore the fact that the Tunisian opposition was also often quite divided.

interim government that was to organize elections for a new interim congress, following which it would hand over power.

Summary of Findings

Tunisia's first post-uprising government, which was in place from January 14, 2011 through the completion of elections for a National Constituent Assembly (NCA) and the handover to a new government that November/December, exhibited several notable features. The TPA's actors played a "bridging" role between revolutionaries and old regime members. This meant, for example, that individuals considered close to the old system, including Mohammed Ghannouchi, Fouad Mebazza, and Béji Caïd Essebsi, managed to play key roles in the decisions that were made during those critical days, including the shape of the interim governing structures and the steps in the immediate phases of the transition process. Both the fact that these old guard members were included in these decision-making processes as well as the decisions themselves would matter going forward. Tunisia's actors also incorporated Tunisia's civil society and worked under a shared vision of building a democratic political system.

A key feature of the TPA's institutions was that they – similar to its actors – attempted to bridge the old and the new. The TPA preserved some of the rules and structures used under the old regime – ranging from big overarching principles like the preservation of a constitutional order, down to much smaller but no less important elements like the map of electoral districts – while discarding institutions especially representative of the cruel authoritarian ways of the past. Much of the TPA's institutional structure was also a hybrid in this sense – the TPA preserved the use of laws and legal texts to frame governing but adopted a new, "revolutionary" way of writing these texts through the Ben Achour Commission, which included previously marginalized groups as well as independent experts and national personalities. Finally, some institutions from the old regime, such as the judiciary, were simply frozen under the TPA. Although a small team of legal experts devoted considerable energy to drafting the texts that would reform the judicial branch, this and other such important decisions were left for future governments (both interim and permanent) to take.

The TPA's institutions also provided a relatively cohesive set of structures through which these interim governing officials could work.

For example, the five new independent commissions created – the Ben Achour (political reform) Commission, the Bouderbala and Amor (fact-finding) Commissions, the INRIC (media reform commission), and the ISIE (electoral management commission) – served critical roles in the planning and organizing for later phases. Importantly, members of these commissions also made sure to *limit* this planning for the future, as a way of preserving their own legitimacy and, whether consciously or not, avoiding blame for poor decisions. Meanwhile, the interim cabinet of Caïd Essebsi worked to keep basic state functions running on a day-to-day basis.

Finally, the TPA adopted several strategies to justify its own existence and decisions and to prevent it from being toppled before achieving its goals (in other words, strategies to secure legitimacy). These included working through consensus, emphasizing inclusion, drawing on historical traditions, abiding by democratic principles, and adapting to rapidly changing conditions. These various ways of overcoming constraints in order to fulfill its (self-determined) mandate contributed to the TPA's success in completing that mandate. The strategy of working by consensus was particularly important because it helped demonstrate that the TPA was not a dictator in disguise, and to reassure all groups that they now had a voice in politics. No strategy worked perfectly – this was demonstrated by the severe friction between certain members and parts of the TPA (sometimes even within commissions[5]), as well as the ongoing public protests throughout its tenure. But by and large, the TPA was a first interim government that laid the groundwork, in many ways, for an (albeit tumultuous) continued transition from authoritarian rule.

As Chapter 3 showed, the TPA also dealt with many challenges, and the ways it dealt with these challenges – as well as the actors, institutions, and strategies of the TPA themselves – heavily influenced the next phases of attempted transition. Like any interim government that is self-appointed, rather than elected or appointed by an outside party, the TPA was challenged to establish its legitimacy and claim that it was

---

[5] As mentioned in Chapters 2 and 3, many of the commissions had a bifurcated executive-legislative structure (that is, a consultative council and an implementation arm); sometimes lack of clarity about roles would cause these two parts of the same commission to come into conflict.

representative of the Tunisian people.[6] In addition, the TPA was challenged by the fact that Tunisians were, despite Bourguiba's efforts, not united around a common vision of their national identity.[7] It was further challenged by the need for immediate reforms in several sectors, such as media, elections, and the judiciary, and by the tricky question of how much to allow members of the former regime to participate in future political life.

The TPA found several approaches to managing these challenges, for instance, by broadening its representation through civil society organizations such as the General Tunisian Workers' Union (UGTT) and Tunisian Human Rights League (LTDH). Nonetheless, the TPA was only partially able to overcome most of the challenges it faced. Most notably, and in part because of its inherent limitations (shortage of time, material resources, and vast inexperience), the TPA could do little to mend the divide within Tunisian society over national identity.

The TPA did, however, set a precedent through its use of consensus. The TPA's recognition of the need for actors from all political persuasions, many of whom had never been forced to negotiate with one another, helped it develop a consensual model for the country's new political system. Such decisions proved critically important for the immediate phase of transition that followed. While Tunisian politics and society became highly polarized under the TPA's successor, the NCA/Troika, the reintroduction of individuals, organizations, and principles of the TPA – especially the notion of consensus – helped the NCA overcome its crisis and eventually adopt a new constitution. Similarly, in regard to transitional justice, the TPA was not permanent, so it could not make permanent decisions. As later phases showed – with the introduction in the parliament of the lustration law in 2013–2014, for example – this type of limited decisions also mattered. Still, even in the area of transitional justice, the TPA set important

---

[6] For some interim governments – and this is a big difference between the TPA and NTC – getting that recognition internationally is just as important for its ability to function as getting it domestically (see Rangwala, "The Creation of Governments-in-Waiting"). In the case of the TPA, the most crucial task was the latter, especially at first.

[7] Before, during, and after the TPA, Tunisians have been deeply divided over the role of Islam in the government, given that they are almost all Muslim but that many think religion and politics should be kept strictly separate, while others don't.

precedents and foundations, many of which became codified into laws such as the transitional justice law of December 2013.

Several features of the NTC in Libya looked quite different from those of the TPA. The actors of the NTC were defined by a lack of cohesion. Although the initial core around which the NTC was built comprised mainly judges, lawyers, and intellectuals, it rapidly expanded to a body that included defectors from the old regime, dissidents in exile, military leaders, and representatives of various localities. In part, this disunity stemmed from Libya's fragmented society and history of a weak central state that would command loyalty in addition to traditional loyalties such as to a city and tribe. Moreover, the actors of the NTC were scarcely more powerful than actors outside the NTC who either helped (like the international community, which was itself not always unified) or challenged it.

Unfortunately, the structurally and functionally weak institutions of the NTC did little to create a sense of cohesion. Illustrative of the NTC's overall structural weakness was the fact that it often had little control over the actions of the various municipal transitional councils that formed at the same time. Even more severe was the lack of control over local military councils, especially the Misrata Military Council. All this meant that the NTC – especially compared to the TPA – was scarcely able to operate through clear structures that made its decisions effective. This was exemplified in actions like its half-hearted attempts to reform the judicial system.

The NTC's choices were often very different from those of the TPA, despite the similarity between the two interim governments' mandate – organizing and overseeing free and fair elections for a new interim government. The NTC, at first, prioritized filling a void in governance (while always seeking to reassure Libyans that it was not a dictatorship in disguise). It quickly began to prioritize securing international support as well. Developing a roadmap for transition emerged as a third strategy through which the NTC would work, but, as several scholars have argued, this process was as much an appeal to outside actors as to Libyans.[8] Meanwhile, in order to secure its own legitimacy internally, the NTC used certain strategies for recruitment. These included winning the support of key tribes or recruiting people from Libya's west, since the NTC had begun in and was operating out of the east. However, such recruitment strategies risked creating resentment.

---

[8] E.g. Mundy, *Libya*, 87; Rangwala, "The Creation of Governments-in-Waiting."

Like the TPA, the NTC was wracked with challenges that made it very difficult to carry out its mandate. These challenges were similar, but not by any means identical, to those facing the TPA. The NTC was challenged by the absence of internal trust; by the proliferation of armed groups; by the need for strong leadership and management – a skill which none of its members had been able to cultivate under the former regime; and by the difficulty of protecting human rights in the heavily armed environment where little rule of law had ever existed. The way the NTC handled those challenges were reflected in the phase immediately following the General National Congress (GNC) elections. For example, the passing of laws such as Laws #37 and 38, which protected "revolutionaries" from punishment and limited the political opportunities for people associated with the former regime, served as the basis for the highly controversial 2013 Political Isolation Law (PIL). This, in turn, triggered actions such as Khalifa Haftar's attack on the GNC and the GNC's subsequent refusal to recognize its intended replacement, the House of Representatives (HOR), after it was elected.

Chapter 6 showed how these features of these first interim governments and the ways they dealt with challenges and left legacies for their successors were reflected in events during the next five years in the two countries. Although Tunisia's was by no means an unqualified success story in terms of transition from an authoritarian rule – indeed, few would argue that it has fully "transitioned" today – its trajectory of attempted consensual politics and democratic elections was markedly different from Libya's, which became a civil war.[9] After inaugurating a second republic, Tunisians held elections for their first non-interim, post-uprising government. This government in many ways carried the mark of the TPA. For one thing, it worked through, but also often became deadlocked by, consensual institutions introduced in the 2014 constitution, which mimicked the governing style of the TPA. Additionally, the new heads of state, President Béji Caïd Essebsi and Prime Minister Habib Essid, were both part of the TPA, and, critically, also represented the old guard. This space left for old guard members gradually began to hamper the transitional justice process the TPA had launched and frequently compromised or threatened to

---

[9] It should not be forgotten that Libyan authorities did manage to draft a new constitution; unfortunately it too was heavily flawed and potentially divisive (see Toaldo, "A Constitutional Panacea for Libya?").

compromise the newfound individual liberties that had been codified in the constitution. Thus, the influence of the TPA on later phases of Tunisia's transition from authoritarian rule was often positive but also often led to difficulties and contradictions.

In Libya, the mark of the NTC was also visible in the years following Haftar's attack on the GNC and the establishment of two rival governments in the east and west of the country. The lack of control of armed groups was an important feature of the NTC and its work and helped fuel the conflict that raged after 2014. The dispute over national resources, primarily oil revenue,[10] also recalled the resistance the NTC had met when it decided to move the national capital back to Tripoli from Benghazi. Finally, the heavy involvement of the international community that defined so much of the NTC's work became even more significant during the years following the GNC phase. In something of a parallel to the TPA, when certain actors, principles, and strategies disappeared in the immediate aftermath and then reappeared, the international community's role in Libya briefly receded after the defeat of Qadhafi, only to become increasingly prevalent following the assassination of Ambassador Christopher Stephens in 2012 (also prompted by other events).[11] Just as the impact and effectiveness of the NATO intervention during the war between the opposition (ostensibly represented by the NTC) and Qadhafi is still debated, the involvement of the international community following the NTC has come to be increasingly seen as harmful.[12]

What Have We Learned?

Where Do Interim Governments Come From?

These two case studies of first interim governments reveal a great deal in terms of how much transition processes are shaped by their "starting conditions" and how much they, and especially in their early moments,

---

[10] Several sources also mention contestation over control of water resources.

[11] See McQuinn, "Assessing (In)security after the Arab Spring," 717: others include the attacks against the ambassador of the United Kingdom (June 2012) and the ICRC compound in Benghazi (August 2012). As a reminder, reduction in international support after the fall of Tripoli was also the desire of the NTC.

[12] For example, see Wehrey and Badi, "Libya's Coming Forever War"; Lacher, *Tripoli's Militia Cartel.*

leave room for agents to shape the direction of attempted transitions. Both the TPA and the NTC governed, in many ways, under the shadow of the past. The great contrasts between the two countries' historical state-societal relations, state institutions, and the space that had been left for developing strategies for leading a transition from authoritarian rule helps understand some of the differences between the TPA and the NTC and between the two interim governments' behavior. Yet, as the preceding analysis shows, the uprisings of 2011 also left plenty of space for actors in these two first interim governments to make decisions that would shape things going forward.

The TPA included many actors who had emerged from or were a product of the outgoing political system. Some were former (or current) statesmen, and some were longstanding members of the opposition. Many were legal experts or civil society or human rights activists coming out of Tunisia's traditional legal school and having benefited from its exposure to international activism. Other TPA actors were new to the political scene but had played an important role during the uprising. Collectively, these actors' history mattered – their history of working together, their experiences in learning about and fighting for democratic reforms, and so forth. Indeed, Libya's NTC could not have comprised the same set of actors due to the differences in its preceding social and political structures.

Yet the membership of the TPA was not preordained. Whether Mohammed Ghannouchi would remain the interim prime minister was initially unclear, along with the members of his first and second interim cabinets. His replacement – which was also initially uncertain, perhaps even a bit of an accident[13] – in turn mattered greatly, because this individual would eventually become the first president under the second Tunisian Republic. In other words, first interim governments are unique because their precise composition is almost entirely unpredictable.[14]

---

[13] In the interviews I conducted, it was not fully clear who proposed Caïd Essebsi to serve as the interim prime minister and why the proposal was generally accepted.

[14] Although it may be supposed that preexisting features of a political system at the time of a revolution, especially the role of the military and the role of the opposition, can help explain the question of who takes over during an authoritarian collapse, this is far from certain, as cases such as Algeria and Sudan in 2019 suggest.

The same is true of the TPA's institutions and its strategies. Although both were in many ways based on Tunisia's historical legacies – its strong legal tradition, its use of dialogue and negotiation, and its reformist visions – in other ways they were characterized by a determination to break with that past. That determination led to features such as the unwieldy structure of the TPA (in its fierce efforts to avoid domination of the legislative body by a single party and to end previous exclusionary practices) and for the adoption of a new constitution entirely.[15]

For the NTC, the situation was the same. Its actors very much reflected the conditions it inherited. Many were members of the opposition – whether intellectuals or Islamists – who had gone into exile, or else who had been back inside Libya trying to find ways to push their agenda.[16] The NTC also included several military figures and others who had defected. Yet, as many observers have noted, that a group of Libyan lawyers and judges would form a council that would become the face of the uprising, and that this council would – albeit imperfectly – incorporate Libyans from a variety of backgrounds in order to defeat the old regime and guide a transition process was utterly unpredictable.[17]

As for the NTC's institutions and strategies, the rules and structures through which the NTC worked were not a complete break with the ways of the past. The interminable meetings and absence of a single commanding authority – as well as a lack of trust – were also the result of the *Jamahouriya* governing system that had come before. Yet the NTC also adopted critical decisions about the country's political institutions – how to organize the security apparatus (a fated decision that many link to the nature of the fighting that followed), where to base the country's capital, and how to handle members of the former regime. Although the NTC was constrained when it faced important decisions – such as decisions around the timing of elections, or how to engage fighters in a Demobilization, Disarmament, and Reintegration (DDR)

---

[15] Some actors have said that with hindsight, the need for writing an entirely new constitution gets called into question (interview, December 24, 2014).

[16] For more detail on the role of the Libyan diaspora network, see Alunni, "Long-Distance Nationalism and Belonging in the Libyan Diaspora."

[17] E.g. Vandewalle (in Kamrava, ed.), "Beyond the Civil War in Libya," 438.

218

Conclusions

process[18] – it was not forced into them (or at least not always). It made distinct choices – such as the choice to amend Article 30 of its Constitutional Declaration – which carried severe repercussions.

What Impact Do First Interim Governments Have?

Thus, the TPA and the NTC affected in many ways the immediate processes that occurred after them and the longer transitional experiences that played out. In Tunisia, for instance, the TPA's actions around transitional justice – a key issue and challenge – proved highly influential. In drafting the electoral law that governed the first post-uprising elections, the TPA set a precedent of trying to exclude or limit the role of former regime members based on their role within the former ruling party, rather than their simple association with the party. Although the TPA could not guarantee that the deputies in its successor body, the NCA, would follow its example, the general spirit of this type of decision did carry forward into the period of the NCA/Troika and beyond, with the most clear manifestation lying in the failure of the proposed lustration law in 2014.[19] Many such decisions taken by the TPA – without knowledge or perhaps even consideration of their future effects – ended up influencing the politics of the later phases.

The NTC too – its actors, institutions, and strategies, as well as its dealing of the challenges it faced – left a tremendous impact on what was to come after it. Even the presence within the NTC's military leadership of individuals such as Khalifa Haftar would have important implications for Libyan (dis)unity, as the years between 2014 and 2019 showed. The NTC also shaped the phase immediately following its tenure through decisions such as conceding to "revolutionary" fighters' demand for salaries. This gave these fighters more strength to resist any reintegration of former security forces, caused others to take up arms in a bid to become a paid member of these new official security structures, and continued to weaken civilians' control over the militia.[20]

---

[18] See Pack et al., *Libya's Faustian Bargains*, 44–45; Cole and McQuinn, eds., *The Libyan Revolution*, 135.

[19] As discussed in Chapter 6, several other events, such as the Economic Reconciliation Law of 2017, indicated a disappearance of that spirit. Thus, the TPA's impact, while firmly established, was also limited.

[20] See McQuinn, "Assessing (In)security after the Arab Spring," 718–719.

Contributions

In sum, this study has shown that first interim governments face choices that can have a great impact on later phases of transition, even if these interim governments do not emerge on a tabula rasa. First interim governments are important because they represent a bridge between the old and the new. Many scholars have sought to identify the ways existing structures carried forward into the post-2011 attempted transitions in the Middle East and North Africa;[21] others have focused on understanding agents' roles.[22] Yet few studies examine how the old and the new came together during and after these uprisings; this study helps fill that gap.

"Zooming in" on the phase in which first interim governments operate reveals many of the more subtle ways transitions get shaped (as well as the more prominent ones, such as whether a bargain is struck between factions of the political elite).[23] For example, studying not only the question of whether or not new elections are held in a case of attempted transition from authoritarian rule but also devoting attention to *how* the rules for those elections get set provides important insight. If taken too hastily, as the case of Libya suggests, these decisions may end up being subversive to the attempted transition by empowering certain actors whose interests and beliefs may not align with the goals of the transition.[24] Similarly, if done too inclusively, as in the case of Tunisia, precedents may be set (and new voting bodies will get elected) that hold the potential to make future governing very difficult.

Furthermore, "zooming in" allows us to see the ways lack of democratic experience within first interim governments can interfere with attempted transition processes, even among well-intentioned actors. The ways the TPA (and its successor, the NCA/Troika) struggled to establish an independent media sector provide a telling example. On the one hand, the right to freedom of expression – including freedom of the press – was an extremely important gain for Tunisians following the toppling of Ben Ali. The TPA knew it risked sabotaging itself by

---

[21] E.g. Brownlee et al., *The Arab Spring: Pathways of Repression and Reform.*
[22] Boduszynski and Henneberg, "Explaining Divergent Pathways of Post-Arab Spring Change," (unpublished).
[23] O'Donnell and Schmitter, *Transitions from Authoritarian Rule.*
[24] See Wehrey, "After Gaddafi," 6.

imposing what could be perceived as unfair restrictions on the new media outlets that were rapidly emerging. Yet, as discussed in Chapter 3, the very same journalists who had worked for so long to resist the repression of Ben Ali demonstrated a lack of understanding in the need for fair and democratic procedures to guide the media. This type of a challenge – especially prevalent during the initial phases of transition, when the authoritarian ways of the past still weigh heavily on everyday practices – exemplifies the reasons transitions from authoritarian rule are so difficult.[25]

This points to still a third takeaway from the study of first interim governments: the question of which types of decisions will have the most impact in later phases of attempted transition from authoritarian rule. Interim governments, more so than other governments, by nature have limited time and resources at their disposal. Thus, they – like all governments – must prioritize. Should they *always* prioritize organizing elections, or should they perhaps prioritize something like securing national unity, or DDR?[26] And whatever they choose to prioritize, how should they go about doing that? Is consensus the best model, or was it more appropriate for the Tunisian case given its history? The two-case comparison presented here suggests that each case of first interim government – precisely *because* it inherits certain particular structures and legacies from the past – is different. This in turn suggests that proposing a formula for interim governments to follow as they form and carry out their work is extremely difficult, if not impossible.

Finally, it is important to remember that, despite their importance, first interim governments are sharply limited in what they can influence in regards to later phases of transition. When the TPA (especially the Ben Achour Commission) chose a Proportional Representation (PR) with largest remainders system for the NCA elections, its members likely believed such a system was appropriate for that moment – that is, for the election of a constituent assembly, which should theoretically be as inclusive of as many voices as possible. It had no way of ensuring that future legislators would choose electoral systems more

---

[25] For more on the challenges of reforming the media sector, see Haugbølle, "Rethinking the Role of the Media in the Tunisian Uprising," in Gana, ed., *The Making of the Tunisian Revolution*, 159–180.

[26] One of the first important scholars of democratic transition, Dankwart Rustow, made the case for national unity as a "background condition." See Rustow, "Transitions to Democracy: Toward a Dynamic Model."

appropriate for permanent legislative bodies. Similarly, in drafting the September 15th document, the TPA tried to define a mandate for its successor, but because it was no longer in charge, it could not force its successor to follow that mandate. Indeed, this is what makes transitions so exciting to study – their potential to surprise us.

Therefore, the comparison of these two cases does not simply provide a list of what a first interim government should or should not look like or do in order to guarantee a successful transition from authoritarian rule.[27] If the NTC had made surrounding decisions differently, for example, perhaps its choice of a roadmap by which a constitutional assembly would be formed separately from the new interim legislature to govern, the second transition phase would have worked well. In other words, this book does not argue that the TPA made the right decisions while the NTC did things wrong. What the comparison does is offer insight into an understanding of the agenda first interim governments may adopt and the ways in which the decisions and actions on these agenda items can matter.

Toward a Theory of Interim Governments

This study of the TPA in Tunisia and the NTC in Libya highlights the important role first interim governments can play as a society attempts to transition from authoritarian rule. The study further suggests that a more systematic compiling of evidence could provide additional insight into the precise parameters of this role: that is, the areas in which first interim governments can have the most influence and the actual extent to which they can shape the transition once they have completed their tenure.[28]

A few key elements of first interim governments make them unique from any other government (whether interim or permanent). The first of these is the role they play in bridging the old and the new, or balancing continuity and change – a critical balance during any transition. As the cases of both the NTC and the TPA show, a first interim

---

[27] Indeed, even the notion of how to measure a successful transition is debatable.
[28] As noted in the introduction, such a task was begun in Shain and Linz's 1995 volume *Between States*, but to my knowledge little work on the subject has since been conducted, with the exception of some attention to cases of internationally administered interim governments such as the Coalition Provisional Administration (CPA) in Iraq.

government may be one of the few mechanisms able to recognize and incorporate revolutionary demands without alienating or excluding those who may have had a role in the authoritarian regime but whose contribution to the new regime could be important. Managing this tension between continuity and change will continue beyond the tenure of first interim governments, but only *first* interim governments have the opportunity to strike the right balance from the outset.

In addition, first interim governments are unique in that they source their legitimacy neither from democratic elections (as their immediate successor presumably will) nor from any other kind of established social contract that may define an authoritarian regime, in which political participation is limited but certain economic or security guarantees are extended in exchange. First interim governments must therefore reassure the governed that they are *the* (legitimate) body capable of fulfilling this mandate – a task not required of other governments.

Moreover, in many instances, these interim governments must become accepted by the international community in order to fulfill their goals.[29] In the current era, states engage on the basis of liberal democratic principles (although some suggest this may be changing).[30] To become a first interim government that engages constructively with other governments outside the country, first interim governments must convince the interlocuters of these credentials. What is also uniquely challenging to first interim governments in this quest to establish external legitimacy, however, is that these credentials may not be the same ones that will allow the first interim government to establish *internal* legitimacy.[31] Therefore, balancing internal and external legitimacy can sometimes be a complicated requirement for first interim governments.

Thirdly, in addition to managing a general transition from authoritarian rule, first interim governments also frequently operate in a situation of conflict or post conflict. This suggests that beyond the mandate of organizing first elections, they are tasked with getting people to agree to the new power-sharing rules. Even if first interim

---

[29] At the time of this writing, gaining the support of the international community appears to be the priority of the self-proclaimed interim government in Venezuela, led by Juan Guiado of the *Voluntad Popular*.

[30] E.g. Diamond and Plattner, eds., *Democracy in Decline*.

[31] See Rangwala, "The Creation of Governments-in-Waiting."

governments do not themselves set these rules (typically in the form of a new constitution), they are usually charged with devising some kind of system that, in theory, should prevent the society from reverting to conflict. Even in the situation of a relatively peaceful attempted transition from authoritarian rule, like Tunisia, the old rules have clearly been rejected, and any failure to establish a roadmap for replacing them – however tentative – will likely cause chaos to ensue.

In sum, first interim governments are unique because they must bridge the old and the new, secure both internal and external legitimacy, and establish some kind of (even if temporary) agreed-upon power-sharing rules. All three features mean that first interim governments are both shaped by the past and shapers of the future, and that they have a relationship to future stages of transition. Without a first interim government capable of these three things, a transition from authoritarian rule cannot go forward. Therefore, the task of developing a theory about interim governments requires us to figure out how we can more precisely define and measure this relationship to future governments and the future governing system. The two central research questions in this book – how do first interim governments get shaped (that is, to what extent do they inherit the structures of the past and to what extent do they reshape those structures) and how do they impact what lies ahead (what is the extent of their influence on future stages of transition) – and the two case studies it has examined point to a more comprehensive research agenda for students of democratic transition to adopt. In the next section, I suggest a tentative research program/agenda for studying this.

The following set of research questions belong on this agenda:

(1) Who is part of the first interim government?

Although first interim governments are often composed of "dissidents in waiting" (usually closely connected with the protest movement[32]), the above comparison and a brief glance around the world (even the MENA region alone) today shows the variety of actors that first interim governments can comprise. In Egypt, for instance, the body that declared itself in charge of organizing elections in the wake of President Hosni Mubarak's ousting in early 2011 was the Egyptian

---

[32] For example, see Rangwala, "The Creation of Governments-in-Waiting" and Alunni, "Long-Distance Nationalism and Belonging in the Libyan Diaspora."

military's Supreme Council of the Armed Forces (SCAF). This was an unsurprising event for many.[33] Yet in countries with a similar tradition of heavy military involvement in politics, such as Algeria, the unexpected resignation of longstanding president Abdelaziz Bouteflika in spring 2019 did not produce a similar situation. Instead (despite the suspected or overt continued involvement of top generals in decision-making), remaining authorities chose to follow constitutional procedures similar to Tunisia in January 2011 (before the departure of Mohammed Ghannouchi and the decision to abrogate the 1959 constitution).[34] Meanwhile, in Sudan, after protests led to the removal of President Omar al-Bashir, the military moved to form a transition council ostensibly like the one in Egypt, but – unlike the experience of its northern neighbor – was not accepted by protestors. Still other actors, including religious or other traditional leaders, may have a role in the first interim government depending on the circumstances.

(2) How does the first interim government structure itself?

Even once an accepted group of actors manages to establish itself as the temporary legitimate authority, it must figure out ways to organize itself. Here, too, the first interim government will typically be working to bridge the old and the new, to secure its own legitimacy, and to get buy-in for some kind of new rule-setting process. Should it model itself on structures from the old regime (for example, by filling existing ministerial posts with new figures) or invent something new (a transitional council filled with revolutionaries, for instance)? This question becomes especially murky when the military is involved because of the importance of the military as a state institution and the connections it may have to other institutions (such as the intelligence services). Nonetheless, in figuring out how it will ensure the provision of security and other public goods, first interim governments face many choices.

(3) How does the first interim government go about fulfilling its mandate?

A first interim government must determine how it will go about achieving its goals. Should it make all decisions by vote? Open its

---

[33] See Anderson, "Demystifying the Arab Spring."
[34] Also like in Tunisia, Algerians continue to protest this interim government, insisting on the departure of the entire "system."

proceedings to the public? Establish participatory measures such as a national dialogue or inclusive constitutional reform process? Or operate behind closed doors? For some first interim governments, even these decisions may be considered outside their mandate or capabilities. The NTC, for instance, hardly knew how to go about trying to be the temporary custodian of Libya's attempted transition from authoritarian rule, besides simply scrambling to fill a void. Because first interim governments operate without any established agenda, let alone by laws or rules, understanding how they choose to go about their work is informative.

(4) What choices do first interim governments make?

During the transition from authoritarian rule, first interim governments face many choices. To begin with, all first interim governments almost always make choices about the holding of democratic elections. This is not only a choice of when, but how. Because they are *by definition* not working in systems where free and fair elections are a systematic occurrence (even if elections may be), holding elections according to the existing election system (if one exists) will most likely not be sufficient for the first interim government to be considered legitimate.[35] Moreover, what type of body gets elected, and according to what precise rules, also has implications for later phases of transition. Thus, choices around the timing and nature of "founding elections" are critical for the eventual establishment of democracy.[36]

As the preceding study showed, however, first interim governments face a host of other dilemmas and decisions beyond the organization of elections. These include, but are not limited to, decisions around critical processes such as transitional justice and how to treat members of the former regime politically;[37] whether or not to revise the

---

[35] The case of Algeria in 2019 points to this. After popular protests led to the resignation of long-standing president Abdelaziz Bouteflika in April, the interim leadership, working under the direction of the army, declared elections according to the old system. This plan was roundly rejected by protestors, forcing elections to be postponed from July to December in an environment of increasing repression.

[36] See Plattner, "Liberalism and Democracy: Can't Have One without the Other."

[37] This is what Shain and Linz call "evening the score." As they discuss, striking the right balance on this question was a key factor that led to the demise of Kerensky's provisional government in Russia in 1917. Shain and Linz, *Between States*, 97.

constitution; how to deal with the international community; and how much to engage in economic reforms (the need for which is frequently a driver of the movements that challenge authoritarian regimes in the first place).[38] Even the extent of their own authority – for example, should the members be allowed to participate in the elections they are organizing, or will this diminish their credibility? – is a choice first interim governments must make.

(5) Where do the decisions of the first interim governments reappear following the end of their tenure?

As the above discussion suggests, a first interim government's ability – or inability– to bridge the old and the new systems, secure legitimacy, and establish new rules for governing help shape its relationship to the future. A shared sense of working for the greater good of the nation established by a first interim government may entice otherwise competitors to cooperate (as the Tunisian National Dialogue showed). Conversely, the failure to promote a sense of national unity may reproduce itself in later processes of transition breakdown. Asking thus how renewed conflict (even if not violent) or cooperation in later phases of attempted transition relate back to decisions by the first interim government can inform why this breakdown or unity occurs. Such a research agenda further calls for an examination of how "new rules" that were set in motion by the first interim governments play out in later phases. Can situations of "gridlock"[39] be traced back to the first transition moment, à la Tunisia? How might patterns in voter participation rates in later phases be explained by earlier events, including decisions by the first interim government? (Such decisions include how widely to exclude former regime members or what type of electoral system to adopt.) Where might reforms in certain sectors – media, security, economic – have their origins? The possibilities for finding traces or even more concrete impacts of decisions made by first interim governments are numerous.

The above research agenda calls for the collection of systematic evidence on the choices, actors, institutions, and strategies that define first interim governments around the world. With more data, scholars

---

[38] See Cammett et al., *A Political Economy of the Middle East*; Alexander, *From Stability to Revolution*, 106–129.

[39] Such as in Tunisia eight years after the uprising (see Brumberg, "Confronting Gridlock and Fragmentation").

can more rigorously test the propositions put forth in this book: First interim governments are constrained by the authoritarian past from which they emerged, *and* they can have a fundamental impact on future stages of transition.[40] They are also, by nature of being temporary and of having restricted authority, limited in the amount of impact they can have going forward. Finally, the book has suggested that certain decisions by first interim governments *may* be more promising for guaranteeing a successful transition from an authoritarian rule (although the book does not claim that either Tunisia or Libya represents such a case). A farther reach back into history and a broader geographical lens could produce a rich dataset on first interim governments' possibilities and limits, from which many enriching studies can emerge.

---

[40] In 2019, the world has witnessed a spate of popular uprisings that have forced leaders out of office and created space for potential interim governing structures. This includes several cases mentioned above, namely Sudan, Algeria, and Venezuela, as well as Puerto Rico, Bolivia, and Lebanon. In several other countries, including most prominently Hong Kong but also Egypt, Cameroon, Chile, Ecuador, Guinea, Iran, Iraq, and Nicaragua, protestors have been taking to the streets in opposition to the governing system under which they live, leading to protracted struggles between them and the leadership.

Appendix A
Tunisia Chronology

Dates	Events	Structure of Government
Tunisian Provisional Administration (TPA)		
January–February 2011	Constitutional procedures first bring old-guard members into interim cabinet, following which decision is taken to abrogate existing constitution. Béji Caïd Essebsi becomes interim prime minister at end of February, replacing Mohammed Ghannouchi.	First and second interim "national unity" cabinets led by Ghannouchi. Political reform commission under Ben Achour, originally expert core. Bouderbala, Amor, and Labidi commissions.
March–October 2011	Daily governing and overseeing the organization of National Constituent Assembly (NCA) elections.	Cabinet under leadership of interim prime minister Caïd Essebsi. Ben Achour Commission for political reform comprising expert core and National Council for the Protection of the Revolution. Other interim commissions for investigation (Bouderbala Commission, Amor

(cont.)

Dates	Events	Structure of Government
		Commission), media reform (INRIC) and Electoral Reform Commission (ISIE)
October–December 2011	Transition of power from TPA to elected NCA; formation of new coalition government.	Transition

National Constituent Assembly (NCA)/Troika

Dates	Events	Structure of Government
January 2012– August 2013	Ongoing constitution drafting and debate over sectoral reforms. Sharp deterioration in security and economic conditions. Series of high-profile political assassinations. NCA eventually reaches impasse; Troika loses legitimacy as conditions decline.	National Constituent Assembly (NCA) in charge of drafting constitution. Troika (coalition of Enahda and two secular parties) leads governing.
August–December 2013	Quartet of civil-society organizations leads National Dialogue to overcome political stalemate. After much negotiation, Troika replaced by caretaker government.	Quartet
January–October 2014	New constitution adopted in January 2014. Preparation for new presidential and parliamentary elections.	Caretaker government led by Mehdi Joma. NCA resumes role as interim legislative body.
October–December 2014	Presidential and parliamentary elections held.	Transition

(*cont.*)

Dates	Events	Structure of Government
2015–2019 Government		
January 2015–June 2016	High-profile security incidents occur. Government passes few meaningful reforms. Nida Tounis, which holds the highest number of seats in Parliament, begins to fracture. Transitional justice process continues.	President Caïd Essebsi. Cross-ideological coalition in Parliament and government, with Prime Minister Essid at helm. Several independent commissions (transitional justice, media regulation, individual liberties, judicial independence) called for in constitution, at varied stages of development.
July/August 2016–June 2018	Carthage declaration forms broader governing coalition, sets new governing priorities, and replaces the prime minister. Progressive laws on women's rights passed. Delayed municipal elections eventually bring new local councils to power. Work on transitional justice and judicial reform progresses haltingly.	President Caïd Essebsi. Cross-ideological coalition in Parliament and government, with Prime Minister Chahed at helm.
July 2018–June 2019	Increasing rivalry between President Caïd Essebsi and Prime Minister Chahed eventually leads to end of governing coalition and	Chahed government continues but with shifting coalitions and allegiances. Independent commissions,

(*cont.*)

Dates	Events	Structure of Government
	partnership between secular Nida Tounis and Enahda. ISIE begins preparation for fall 2019 elections. Transitional Justice Commission concludes work.	including new ISIE 2 (electoral commission).

Appendix B
Libya Chronology

Date	Description of Events	Structure of Government
National Transition Council (NTC)		
February–October 2011	In response to popular anti-government uprising, National Transition Council (NTC) attempts to lead military effort to defeat Qadhafi's army, preside over national-level governance, and draft Constitutional Declaration. Qadhafi killed in October.	NTC comprising executive council (led by Mahmoud Jibril), council of representatives from around the country (led by Mustafa Abd-al) Jalil, and military wing.
November 2011–July 2012	Abdelrahman al-Kib named new prime minister; elections for new legislature and Constitution Drafting Assembly planned for summer 2012. Establishing monopoly over legitimate use of force proves exceedingly difficult for NTC.	Al-Kib government. National and local representative councils. Weak Supreme Security Council (SSC) and Libya Shield Forces meant to act as state policing units and national guard, respectively. Locally based militia continue to operate either as part of or separately from these official entities.

(cont.)

Date	Description of Events	Structure of Government
July 2012	Elections for General National Congress (GNC) to replace NTC as legislative body and to organize elections for Constitution Drafting Assembly.	

General National Congress (GNC)

Date	Description of Events	Structure of Government
July 2012–January 2014	GNC forms government, organizes elections for Constitution Drafting Assembly (CDA). Threats to security (assassination of American diplomats and kidnappings of prime minister) and transitional justice (such as adoption of Political Isolation Law).	GNC. Government led by Premier Ali Zeidan (preceded by Mustafa Abushagur and succeeded by Abdullah al-Thinni). Competing militia back different political entities/individuals.
February–August 2014	CDA elected (with low turnout) in February. Forces led by General Khalifa Haftar launch successive attacks on GNC. Coalition of mostly Islamist and Misratan-based forces form anti-Haftar coalition in response. Elections held in June (very low turnout) for new legislative body (House of Representatives, HOR), which is forced to take its seat in the east	GNC Constitution Drafting Assembly (CDA)

(*cont.*)

Date	Description of Events	Structure of Government
	(Tobruk) because GNC refuses to recognize it. Supreme Court rules HOR invalid.	

Competing Governments of 2014–2019

Date	Description of Events	Structure of Government
August 2014–December 2015	International community seeks to mediate solution among political rivals amid declining security conditions and increasing competition over oil and economic resources. Libyan Political Agreement (LPA) signed in Skhirat, Morocco, on 17 December 2015.	GNC based in Tripoli. HOR based in Tobruk. CDA based in Tripoli.
January 2016–April 2019	Internationally backed Government of National Accord (GNA) forms based on LPA. Existing bodies claiming to be legitimate government refuse to cooperate. Conflict among local armed groups intersects with national-level political and military conflicts. In a culmination of a series of clashes in Tripoli, major fighting breaks out around the capital in September	Weak/incomplete GNA based in Tripoli, comprising High State Council and Presidency Council. HOR based in Tobruk. Parts of rump GNC continuing to operate.

(*cont.*)

Date	Description of Events	Structure of Government
	2018 as new brigades, empowered by international attempts to eradicate extremist groups (ISIS and al-Qaeda), attack the Tripoli-based government.	
April–June 2019	Devastating fighting in/ around Tripoli following attack led by Khalifa Haftar.	

Bibliography

Abderrazak, Lejri. "Effets dévastateurs et révélateurs suite à la polémique soulevée par les affirmations explosives de Farhat Errajhi." *Nawaat*, May 9, 2011. http://nawaat.org/portail/2011/05/09/effets-devastateurs-et-revelateurs-suite-a-la-polemique-soulevee-par-les-affirmations-explo sives-de-farhat-errajhi/.

Ahmida, Ali. *The Making of Modern Libya*, 2nd ed. Albany: State University of New York Press, 2009.

Ahram, Ariel. *Break All the Borders*. New York: Oxford University Press, 2019.

Al-Ali, Zaid. "Libya's Interim Constitution: An Assessment." *OpenDemocracy*, October 5, 2011. www.opendemocracy.net/en/libyas-interim-con stitution-assessment/.

Alexander, Christopher. *Tunisia: Stability and Reform in the Modern Maghreb*. New York: Routledge, 2010.

Tunisia: From Stability to Revolution in the Maghreb. New York: Routledge, 2016.

Al-Hilali, Amel. "Tunisia in Limbo after Essebsi Ends Enahda Alliance." *Al-Monitor*, October 5, 2018. www.al-monitor.com/pulse/originals/ 2018/10/tunisia-caid-essebsi-ends-alliance-ennahda-nidaa-tunis.html.

Al-Toraifi, Adel. "Mustafa Abdel-Jalil on Libya's Revolution." *Asharq Al-Awsat* (English), October 21, 2013. http://english.aawsat.com/ 2013/10/article55319876.

Alunni, Alice. "Long-Distance Nationalism and Belonging in the Libyan Diaspora (1969–2011)." *British Journal of Middle Eastern Studies* 46, no. 2 (2019): 242–258.

Amnesty International. *Libya: Civilians Caught in the Crossfire As Militias Battle for Tripoli*. London: Amnesty International, October 22, 2019. www.amnesty.org/en/latest/news/2019/10/libya-civilians-caught-in-the-crossfire-as-militias-battle-for-tripoli/.

Libya's Dark Web of Collusion: Abuses against Europe-Bound Refugees and Migrants. London: Amnesty International, December 11, 2017. www.amnesty.org/en/documents/mde19/7561/2017/en/.

They Never Tell Me Why: Arbitrary Restrictions on Movement in Tunisia. London: Amnesty International, October 24, 2018. www.amnesty.org/en/documents/mde30/8848/2018/en/.

Tunisia: Attempts to Obstruct Work of Truth and Dignity Commission Undermine Victims' Rights and Threaten Transitional Justice. London: Amnesty International, April 17, 2018. www.amnesty.org/en/documents/mde30/8221/2018/en/.

Anderson, Lisa. "Demystifying the Arab Spring." *Foreign Affairs* 90, no. 3 (2011): 2–7.

"Lawless Government and Illegal Opposition: Reflections on the Middle East." *Journal of International Affairs* 40, no. 2 (1987): 219–232.

The State and Social Transformation in Tunisia and Libya 1830–1980. Princeton, NJ: Princeton University Press, 1986.

"'They Defeated Us All': International Interests, Local Politics, and Contested Sovereignty in Libya." *Middle East Journal* 71, no. 2 (2017): 229–247.

Arieff, Alexis. *Political Transition in Tunisia.* Washington, DC: Congressional Research Service, February 2, 2011.

Political Transition in Tunisia. Washington, DC: Congressional Research Service, June 27, 2011.

Arieff, Alexis and Carla E. Humud. *Political Transition in Tunisia.* Washington, DC: Congressional Research Service, January 29, 2014.

Ashour, Omar. *Libyan Islamists Unpacked: Rise, Transformation, and Future.* Policy Briefing, Doha: Brookings Doha Center, May 2012.

Attia, Syrine. "Tunisie – Seuil de Représentativité Electorale à 5%." *Jeune Afrique*, November 19, 2018.

Ayubi, Nazih. *Over-Stating the Arab State: Politics and Society in the Middle East.* London: I. B. Tauris, 1995.

Baccouche, Néji. "Les Droits Economiques et Sociaux et la Constitution." In *La Constitution de la Tunisie: Processus, Principes, et Perspectives.* Tunis: UNDP, September 26, 2016. www.tn.undp.org/content/tunisia/fr/home/library/democratic_governance/la-constitution-de-la-tunisie-.html.

Barfi, Barak. "Khalifa Haftar: Rebuilding Libya from the Top Down." Research Notes, No. 22. Washington, DC: The Washington Institute for Near East Policy, 2014.

"Transitional National What? Libyans Still Don't Know Who Their New Leaders Are." *The New Republic*, August 31, 2011.

Bayat, Asef. *Revolution without Revolutionaries: Making Sense of the Arab Spring.* Stanford, CA: Stanford University Press, 2017.

Becker, Jo and Scott Shane. "Hillary Clinton, 'Smart Power', and a Dictator's Fall." *New York Times*, February 27, 2016.

Bell, Anthony and David Witter. *The Libyan Revolution: Roots of Rebellion – Part I*. Washington, DC: Institute for the Study of War, 2011.

The Libyan Revolution: Escalation & Intervention – Part 2. Washington, DC: Institute for the Study of War, 2011.

The Libyan Revolution: Stalemate & Siege – Part 3. Washington, DC: Institute for the Study of War, 2011.

The Libyan Revolution: The Tide Turns – Part 4. Washington, DC: Institute for the Study of War, 2011.

Bellin, Eva. "The Robustness of Authoritarianism in the Middle East: Exceptionalism in Comparative Perspective." *Comparative Politics* 36, no. 2 (2004): 139–158.

Benabdelsalem, Sélima. "The Making of a Constitution: A Look Back at Tunisia's Thorny Consensus-Building Process." *Constitution.net*, March 26, 2014. constitutionnet.org/news/making-constitution-look-back-tunisias-thorny-consensus-building-process.

Ben Aicha, Mounir. "Béji Caïd Essebsi, un vieillard tunisien, ancien dictateur, encore assoiffé de pouvoir."*Nawat*, January 2, 2013. http://nawaat.org/portail/2013/01/03/etudebeji-caid-essebsi-un-vieillard-tunisien-ancien-dictateur-encore-assoiffe-de-pouvoir/7/.

Ben Aissa, Mohammed Salah. "La décision relative au refus de prorogation du mandat de l'Instance Vérité et Dignité (IVD) adoptée par l'Assemblée des Représentants du Peuple (ARP) le 26 mars 2018: une illustration des difficultés de mise en œuvre de la justice transitionnelle." Unpublished paper, 2018.

Ben Aissa, Mohamed Salah. "Pouvoir judiciaire et transition en Tunisie." Unpublished conference paper, 2014.

Ben Hafaiedh, Abdelwahab and I. William Zartman. "Tunisia: Beyond the Ideological Cleavage: Something Else." In *The Arab Spring: Negotiating in the Shadow of the Intifadat*, edited by I. William Zartman, 50–79. Athens: University of Georgia Press, 2015.

Ben Romdhane, Mahmoud. *Tunisie: La Démocratie en Quête d'Etat*. Tunis: Sud Editions, 2018.

Bertlesmann Stiftung. *BTI 2016 Country Report – Tunisia*. Gütersloh: Bertelsmann Stiftung, 2016.

BTI 2018 Country Report – Libya. Gütersloh: Bertelsmann Stiftung, 2018.

Blaise, Lilia. "Interview avec Riadh Ferjani." *Huff Post Maghreb*, January 29, 2014. www.huffpostmaghreb.com/2014/01/29/riadh-ferjani-haica-inter_n_4685535.html.

Blanchard, Christopher. *Libya: Unrest and US Policy*. Washington, DC: Congressional Research Service. June 6, 2011.

Libya: Unrest and US Policy. Washington, DC: Congressional Research Service. August 26, 2011.

Libya: Unrest and US Policy. Washington, DC: Congressional Research Service. September 9, 2011.

Libya: Unrest and US Policy. Washington, DC: Congressional Research Service. September 14, 2012.

Libya: Transition and US Policy. Washington, DC: Congressional Research Service. August 3, 2015.

Blaydes, Lisa. *Elections and Distributive Politics in Mubarak's Egypt*. New York: Cambridge University Press, 2010.

Boduszynski, Mieczyslaw and Sabina Henneberg. "Explaining Divergent Pathways of Post-Arab Spring Change." Paper presented at the Eleventh Annual Conference of the Association for the Study of the Middle East and Africa (ASMEA), Washington, DC, November 3, 2018.

Bodusyznski, Mieczyslaw and Christopher Lamont. "Who Controls Libya's Airports Controls Libya." *Foreign Policy*, April 24, 2019. https://foreignpolicy.com/2019/04/24/who-controls-libyas-air ports-controls-libya-haftar-mitiga-conflict-airstrikes/.

Boduszynski, Mieczyslaw and Marieke Wierda, "Political Exclusion and Transitional Justice: A Case Study of Libya." In *Transitional Justice in the Middle East and North Africa*, edited by Sriram, Chandra Lekha, 141–160. New York: Oxford University Press, 2016.

Boguslavsky, Anna. "The African Union and the Libyan Crisis." *International Affairs: A Russian Journal of World Politics, Diplomacy & International Relations* 58, no. 1 (2012): 71–81.

Boubekeur, Amel. "Islamists, Secularists, and Old Regime Elites in Tunisia." *Mediterranean Politics* 21, no. 1 (2016): 107–127.

Bratton, Michael and Nicholas van de Walle. *Democratic Experiments in Africa: Regime Transitions in Comparative Perspective*. New York: Cambridge University Press, 1997.

Brownlee, Jason, Tarek E. Masoud, and Andrew Reynolds. *The Arab Spring: Pathways of Repression and Reform*. Oxford: Oxford University Press, 2015.

Brumberg, Daniel. "Confronting Gridlock and Fragmentation: Impressions from Tunisia's Democratic Transition." Washington, DC: Project on Middle East Democracy, February 2017. https://pomed.org/wp-content/uploads/2017/02/Gridlock_Fragmentation_Tunisia_QA.pdf?x37106.

Brynen, Rex, Peter Moore, Bassel F. Salloukh, and Marie-Joelle Zahar. *Beyond the Arab Spring: Authoritarianism and Democratization in the Arab World*. Boulder, CO: Lynne Rienner Publishers, 2012.

Byrne, Eileen. "Tunisia Clinches Deal on Road to Democracy." *Financial Times*, September 13, 2011.

Cammett, Melanie, Ishac Diwan, Alan Richards, and John Waterbury. *A Political Economy of the Middle East*, 4th ed. Boulder, CO: Westview Press, 2015.

Campbell, Les. *Notes from Benghazi: Libyans Hungry for Information and Help*. Washington, DC: National Democratic Institute, May 13, 2011. www.ndi.org/notes-from-Benghazi-Libya.

Canal +. "Special Investigation – Gaz et pétrole guerres secrètes." 2013. www.canalplus.f/c-infos-documentaires/pid3357-c-special-investigation .html?vid760326. Accessed July 31, 2013.

Capoccia, Giovanni and Daniel Ziblatt. "The Historical Turn in Democratization Studies: A New Research Agenda for Europe and Beyond." *Comparative Political Studies* 43, no. 8/9 (2010): 931–968.

Carey, John. "Electoral Formula and the Tunisians Constituent Assembly." May 9, 2013. Unpublished Paper.

"Why Tunisia Remains the Arab Spring's Best Bet." August 27, 2013. Paper Draft.

Carey, John M. and Andrew Reynolds. "The Impact of Election Systems." *Journal of Democracy* 22, no. 4 (2011): 36–47.

Carey, John M. and Matthew Soberg Shugart, "Incentives to Cultivate a Personal Vote: A Rank Ordering of Electoral Formulas." *Electoral Studies* 14 (1995): 417–439.

Carter Center. *Libya's Constitutional Drafting Assembly Elections: Final Report*. Atlanta, GA: The Carter Center, 2014.

National Constituent Assembly Elections in Tunisia: Final Report. Atlanta, GA: The Carter Center, 2011.

Cavatorta, Francesco and Vincent Durac. *Civil Society and Democratization in the Arab World: The Dynamics of Activism*. Routledge Studies in Middle Eastern Politics. London; New York: Routledge, 2011.

Cavatorta, Francesco and Fabio Merone. "Post-Islamism, Ideological Evolution and 'La Tunisianité' of the Tunisian Islamist Party al-Nahda." *Journal of Political Ideologies* 20, no. 1 (2015): 27–42.

"Chafik Sarsar – ISIE: Les vrais raisons d'une démission et ses enjeux." *Leaders*, May 9, 2017.

Cheibub, Jose Antonio. *Presidentialism, Parliamentarism, and Democracy*. New York: Cambridge University Press, 2007.

Cherif, Yousef. "Can Tunisia's Democracy Survive?" *Project Syndicate*. January 9, 2019. www.project-syndicate.org/commentary/tunisian-democracy-in-crisis-by-youssef-cherif-2019-01?barrier=accesspaylog.

Chick, Kristen. "Why Tunisia's Interim Government May Not Fly with Protesters." *The Christian Science Monitor*, January 17, 2011.

Chivvis, Christopher S. *Toppling Qaddafi: Libya and the Limits of Liberal Intervention*. New York: Cambridge University Press, 2014.

Chollet, Derek and Benjamin Fishman. "Who Lost Libya?" *Foreign Affairs*, 94, no. 3 (2015).

Chomiak, Laryssa. "What Tunisia's Historic Truth Commission Accomplished – And What Went Wrong." *Washington Post – The Monkey Cage*, January 16, 2019. www.washingtonpost.com/news/monkey-cage/wp/2019/01/16/heres-what-we-can-learn-from-tunisias-post-revolution-justice-commission/?noredirect=on&utm_term=.6391be2915a5.

Chorin, Ethan. *Exit the Colonel*. New York: Public Affairs, 2012.

Chouikha, Larbi. "La difficile entreprise de réformer les médias en Tunisie." *Communication* 32, no. 1 (2013).

"L'instance supérieure indépendante pour les élections et le processus électoral tunisien: Un témoignage de l'intérieur." *Confluences Mediterranée* 3 (2012) : 171–185.

"Chronology: January 15, 2011–April 15, 2011." *Middle East Journal* 65, no. 3 (Summer 2011): 457–500.

"Chronology: April 16, 2014–July 15, 2012." *Middle East Journal* 66, no. 4 (Autumn 2012): 683–721.

"Chronology: January 15, 2014–April 15, 2014." *Middle East Journal* 68, no. 3 (Summer 2014): 436–464.

"Chronology: April 16, 2014–July 15, 2014." *Middle East Journal* 68, no. 4 (Autumn 2014): 604–632.

"Chronology: July 16, 2018–October 15, 2018." *The Middle East Journal* 73, no. 1 (Winter 2019): 113–148.

Cole, Peter and Brian McQuinn. *The Libyan Revolution and Its Aftermath*. New York: Oxford University Press, 2015.

Collier, David and Ruth Berins Collier. *Shaping the Political Arena: Critical Junctures, the Labor Movement, and Regime Dynamics in Latin America*. Princeton, NJ: Princeton University Press, 1991.

Coupe, Jeffrey and Hamadi Redissi. "Tunisia." In *The Middle East*, 13th ed., edited by Ellen Lust, 789–829. Los Angeles, CA: Sage/CQ Press, 2014.

Daragahi, Borzou. "Libya: From Euphoria to Breakdown." *Adelphi Series* 55, no. 452 (2015): 39–58.

Dawisha, Adeed Isam and I. William Zartman. *Beyond Coercion: The Durability of the Arab State*. Florence: Taylor & Francis, 1988.

Dermech, A. "Magistrature – le conseil supérieure désormais opérationnel." *La Presse Tunisie*, December 30, 2016.

De Waal, Alex. "African Roles in the Libyan Conflict of 2011." *International Affairs* 89, no. 2 (2013): 365–379.

Diamond, Larry and Marc F. Plattner, eds. *Democratization and Authoritarianism in the Arab World*. Baltimore: Johns Hopkins University Press, 2014.

eds. *Democracy in Decline?* Baltimore: Johns Hopkins University Press, 2015.

Di Palma, Guiseppe. *To Craft Democracies: An Essay on Democratic Transition.* Berkeley: University of California Press, 1990.

Diwan, Ishac, ed. *Understanding the Political Economy of the Arab Uprisings.* Singapore; New Jersey: World Scientific, 2014.

Doherty, Megan. "Building a New Libya: Citizen Views on Libya's Electoral and Political Process." *National Democratic Institute.* Washington, DC: National Democratic Institute, May 22, 2012.

Dwyer, Kevin. *Arab Voices: The Human Rights Debate in the Middle East.* Berkeley: University of California Press, 1991.

Economist Intelligence Unit. *Libya – Country Report.* London: Economist Intelligence Unit, February 2011.

Libya – Country Report. London: Economist Intelligence Unit, March 2011.

Libya – Country Report. London: Economist Intelligence Unit, April 2011.

Libya – Country Report. London: Economist Intelligence Unit, July 2011.

Libya – Country Report. London: Economist Intelligence Unit, August 2011.

Libya – Country Report. London: Economist Intelligence Unit, April 2012.

Libya – Country Report. London: Economist Intelligence Unit, May 2012.

Libya – Country Report. London: Economist Intelligence Unit, July 2012.

Libya – Country Report. London: Economist Intelligence Unit, May 2015.

Tunisia – Country Report. London: Economist Intelligence Unit, February 2011.

Tunisia – Country Report. London: Economist Intelligence Unit, June 2011.

Tunisia – Country Report. London: Economist Intelligence Unit, July 2011.

Tunisia – Country Report. London: Economist Intelligence Unit, February 2015.

El-Houssi, Leila, Alessia Melcangi, Stefano Torelli, and Massimiliano Cricco, eds. *North African Societies after the Arab Spring: Between Democracy and Islamic Awakening.* Newcastle: Cambridge Scholars Publishing, 2016.

Elkins, Zachary. "Constitutional Engineering." In *International Encyclopedia of Political Science*, edited by Badie, Bertrand, Dirk Berg-Schlosser, and Leonardo Morlino, 414–416. Thousand Oaks, CA: SAGE Publications, 2011.

Elloumi, Mohamed. "Les Gouvernements Provisoires en Tunisie du janvier au 23 octobre." Unpublished Master's Thesis, Université Tunis El Manar, 2011.

Elster, Jon. *Closing the Books: Transitional Justice in Historical Perspective.* Cambridge: Cambridge University Press, 2004.

Elster, Jon, ed. *The Roundtable Talks and the Breakdown of Communism.* Chicago: University of Chicago Press, 1996.

Entelis, John P. "Republic of Tunisia." In *The Government and Politics of the Middle East and North Africa*, 6th ed., edited by Long, David E., Bernard Reich, and Mark Gasiorowski, 509–536. Boulder, CO: Westview Press, 2011.

Erdle, Steffen. *Ben Ali's "New Tunisia" (1987–2009): A Case Study of Authoritarian Modernization in the Arab World.* Berlin: Klaus Schwarz, 2010.

Erlanger, Stephen. "Thinker Led the President to War." *International Herald Tribune*, April 2, 2011.

Feuer, Sarah. "*A National Unity Government for Tunisia.*" Washington, DC: The Washington Institute for Near East Policy, August 12, 2016.

Fitzgerald, Mary. "Introducing the Libyan Muslim Brotherhood." *Foreign Policy*, November 2, 2012.

Francisco, Ronald A. *The Politics of Regime Transition.* Boulder, CO: Westview Press, 2000.

Frosini, Justin Orlando and Francesco Biagi, eds. *Political and Constitutional Transitions in North Africa: Actors and Factors.* London: Routledge, 2015.

Gana, Nouri, ed. "*The Making of the Tunisian Revolution: Contexts, Architects, Prospects.*" Edinburgh: Edinburgh University Press, 2013.

Gaub, Florence. "The Libyan Armed Forces between Coup-Proofing and Repression." *Journal of Strategic Studies* 36, no. 2 (2013): 221–244.

Gaynor, Tim and Taha Zargoun. "Gaddafi Caught Like 'Rat' in a Drain, Humiliated and Shot." *Reuters*, October 21, 2011. www.reuters.com/article/us-libya-gaddafi-finalhours-idUSTRE79K43S20111021.

Gazzini, Claudia. "Was the Libya Intervention Necessary?" *Middle East Report* no. 261 (December 2011): 2–9.

Ghariri, Ghazi. "El Haia el oulia l'il tahqeeq el ahdaf a-thawra, islah e-siasia, wa intiqalia el demokratie" (The High Commission for Realization of the Objectives of the Revolution, Political Reform, and the Democratic Transition) in "Taqdeem el intiqalia el demokratia vi Tunis baad thalath senuwat" (Presentation of the Democratic Transition in Tunis After Three Years), edited by Ghazi Ghariri, 11–27. Tunis: Kondrad Adenauer Stiftung, 2014.

Ghilès, Francis. "Tunisia Has Made Strides in Democratic Transition: Can It Get the Economy Right?" *Informed Comment*, April 8, 2014. www.juancole.com/2014/04/tunisia-democratic-transition.html.

Tunisia: Secular Social Movements Confront Radical Temptations: Barcelona: Center for International Affairs (CIDOB), 2012.

Gobe, Eric. "Of Lawyers and Samsars: The Legal Services Market and the Authoritarian State in Ben'Ali's Tunisia (1987–2011)." *The Middle East Journal* 67, no. 1 (2013): 44–62.

Gobe, Éric and Michaël Béchir Ayari. "Les avocats dans la Tunisie de Ben Ali: Une profession politisée?" *L'Année Du Maghreb* no. III (2007): 105–132.

Gray, Doris. "In Search of Righting Wrongs: Women and the Transitional Justice Process in Tunisia." *E-International Relations* 13 (2013).

Gritten, David. "Key Figures in Libya's Rebel Council." *BBC*, August 25, 2011. www.bbc.com/news/world-africa-12698562.

Guittieri, Karen and Jessica Piombo. *Interim Governments: Institutional Bridges to Peace and Democracy?* Washington, DC: United States Institute of Peace, 2007.

Haas, Mark L. and David W. Lesch, eds. *The Arab Spring: Change and Resistance in the Middle East*. Boulder, CO: Westview Press, 2013.

Haggard, Stephan and Robert R. Kaufman. "The Political Economy of Democratic Transitions." *Comparative Politics* 29, no. 3 (1997): 263–283.

Hajji, Lutfi. *Arab Reform Brief: The 18 October Coalition for Rights and Freedoms in Tunisia*: Berlin: Arab Reform Initiative, 2006.

Hamid, Shadi. *Temptations of Power: Islamists and Illiberal Democracy in a New Middle East*. Oxford University Press, 2014.

Harchaoui, Jalel. "La Libye depuis 2015 : entre morcellement et interférences." *Politique étrangère*, 4 (Winter 2018), 133–145.

"Libya's Monetary Crisis." *Lawfare*, January 10, 2018. www.lawfareblog.com/libyas-monetary-crisis.

Harchaoui, Jalel and Matthew Herbert. "Italy Claims It's Found a Solution to Europe's Migrant Problem. Here's Why Italy's Wrong." *Washington Post*, September 26, 2017.

Haugbølle, Rikke Hostrup and Francesco Cavatorta. "Will the Real Tunisian Opposition Please Stand Up? Opposition Coordination Failures Under Authoritarian Constraints." *British Journal of Middle Eastern Studies* 38, no. 3 (2011): 323–341.

Haute Instance Pour la Réalisation des Objectifs de la Révolution, et la Réforme Politique, et la Transition Démocratique. *Moudawalat el-Haiat* (Committee Deliberations), Part I (March–May 2011), Photocopy, Observatoire Tunisien de la Transition Démocratique, Tunis.

Haute Instance Pour la Réalisation des Objectifs de la Révolution, et la Réforme Politique, et la Transition Démocratique. *Moudawalat el-Haiat* (Committee Deliberations), Part II (June–October 2011), Photocopy, Observatoire Tunisien de la Transition Démocratique, Tunis.

Hawthorne, Amy. "*POMED Backgrounder: A Trip Report from Tunisia's 'Dark Regions.'*" Washington, DC: Project on Middle East Democracy, December 2015. https://pomed.org/wp-content/uploads/2015/12/Backgrounder-Hawthorne-Dec-2015.pdf.

Heilbrunn, John R. "The Social Origins of National Conferences in Benin and Togo." *The Journal of Modern African Studies* 31, no. 2 (1993): 277–299

Henneberg, Sabina. "Before and After Bin 'Ali: Comparing Two Attempts at Political Liberalization in Tunisia." *Review of Middle East Studies* 53, no. 2 (2019): 306–320.

"Comparing the First Provisional Administrations in Tunisia and Libya: Some Tentative Conclusions." *The Journal of North African Studies* 24, no. 2 (2019): 226–246.

. "Understanding Charlie Hebdo: Lessons from Tunisia." *SAIS Review of International Affairs*, 2015. www.saisreview.org/2015/01/28/understanding-charlie-hebdo-lessons-from-tunisia/.

Henriksen, Dag and Ann Karin Larssen. *Political Rationale and International Consequences of the War in Libya*. Oxford: Oxford University Press, 2016.

Hibou, Béatrice. Translated by Andrew Brown. *The Force of Obedience: The Political Economy of Repression in Tunisia*. Cambridge, UK; Malden, MA: Polity Press, 2011.

Higley, John and Michael G. Burton. "The Elite Variable in Democratic Transitions and Breakdowns." *American Sociological Review* 54 (1989): 17–32.

Higley, John and Richard Gunther. *Elites and Democratic Consolidation in Latin America and Southern Europe*. Cambridge: Cambridge University Press, 1992.

Hinnebusch, Raymond. "Historical Sociology and the Arab Uprising." *Mediterranean Politics* 19, no. 1 (2014): 137–140.

Horowitz, Donald. "Comparing Democratic Systems." *Journal of Democracy* 1, no. 4 (1990): 73–79.

Hubler, Katharina Owens. "Election Management Bodies in Transitioning Democracies: Tunisia and Egypt." Unpublished Master's Thesis, University of Colorado at Denver, 2012.

Human Rights Watch. *Libya: Revoke Draconian New Law*. New York: Human Rights Watch, May 5, 2012. www.hrw.org/news/2012/05/05/libya-revoke-draconian-new-law.

Libya: Suspend Deaths against Qadhafi Loyalists. New York: Human Rights Watch, October 4, 2013. www.hrw.org/news/2013/10/04/libya-suspend-death-sentences-against-gaddafi-loyalists.

Tunisia: Amnesty Bill Would Set Back Transition. New York: Human Rights Watch, July 14, 2016. www.hrw.org/news/2016/07/14/tunisia-amnesty-bill-would-set-back-transition.

Tunisia: Counterterror Law Endangers Rights. New York: Human Rights Watch, July 31, 2015. www.hrw.org/news/2015/07/31/tunisia-counter terror-law-endangers-rights#.

Huntington, Samuel. *The Third Wave: Democratization in the Late Twentieth Century.* Norman, OK: Oklahoma University Press, 1991.

Ibrahim, Suleiman and Jan Michiel Otto. *Resolving Real Property Disputes in Post-Qadhafi Libya, in the Context of Transitional Justice: Final Report of a Libyan-Dutch Collaborative Research Project.* Leiden: Van Vollenhoven Institute, 2017.

Instance Nationale pour la Reforme de l'Information et de la Communication (INRIC). *General Report.* Tunis: Imprimière Boussaa, 2012.

Institute for Integrated Transitions. *Inside the Transition Bubble: International Expert Assistance in Tunisia.* Barcelona: Institute for Integrated Transitions, 2013.

International Crisis Group. *Addressing the Rise of Libya's Madkhali-Salafis.* Brussels: International Crisis Group, 2019.

After the Showdown in Libya's Oil Crescent. Brussels: International Crisis Group, 2018.

Divided We Stand. Brussels: International Crisis Group, 2012.

Getting Geneva Right. Brussels: International Crisis Group, 2015.

Holding Libya Together. Brussels: International Crisis Group, 2011.

The Libyan Political Agreement. Brussels: International Crisis Group, 2016.

Popular Protests in North Africa/the Middle East (IV): Tunisia's Way. Brussels: International Crisis Group, 2011.

Popular Protests in North Africa/the Middle East (V): Making Sense of Libya. Brussels: International Crisis Group, 2011.

Restoring Public Confidence in Tunisia's Political System. Brussels: International Crisis Group, 2018.

Stemming Tunisia's Authoritarian Drift. Brussels: International Crisis Group, 2018.

Trial by Error. Brussels: International Crisis Group, 2013.

International Foundation for Electoral Systems (IFES). *Tunisia – First Round Presidential Elections: Frequently Asked Questions.* Washington, DC: IFES, January 24, 2014.

International Monetary Fund. *Statement at the End of an IMF Staff Review Mission to Tunisia*, April 9, 2019. www.imf.org/en/News/Articles/2019/04/09/pr19109-tunisia-statement-at-the-end-of-an-imf-staff-review-mission-to-tunisia. Accessed May 19, 2019.

"Tunisia: At a Glance." www.imf.org/en/Countries/TUN. Accessed May 19, 2019.

Irish, John. "Egypt, Qatar Trade Barbs at UN on Libya Conflict Interference." *Reuters*, September 24, 2019. https://uk.reuters.com/article/uk-egypt-libya/egypt-qatar-trade-barbs-at-u-n-on-libya-conflict-interference-idUKKBN1W9242.

Joseph, Richard. "Challenges of a 'Frontier' Region." *Journal of Democracy* 19, no. 2 (2008): 94-108.

"Joint Open Letter: Appeal to the Government to Put an End to the Widespread Impunity," March 13, 2018. www.hrw.org/news/2018/03/13/joint-letter-appeal-government-put-end-widespread-impunity#.

Kao, Kristen and Ellen Lust. *Why Did the Arab Uprisings Turn Out As They Did? A Survey of the Literature.* Washington, DC: Project on Middle East Democracy, 2017. https://pomed.org/pomed-snapshot-why-did-the-arab-uprisings-turn-out-as-they-did-a-survey-of-the-literature/.

Kienle, Eberhard and Nadine Sika, eds. *The Arab Uprisings: Transforming and Challenging State Power.* London, New York: I. B. Tauris, 2015.

Kirkpatrick, David. "One of Libya's Rival Governments Moves to Control Oil Revenue." April 5, 2015. www.nytimes.com/2015/04/06/world/middleeast/one-of-libyas-rival-governments-moves-to-control-oil-revenue.html?partner=bloomberg.

Kubinec, Robert and Sharan Grewal. "When National Unity Governments are Neither National, United, nor Governments: The Case of Tunisia." 2018. Unpublished Paper.

Kuperman, Alan J. "A Model Humanitarian Intervention? Reassessing NATO's Libya Campaign." *International Security* 38, no. 1 (2013): 105–136.

Lacher, Wolfram. "Families, Tribes, and Cities in the Libyan Revolution." *Middle East Policy* XVIII, no. 4 (2011): 140–154.

Fault Lines of the Revolution: Political Actors, Camps, and Conflicts in the New Libya. Berlin: Stiftung Wissenschaft und Politik, May 2013.

"Libya's Conflict Enters a Dangerous New Phase." Berlin: Stiftung Wissenschaft und Politik, February 2019.

"Libya's Transition: Towards Collapse." Berlin: Stiftung Wissenschaft und Politik, May 2014.

Tripoli's Militia Cartel: How Ill-Conceived Stabilisation Blocks Political Progress, and Risks Renewed War. Berlin: Stiftung Wissenschaft und Politik, April 2018.

"Was Libya's Collapse Predictable?" *Survival* 59, no. 2 (2017): 139–152.

Lamont, Christopher, " Contested Governance: Understanding Justice Interventions in Post-Qadhafi Libya." *Journal of Intervention and Statebuilding* 10, no. 3 (2016): 328–399.

"Transitional Justice and the Politics of Lustration in Tunisia." Washington, DC: Middle East Institute, December 28, 2013. www.mei.edu/content/transitional-justice-and-politics-lustration-tunisia.

Lemarchand, René. "Non-State Politics in Post-Qadhafi Libya." In *North African Societies After the Arab Spring*, edited by Leila El-Houssi, Alessia Melcangi, Stefano Torelli, and Massimiliano Cricco, 183–196. Newcastle: Cambridge Scholars Publishing, 2016.

"Libya Opposition Vow Free, Fair Vote." *News24.Com*, March 29, 2011. www.news24.com/Africa/News/Libya-opposition-vow-free-fair-vote-20110329.

Linn, Rachel. "'Change with Continuity:' The Equity and Reconciliation Commission and Political Reform in Morocco." *Journal of North African Studies* 16, no. 1 (2011): 1–17.

Linz, Juan J. and Alfred Stepan. *Problems of Democratic Transition and Consolidation: Southern Europe, South America, and Post-Communist Europe.* Baltimore: Johns Hopkins University Press, 1996.

Lijphart, Arend. "The Political Consequences of Electoral Laws: 1945–85." *American Political Science Review* 84, no. 2 (1990).

Lister, Tim and Nada Bashir. "She's One of the Most Prominent Female Politicians in her Country. A Few Days Ago, She Was Abducted from Her House." *CNN*, July 20, 2019. https://edition.cnn.com/2019/07/20/africa/libya-sergewa-intl/index.html.

Lust, Ellen. *Voting for Change: The Pitfalls and Possibilities of First Elections in Arab Transitions.* Brookings Doha Center-Stanford Project on Arab Transitions, May 9, 2012.

Lust, Ellen, Gamal Soltan, and Jacob Wichmann. "After the Arab Spring: Islamism, Secularism, and Democracy." *Current History* 111, no. 749 (2012).

Lust-Okar, Ellen. "Divided they Rule: The Management and Manipulation of Political Opposition." *Comparative Politics* 36, no. 2 (2004): 159–179.

Lust-Okar, Ellen and Saloua Zerhouni. *Political Participation in the Middle East.* Boulder, CO: Lynne Rienner Publishers, 2008.

Lynch, Marc. *The Arab Uprising: The Unfinished Revolutions of the New Middle East.* New York: Public Affairs, 2012.

Lynch, Marc, ed. *The Arab Uprisings Explained: New Contentious Politics in the Middle East.* Columbia Studies in Middle East Politics. New York: Columbia University Press, 2014.

Maghur, Azza K. *A Legal Look into the Libyan Supreme Court Ruling.* Washington, DC: Atlantic Council, December 8, 2014.

Mahfoudh, Haykel Ben. *Security Sector Reform in Tunisia Three Years into the Democratic Transition.* Berlin: Arab Reform Initiative, July 2014.

Martinez, Luis. *The Libyan Paradox.* New York: Columbia University Press in association with the Centre d'etudes et de recherches internationales, 2007.

Masri, Safwan. *Tunisia: An Arab Anomaly.* New York: Columbia University Press, 2017.

Mattes, Hanspeter. "Challenges to Security Sector Governance in the Middle East: The Libyan Case." Conference Paper, Geneva Centre for the Control of Armed Forces (DCAF), July 12–13, 2004.

"Libya Since 2011: Political Transformation and Violence." *Middle East Policy*, XXIII, no. 2 (2016): 59–75.

McCarthy, Rory. *Inside Tunisia's Al-Nahda: Between Politics and Preaching.* New York: Cambridge University Press, 2018.

McCurdy, Daphne. *Backgrounder: Previewing Libya's Elections.* Washington, DC: Project on Middle East Democracy, July 5, 2012.

McGreal, Christopher. "Libyan Rebel Efforts Frustrated by Internal Disputes Over Leadership." *The Guardian*, April 3, 2011.

McGuire, James W. "Interim Governments and Democratic Consolidation: Argentina in Comparative Perspective." In *Between States*, edited by Yossi Shain and Juan Linz, 179–210.

McQuinn, Brian. "Armed Groups in Libya: Typology and Roles." *Small Arms Survey* no. 18 (2012).

"Assessing (In)security after the Arab Spring: The Case of Libya." *PS: Political Science & Politics* 46, no. 4 (2013): 716–720.

Megerisi, Tarek. *Adapting to the New Libya.* Washington, DC: Carnegie Endowment for International Peace, May 2, 2019.

"Can Germany Stop Libya Becoming the New Syria?" European Council on Foreign Relations, September 24, 2019.

"The Promise of Palermo: Uniting the Strands of Europe's Libya Policy." European Council on Foreign Relations, November 8, 2018.

Merone, Fabio. "Enduring Class Struggle in Tunisia: The Fight for Identity Beyond Political Islam." *British Journal of Middle Eastern Studies* 42, no. 1 (2015): 74–87.

Mersch, Sarah. *"Tunisia's Compromise Constitution."* Washington, DC: Carnegie Endowment for International Peace, January 21, 2014.

Mezran, Karim. *"Libya Has Successful Elections but Not Yet Democracy."* Washington, DC: Atlantic Council, July 10, 2012.

Negotiation and Construction of National Identities. International Negotiation Series. Vol. 3. Leiden, The Netherlands; Boston: Martinus Nijhoff Publishers, 2007.

"Negotiating a Solution to the Security Problem in Libya." Washington, DC: Atlantic Council, June 11, 2012.

Mezran, Karim and Alice Alunni, "Libya: Negotiations for Transition." In *The Arab Spring: Negotiating in the Shadow of the Intifadat*, edited by I. William Zartman, 252–256. Athens: University of Georgia Press, 2015.

Mezran, Karim and Fadhel Lamen. "Security Challenges for Libya's Quest for Democracy." Washington, DC: Atlantic Council, September 12, 2012.

Mezran, Karim and Duncan Pickard. "Negotiating Libya's Constitution." Washington, DC: Atlantic Council, January 22, 2014. www.atlanticcouncil.org/publications/issue-briefs/negotiating-libya-s-constitution.

Mrad, Hatem and Fadhel Moussa, eds. *La Transition Démocratique à la Lumière des Expériences Comparées: Colloque Internationale Tenue Le 5-6-7 Mai 2011 à Tunis*. Tunis: Association Tunisienne d'Etudes Politiques, 2012.

Mundy, Jacob. *Libya*. Hot Spots in Global Politics. Cambridge, UK; Malden, MA: Polity Press, 2018.

Murphy, Emma. *Economic and Political Change in Tunisia*. New York: St. Martin's Press, 1999.

"The Tunisian Elections of October 23, 2011: A Democratic Consensus." *Journal of North African Studies* 18, no. 2 (2013): 231–247.

"The Tunisian Uprising and the Precarious Path to Democracy." *Mediterranean Politics* 16, no. 2 (2011): 299–305.

Norton, Augustus R., ed. *Civil Society in the Middle East*. Leiden; New York: Brill, 1996.

Nouira, Asma. "Tunisia's Local Elections: Entrenching Democratic Practices." Arab Reform Initiative, May 2018.

O'Donnell, Guillermo A. and Philippe C. Schmitter. *Transitions from Authoritarian Rule*. Baltimore: Johns Hopkins University Press, 1986.

"Ordinance." In Oxford English Dictionary online. Oxford University Press, 2019.

Pack, Jason. "Fight Over Oil Offers Opportunity to Protect Libya's Wealth." *Al-Monitor*, June 29, 2018. www.al-monitor.com/pulse/originals/2018/06/resolve-fight-oil-libya.html.

Pack, Jason, ed. *The 2011 Libyan Uprisings and the Struggle for the Post-Qadhafi Future*. New York: Palgrave Macmillan, 2013.

Pack, Jason and Haley Cook. "The July 2012 Libyan Election and the Origin of Post-Qadhafi Appeasement." *The Middle East Journal* 69, no. 2 (2015): 171–198.

"Libya's Happy New Year." *Majalla*. December 31, 2013. https://eng.majalla.com/2013/12/article55247722/libya%E2%80%99s-happy-new-year.

Pack, Jason and Barak Barfi. *In War's Wake: The Struggle for a Post-Qadhafi Libya*. Washington, DC: Washington Institute for Near East Policy, February 2012.

Pack, Jason, Karim Mezran, and Mohamed Eljarh. *Libya's Faustian Bargains: Breaking the Appeasement Cycle*. Washington, DC: Atlantic Council of the United States, May 5, 2014.

Pargeter, Alison. "Libya: Reforming the Impossible?" *Review of African Political Economy* 33, no. 108 (2006): 219–235.

Libya: The Rise and Fall of Qadhafi. New Haven: Yale University Press, 2012.

Perkins, Kenneth J. *Historical Dictionary of Tunisia*. African Historical Dictionaries. Vol. 45. Metuchen, NJ: Scarecrow Press, 1989.

A History of Modern Tunisia. Cambridge, UK; New York: Cambridge University Press, 2004.

Petkanas, Zoe. "Emerging Norms: Writing Gender in the Post-Revolution Tunisian State." In *Women and Social Change in North Africa: What Counts as Revolutionary?*, edited by Gray, Doris and Nadia Sonneveld, 353–377. Cambridge: Cambridge University Press, 2018.

Pickard, Duncan. *Identity, Islam, and Women in the Tunisian Constitution*. Washington, DC: Atlantic Council, January 24, 2014.

Tunisia's New Constitutional Court. Washington, DC: Atlantic Council, April 2015.

Plattner, Marc F. "Liberalism and Democracy: Can't Have One without the Other." *Foreign Affairs* 77, no. 2 (1998): 171–180.

"Pourquoi Habib Essid est presenti pour la presidence du gouvernement. " *Leaders*. January 4, 2015. www.leaders.com.tn/article/15961-pour quoi-habib-essid-est-pressenti-pour-la-presidence-du-gouvernement.

Proctor, Bill and Ikbal Ben Moussa. *Tunisia's Constituent Assembly's By-Laws: A Brief Analysis*. International Institute for Democracy and Electoral Assistance (International IDEA), 2012. www.idea.int/publications/cata logue/tunisian-constituent-assembly%E2%80%99s-laws-brief-analysis.

Rangwala, Glen. "The Creation of Governments-in-Waiting: The Arab Uprisings and Legitimacy in the International System." *Geoforum* 66 (2015): 215–223.

Redissi, Hamadi, Asma Nouira, and Abdelkader Zghal. *La Transition Démocratique En Tunisie : Etat Des Lieux. Vol. I : Les Acteurs*. Tunis: Diwen Editions, 2012.

La Transition Démocratique En Tunisie : Etat Des Lieux. Vol. II : Les Thématiques. Tunis: Diwen Editions, 2012.

Reporters without Borders. "Reporters without Borders in Tunisia: A New Freedom that Needs Protecting." Accessed May 26, 2019. https://rsf.org/en/news/reporters-without-borders-tunisia-new-freedom-needs-protecting.

Roberts, Hugh. "Who Said Qadhafi Had to Go?" *The London Review of Books* 33, no. 22 (2011): 8–11.

Rose, Richard, William Mishler, and Christian Haerpfer. *Democracy and Its Alternatives: Understanding Post-Communist Societies*. Baltimore: Johns Hopkins University Press, 1998.

Russo, Francesca and Simone, Santi. *Non Ho Più Paura : Tunisi, Diario Di Una Rivoluzione*. Roma: Gremese, 2011.

Rustow, Dankwart. "Transitions to Democracy: Toward a Dynamic Model." *Comparative Politics* 2, no. 3 (1970): 337–363.

Salamé, Ghassan, ed. *Democracy without Democrats? The Renewal of Politics in the Muslim World*. London: I. B. Taurus, 1994.

   ed. *The Foundations of the Arab State*. London, New York: Croom Helm, 1987.

Saleh, Hanan. "Militias and the Quest for Libyan Unity." New York: Human Rights Watch, October 27, 2015. www.hrw.org/news/2015/10/27/militias-and-quest-libyan-unity#

Sanallah, Mustapha. "How to Save Libya from Itself? Protect Its Oil from Its Politics." *New York Times*, June 19, 2017.

Sawani, Youssef Mohammad. "Post-Qadhafi Libya: Interactive Dynamics and the Political Future." *Contemporary Arab Affairs* 5, no. 1 (2012): 1–26.

Schlumberger, Oliver, ed. *Debating Arab Authoritarianism: Dynamics and Durability in Nondemocratic Regimes*. Stanford, CA: Stanford University Press, 2007.

Schraeder, Peter J. and Hamadi Redissi. "Ben Ali's Fall." *Journal of Democracy* 22, no. 3 (2011): 5–19.

Seely, Jennifer C. *The Legacies of Transition Governments: Post-Transition Dynamics in Benin and Togo*. New York: Palgrave-MacMillan, 2009.

Shain, Yossi, Juan J. Linz, and Lynn Berat. *Between States: Interim Governments and Democratic Transitions*. New York: Cambridge University Press, 1995.

Sisk, Timothy. *Democratization in South Africa: The Elusive Social Contract*, Princeton: Princeton University Press, 1995.

Sriram, Chandra Lekha, ed. *Transitional Justice in the Middle East and North Africa*, 83–101. New York: Oxford University Press, 2016.

Stephen, Christopher. "The Libya Paradox." *The Libya Herald*, July 7, 2017. www.libyaherald.com/2017/07/07/the-libya-paradox/.

Stephen, Christopher and L. Harding. "Libyan PM Snubs Islamists with Cabinet to Please Western Backers." *The Guardian*, November 22, 2011.

St John, Ronald Bruce. "From the 17 February Revolution to Benghazi: Rewriting History for Political Gain." *Journal of North African Studies* 21, no. 3 (2016): 357–378.

Libya: From Colony to Revolution, 3rd ed. London: Oneworld, 2017.

Storm, Lise. *Party Politics and Prospects for Democracy in North Africa. Studies on North Africa*. Boulder, CO: Lynne Rienner Publishers, 2014.

Tavana, Daniel, and Alex Russell. "Previewing Tunisia's Parliamentary and Presidential Elections." Washington, DC: Project on Middle East Democracy, October 2014.

Tavana, Daniel L. " Preparing to Draft a New Social Contract: Tunisia's National Constituent Assembly Election, 2011." Princeton University: Innovations for Successful Societies, https://successfulsocieties.princeton .edu/publications/preparing-draft-new-social-contract-tunisias-national-constituent-assembly-election.

Tempelhof, Susanne Tarkwoski and Manal Omar. *Stakeholders of Libya's February 17 Revolution*. Washington, DC: United States Institute of Peace (January 2012).

Teitel, Ruti G. *Transitional Justice*. New York: Oxford University Press, 2000.

Tessler, Mark and Michael Robbins. "Political System Preferences of Arab Publics." In *The Arab Uprisings Explained: New Contentious Politics in the Middle East*, edited by Marc Lynch, 247–296. New York: Columbia University Press, 2014.

Toaldo, Mattia. "A Constitutional Panacea for Libya?" Washington, DC: Carnegie Endowment for International Peace, August 22, 2017.

Tolbert, David. "Tunisia's Black Book: Transparency or Witch-hunt?" *Al Jazeera*, December 9, 2013.

"Tunisia's Interior Minister Sacked." *The Telegraph*, January 12, 2011. www.telegraph.co.uk/news/worldnews/africaandindianocean/tunisia/ 8255408/Tunisias-interior-minister-sacked.html.

"Tunisia's Municipal Elections – The View from Tunis." Washington, DC: Project on Middle East Democracy, May 2018. https://pomed.org/wp-content/uploads/2018/05/Tunisia_QA_FINAL.pdf?x37106.

United Nations Development Program (UNDP). *Résumé du rapport de la commission d'investigation sur les abus enregistres au cours de la période allant du 17 décembre 2010 jusqu'à l'accomplissement de son objet*. Tunis: UNDP, 2013.

United States Department of State. "Annual Human Rights Report 2018," March 13, 2019. www.state.gov/reports/2018.

Vandewalle, Dirk. "Beyond the Civil War in Libya." In *Beyond the Arab Spring: The Evolving Ruling Bargain in the Middle East*, edited by Mehran Kamrava, 437–457. New York: Oxford University Press, 2014.

A History of Modern Libya, 2nd ed. New York: Cambridge University Press, 2012.

"Rebel Rivalries in Libya." *Foreign Affairs*, August 18, 2011. www
  .foreignaffairs.com/articles/68198/dirk-vandewalle/rebel-rivalries-in-libya.
Volpi, Frédéric. *Revolution and Authoritarianism in North Africa*. London:
  Hurst & Company, 2017.
Waltz, Susan E. *Human Rights and Reform: Changing the Face of North
  African Politics*. Berkeley: University of California Press, 1995.
  "Tunisia's League and the Pursuit of Human Rights." *Maghreb Review* 14,
  no. 3 (1989): 214.
Weber, Max. "The Types of Legitimate Domination." In *Max Weber:
  Economy and Society*, edited by Roth, Guenther and Claus Wittich,
  212–254. Berkeley: University of California Press, 1978.
  "Politics As a Vocation." In *From Max Weber: Essays in Sociology*,
  translated and edited by H. H. Gerth and C. Wright Mills, 78–88.
  New York: Oxford University Press, 1946.
Wehrey, Frederic. "After Gaddafi: Libya's Path to Collapse." In *The
  Oxford Handbook of Contemporary Middle-Eastern and North Afri-
  can History*, edited by Amal Ghazal and Jens Hanssen (online: January
  2019).
  The Burning Shores: Inside the Battle for the New Libya. New York:
  Farrar, Straus, and Giroux, 2018.
  Electing a New Libya. Washington, DC: Carnegie Endowment for Inter-
  national Peace, July 2, 2012.
  The Struggle for Security in Eastern Libya. Washington, DC: Carnegie
  Endowment for International Peace, September 19, 2012.
  The Wrath of Libya's Salafis. Washington, DC: Carnegie Endowment for
  International Peace, September 12, 2012.
Wehrey, Frederic and Emad Badi. *A Place of Distinctive Despair*. Washing-
  ton, DC: Carnegie Endowment for International Peace, 2018.
  "Libya's Coming Forever War: Why Backing One Militia against Another
  Is Not the Solution." *War on the Rocks*, May 15, 2019. https://
  warontherocks.com/2019/05/libyas-coming-forever-war-why-backing-
  one-militia-against-another-is-not-the-solution/.
Wehrey, Frederic and Anouar Boukhars. *Salafism in the Maghreb: Politics,
  Piety, and Militancy*. New York: Oxford University Press, 2019.
Wehrey, Frederic and Jalel Harchaoui. "Is Libya Finally Ready for Peace?"
  Foreign Affairs, November 30, 2018.
Widner, Jennifer A. "Political Parties and Civil Societies in Sub-Saharan
  Africa." In *Democracy in Africa: The Hard Road Ahead*, 65–81. Boul-
  der, CO: Lynne Rienner, 1997.
Willis, Michael J. *Politics and Power in the Maghreb: Algeria, Tunisia and
  Morocco from Independence to the Arab Spring*. New York: Columbia
  University Press, 2012.

Wolf, Anne. *Political Islam in Tunisia: The History of Enahda*. Oxford: Oxford University Press, 2017.

Yerkes, Sarah and Zeineb Ben Yehmed. *Tunisia's Revolutionary Goals Remain Unfulfilled*. Washington, DC: Carnegie Endowment for International Peace, December 2018.

Yousfi, Héla. *L'UGTT, une passion Tunisienne: Enquête sur les syndicalistes en révolution, 2011–2014*. Tunis: Institut de recherche sur la Maghreb contemporaine, 2015.

Zartman, I. William, ed. *Tunisia: The Political Economy of Reform*. Boulder, CO: Lynne Rienner, 1991.

    ed. *Arab Spring: Negotiating in the Shadow of the Intifadat*. Athens: University of Georgia Press, 2015.

Zoubir, Yahia H. and Erzsébet N. Rózsa. "The End of the Libyan Dictatorship: The Uncertain Transition." *Third World Quarterly* 33, no. 7 (2012): 1267–1283.

Index

12/12 movement, 128–129
18 October collective, 64

Abassi, Houcine, 73
Abu Salim massacre, 2, 102
Abushagur, Mustafa, 148–149
Addis Ababa, 139
Afghanistan, 116
Africa, 18, 164
  North, 7–8, 14, 207, 219 (*See also* MENA (Middle East and North Africa))
  Sub-Saharan, 6, 56, 201
African Union (AU), 137–139
AFTURD (Association de la Femme Tunisienne pour la Récherche et le Développment), 43n93
Agence Tunisienne des Communications Externales (ATCE), 75–76, 81
Ahd Joumhouri. See Republican Pact
Ajdabiya, 133, 148
al-Baida, 2, 103, 105, 107–108
al-Qaeda, 136n148, 202–203
Alaqi, Mohamed al-, 110
Algeria, 136n148, 201, 216n14, 224
  1988 protests, 7n21
  2019 protests, 225n35, 227n40
  colonization of, 18n3
  Gouvernement Provisoire de la République Algérienne (GPRA), 118n73
Algiers, 1
Ali, Zaid al-, 141, 142n173
Amazigh, 189–190
American consulate in Benghazi, 151–153, 157
American embassy in Tunis, 69
Amnesty International, 162–163

Amor Commission, 34–38, 61–62, 77, 86, 90–91, 96, 174–175, 182–183, 211
Amor, Abdelfatah, 34
AMT (Tunisian Magistrates' Association), 96n135
Ansar al-Sharia, 151, 154n16, 157, 162
Arab League, 112, 131–133, 137
Arab Spring. *See* Arab uprisings
Arab uprisings, 7–8, 10, 14
Arabian Gulf Oil Company, 129
ARP (People's Representative Assembly), 171, 173, 186–187
Article 105, 178n28. *See also* Tunisian Bar Association
Article 15, 78, 94–95, 180
Article 18, 34n61, 43, 49. *See also* gender parity
Article 28, 23n15
Article 30, 141–142, 218. *See also* National Transition Council (NTC)
Article 56, 20–21
Article 57, 21
Article 8, 34n61
Association de la Femme Tunisienne pour la Récherche et le Développment (AFTURD), 43n93
Association des Magistrats Tunisiens (AMT), 96n135
Association Tunisienne des Femmes Democrates (ATFD), 36, 43n93
ATCE (Tunisian External Communications Agency), 75–76, 81
ATFD (Tunisian Association of Democratic Women), 25n27, 36, 43n93
AU (African Union), 137–139

256

Awjali, Ali al-, 111
Awlad-Suleiman, 200n110

Ban Ki-moon, 130
Bani Walid, 2, 119, 167
bar association. *See* Libyan Bar
    Association; Tunisian Bar
    Association
Barakat, Naji, 111
Bardo National Museum attack, 172,
    182
Bardo Palace sit-in, 71
Barqa Council, 144–145, 154–155
Bashir, Omar al-, 224
Basic Freedoms and Human Rights
    Council (BFHRC), 190, 199
Belaïd, Chokri, 70
Ben Achour Commission, 48, 50,
    53–54, 56, 62, 66–68, 87, 89, 211,
    220
  consensus and, 52
  decree laws and, 30, 40–42, 47, 80
  elections and, 38, 51, 57–58, 83, 94,
    180, 184
  expert core, 52, 63, 73–78, 210
  formation of, 25–27, 33
  media freedom and, 80–82
  representation in, 42–46, 49, 186,
    210 (*See also* gender parity)
Ben Achour, Yadh, 25–26, 32–33,
    44–46, 58, 68
Ben Ali, Zine al-Abidine
  1987 coup, 20, 67n23
  exile and resignation, 1–3, 12,
    17, 20–21, 25, 29, 34, 43,
    209
  government of, 28, 30–31, 40, 42,
    44, 48, 50–51, 53–55, 59, 63–64,
    72, 83, 88–91, 94–95, 180–182,
    184–185
  judiciary under, 75–76, 96
  reforms introduced by, 20, 209
  restrictions on freedom of expression,
    54–55, 63, 75–79, 93, 219–220
Ben Ammar, Rachid, 23–24, 89
Ben Jafar, Mustafa, 22
Ben Sassi, Othman, 113
Ben Yousef, Salah, 19
Benghazi. *See also* American consulate
    in Benghazi

17 February Coalition and, 102–103,
    117
Ansar al-Sharia assault on, 157
Central Bank of, 129, 196
Haftar assault on, 153, 192
National Oil Corporation (NOC) in,
    129, 197 (*See also* National Oil
    Corporation (NOC))
NTC headquarters in, 3, 117, 120,
    122–125, 128–129, 215 (*See also*
    12/12 movement)
  protests in, 2–3, 102
  Qadhafi assault on, 133
Benghazi Council, 103–104, 109
Benin, 10
Bennour, Jamal, 109
Berlin, 194
Berlusconi, Silvio, 130–131
BFHRC (Basic Freedoms and Human
    Rights Council), 190, 199
Bhriri, Nourdine, 96–97
Bilhaj, Abdelhakim, 117, 123, 128,
    136n148, 137n154, 149
Bilhaj, Alamin, 116
Black Book, 93, 97
Bouderbala Commission, 35–36,
    49–50, 61–62, 77, 182, 211
  Truth and Dignity Commission
    (TDC) and, 90, 92, 174–175
Bouderbala, Tawfik, 35–36
Boughaigis, Salwa, 110, 168
Bourguiba, Habib, 18–19, 40, 42, 48,
    53, 55, 63, 78, 180
  liberalization and reform, 30,
    208–209
  overthrow of, 20
  Tunisian national identity and, 18,
    212
Bouteflika, Abdelaziz, 224
Brahim, Ahmed, 22, 24
Brahmi, Mohammed, 71–72
Brazil, 132
Brussels, 134

Caïd Essebsi, Béji, 30–31, 51, 210
  conflict with Yousef Chahed,
    173–174, 177
  death of, 177
  interim cabinet of, 24–26, 48, 56–58,
    62n6, 66, 74–77, 89, 211

Caïd Essebsi, Béji (cont.)
  interim prime ministership of, 24, 31,
    40–41, 44, 50, 57–58, 61, 63,
    74–77, 87, 216n13
  media freedom and, 77–80
  Nida Tounis and, 69–70, 173 (*See
    also* Nida Tounis)
  presidency of, 98, 171, 173–174,
    181, 214
Caïd Essebsi, Hafedh, 173, 177n23
Cameron, David, 130
Carthage Declaration, 173–174
CBL (Central Bank of Libya), 196–198,
  200
CDA (Constitutional Drafting
  Assembly), 15, 148, 161, 189,
  192–193, 196
Central Bank of Benghazi, 129, 196
Central Bank of Libya (CBL), 196–198,
  200
Chad, 111
Chahed, Yousef, 173–174, 177, 184
Chamber of Deputies, 21–23, 29,
  89
Chambi mountains, 72
Charlie Hebdo attack, 172
Chebbi, Ahmed Najib, 22, 24
China, 131–132
Clinton, Hillary, 109, 130n127, 132,
  159
CNPR (National Council for the
  Protection of the Revolution),
  25–27, 48, 87, 89
colonialism. *See also* neocolonialism
  in Algiers by France, 1, 18n3
  in Libya by Italy, 209
Congrès Pour la République (CPR), 22,
  65, 68
Conseil Supérieure de la Magistrature
  (CSM), 174, 178–179
consensus
  lack of, 11n33, 24, 74, 142, 144,
    161, 169, 177, 199
  spirit of, 17, 32–33, 46, 51–52,
    55–56, 58, 65, 68–69, 97–98, 122,
    170, 172, 178–180, 184, 188, 205,
    211–212
Consensus Committee, 179
Constitutional Council, 21, 96
Constitutional Court, 32, 177–179

Constitutional Democratic Rally
  (RCD), 21–24, 28–30, 32n56, 89,
  93–95, 180–181, 184
Constitutional Drafting Assembly
  (CDA), 15, 148, 161, 189,
  192–193, 196
Consultative Support Group, 155–156
CPR (Congrès Pour la République), 22,
  65, 68
CSM (Conseil Supérieure de la
  Magistrature), 174, 178–179
Cyrenaica, 100, 113, 192

Dabbashi, Ibrahim, 104
Day of Rage, 2, 103, 109, 115. *See also*
  February 17 revolution
DDR (Demobilization, Disarmament,
  and Reintegration), 136n149, 150,
  217, 220
de Gaulle, Charles, 1
Deauville, 139
Demobilization, Disarmament, and
  Reintegration (DDR), 136n149,
  150, 217, 220
Democratic Forum for Work and
  Liberties (FDTL), 22, 56, 65, 68
Democratic Patriots Movement, 70
Democratic Progressive Party (PDP),
  22, 24, 56
Derna, 2, 157, 197n100
Destour Sagheer, 34, 47–48, 66, 75
Doha, 124, 135

Eastern Libyan Shield, 157–158
Economic Reconciliation Law, 182
Egypt, 104, 118, 147–148, 177, 192,
  201, 203–204
  1952 revolution, 101, 209
  2007 "bread riots," 7n21
  2011 revolution, 223–224
  2013 protest movement, 71, 73,
    202n119
el-Magariaf, Muhammad, 148
elections. *See* specific governing body
Enahda, 22, 25, 70–73, 82, 179, 183.
  See also Troika
  ban on, 19, 67
  elections and, 46, 65, 68, 98,
    185
  lustration law proposed by, 95

ties to radical Islamist groups, 69,
181
Equity and Reconciliation Commission,
36
Erdogan, Tayyip, 131
ésprit de consensus. *See* consensus
Essid, Habib, 89, 171–173, 181, 214
ethnic groups
Amazigh, 189n68
Farjan, 110
Tebu, 157, 189n68, 199
Touareg, 111, 189n68, 199
Tubu, 111
Zawiya, 122, 133, 157, 164, 200
Ettajdid, 22, 24, 56
Ettakatol (FDTL), 22, 56, 65, 68
EU (European Union), 130, 137, 203
Europe, 18, 48
Eastern, 6, 14
European Parliament, 114
European Union (EU), 130, 137, 203

fact-finding commission on state abuse.
See Bouderbala Commission
Fajr Libya. *See* Libya Dawn
Farjan, 110
FDTL (Ettakatol), 22, 56, 65, 68
February 17 Coalition, 103, 112–113,
117, 123, 155
February 17 revolution, 166. *See also*
Day of Rage
Fezzan, 113, 189n68
Fishman, Benjamin, 160
Fituri, Anwar, 111
Forum Démocratique Pour le Travail et
les Libertés (FDTL), 22, 56, 65, 68
FP (Front Populaire), 71
France, 1, 100, 109, 113, 127,
130–135, 139–140, 158–159, 190,
193, 202–204, 209. *See also*
colonialism
protectorate in Tunisia, 18, 30, 208
Free Libya Armed Forces, 120
Front Populaire (FP), 71

Gabon, 139
Gafsa, 25
Gajiji, Othman, 144
GCC (Gulf Cooperation Council),
131–132, 137

gender parity, 186
in the Amor Commission, 34
in the Ben Achour Commission, 27,
41n88, 43–44, 49, 82–83, 184,
186
in the Bouderbala commission, 36,
90
General National Congress (GNC), 15,
170, 196, 200–201. *See also* Libya
Dawn; Libya Political Agreement
(LPA)
distribution of seats in, 155
elections, 3–4, 116, 142–146, 155,
159, 161, 214
international assistance,
159–160
security, 4, 151–153, 157, 167–168,
199, 203
selection of prime minister, 148–149,
162, 189, 192
split with HOR, 153–154, 162, 167,
190–191, 198
General Tunisian Workers' Union
(UGTT), 1, 19, 22, 25, 27, 43–45,
48, 53–54, 70–74, 173, 178, 184,
212
Geneva, 190
Germany, 132
Ghannouchi, Mohammed
interim cabinet of, 22–23, 31
prime ministership of, 20–26, 28–29,
34–35, 37–38, 53, 56, 59, 89, 210,
216, 224
Ghannouchi, Rachid, 22, 69n29,
174n10, 207n1
Gharyani, Sheikh al-Sadiq al-, 117
Ghazal, Salah, 103n15, 109
Ghoga, Abdel Hafez, 103, 105, 108,
144
Ghwell, Khalifa, 192
GNA (Government of National
Accord), 191–194, 200, 203–204
GNC (General National Congress).
See General National Congress
(GNC)
Government of National Accord
(GNA), 191–194, 200, 203–204
Gulf Cooperation Council (GCC),
131–132, 137
Gumia, Hania al-, 111

Haftar, Khalifa, 111, 195, 197, 205, 218
  control of oil, 192–195, 200
  and international community, 201,
    203–204
  parliamentary attack by, 147,
    153–154, 162, 168, 214–215 (*See
    also* Operation Dignity)
  and tensions within NTC, 125–126
HAICA (High Independent Authority
  for Audio-Visual Communication),
  79–80, 82, 86, 88
Hariati, Mehdia al-, 123
Hariri, Omar al-, 110
Haute Autorité Indépendente de la
  Communication Audiovisuelle
  (HAICA), 79–80, 82, 86, 88
Haute Instance pour la Réalisation des
  Objectifs de la Revolution, la
  Réforme Politique, et la Transition
  Démocratique. *See* Ben Achour
  Commission
High Authority for the Realization of
  the Goals of the Revolution,
  Political Reform, and Democratic
  Transition. *See* Ben Achour
  Commission
High Independent Authority for Audio-
  Visual Communication (HAICA),
  79–80, 82, 86, 88
High Judicial Council (CSM), 174,
  178–179
High National Elections Commission
  (HNEC), 143–144
High State Council, 191–192
HIROR. *See* Ben Achour Commission
HNEC (High National Elections
  Commission), 143–144
Hodeifah, Kamel, 109
HOR (House of Representatives). *See*
  House of Representatives (HOR)
horizontal parity. *See* zipper parity
Houni, Abdelmonem al-, 112
House of Representatives (HOR),
  153–154
  elections, 162, 188, 199
  split with GNC, 162, 168–169,
    188–198, 214
Human Rights Watch, 3n5, 108n31,
  159n40
Huntington, Samuel, 6

ICC (International Criminal Court),
  138, 163
ILE (Independent Local Election
  Authority), 84
IMF (International Monetary Fund),
  19, 183–184
Independent Commission for
  Investigation of Corruption. *See*
  Amor Commission
Independent High Electoral Authority
  (ISIE), 38, 41, 44, 46, 51, 62,
  63n11, 76, 84, 88, 97, 171, 187,
  211
Independent Local Election Authority
  (ILE), 84
Independent Local Electoral Authority
  (IRIE), 84–85
India, 105, 132
INRIC (National Commission for
  Information and Communication
  Reform), 37–38, 47–48, 76–77,
  79–81, 86, 187, 211
Instance d'Equité et Reconciliation. *See*
  Equity and Reconciliation
  Commission
Instance Supérieure Indépendente pour
  les Elections (ISIE), 38–39, 41, 44,
  46, 51, 62, 63n11, 76, 84–86, 88,
  97, 171, 187, 211
Instances Locales pour les Elections
  (ILE), 84
Instances Régionales Indépendentes
  pour les Elections (IRIE), 84–85
International Contact Group, 133
International Criminal Court (ICC),
  138, 163
International Monetary Fund (IMF),
  19, 183–184
IRIE (Instances Régionales
  Indépendentes pour les Elections),
  84–85
ISIE (Independent High Electoral
  Authority), 38–39, 41, 44, 46, 51,
  62, 63n11, 76, 84–85, 88, 97, 171,
  187, 211
ISIS, 202–203
Islamic State. *See* ISIS
Issawi, Ali, 105, 121
Italy, 140, 193, 202–203
  colonization of Libya, 100, 209

Itilaf al-sabatash Febriar, 117, 123. *See also* February 17 Coalition

Jadran, Ibrahim, 192–193, 196, 200
Jalil, Mustafa Abd-al, 107–108,
 145–146, 149
 and formation of NTC, 103,
 105–107, 127–128
 liberation speech, 114, 128
 political weakness of, 124, 126–128,
 156–157
Jamahouriya, 101, 102n11, 103, 217
Jendouba, 72
Jendoubi, Kamel, 39
Jibril, Mahmoud, 108
 and international community, 109,
 130–132, 136, 159
 prime ministership, 108–109, 121,
 124–126, 140, 148–149, 155–156
Jomaa, Mehdi, 72
 government of, 72–74, 97
journalism. *See* press freedom
Jrad, Abdelsalam, 22
Justice and Construction Party, 116,
 148
Justice and Equality Movement, 136
Juweili, Osama, 111, 150–151, 195

Kabir, Sadiq al-, 105n21, 197–198, 200
Kairouan, 25
Karoui, Nabil, 177
Kasbah protests, 23, 25, 35n66, 89
Kib, Abdelrahman al-, 114
 government of, 114, 144n179, 159,
 203
Kufra, 111, 136n150, 157, 164, 200
Kuni, Musa al-, 111
Kuwait, 140

La Marsa, 32
Laabidi, Kamel, 37–38
Laarayedh, Ali, 72
labor unions, 6, 19, 53
Law #26, 165n65
Law #37, 166, 214
Law #38, 165–167, 214
Law #4, 165
LCG (Libya Contact Group), 135–136,
 138–140
León, Bernadino, 190

letters of credit, 198
Lévy, Bernard-Henri, 109, 131–132
LIA (Libyan Investment Authority), 110
Libya, 99–169, 188–205. *See also*
 National Transition Council
 (NTC)
 civil society in, 158
 history of, 100–106
 international involvement in, 109,
 120–127, 129–139, 142–143
 National Assembly, 100–101
 national identity, 101
 oil in (*See* oil in Libya)
 statelessness, 118–119
 tribes of, 100, 107, 154, 164, 193,
 199–200, 205, 213 (*See also* ethnic
 groups)
Libya Contact Group (LCG), 135–136,
 138–140
Libya Dawn, 153, 190
Libya Political Agreement (LPA),
 191–193, 203
Libyan Bar Association, 108, 110, 178
Libyan International Medical
 University, 155
Libyan Investment Authority (LIA), 110
Libyan Islamic Fighting Group (LIFG),
 116–117
Libyan Islamic Movement for Change
 (LIMC). *See* Libyan Islamic
 Fighting Group (LIFG)
Libyan National Planning Council, 108
Libyan Shield Force (LSF), 151, 156
Libyan Supreme Court, 165n62, 190,
 199
Libyan Unionist Party, 155
Libyan Vision, 108
LIFG (Libyan Islamic Fighting Group),
 116–117
Ligue tunisien de droit de l'homme
 (LTDH), 22, 27, 32, 35–36, 44,
 48, 54, 64, 72, 74, 212
LIMC (Libyan Islamic Movement for
 Change). *See* Libyan Islamic
 Fighting Group (LIFG)
little constitution. *See Destour Sagheer*
Loi Fondamentale, 49n111
London, 13, 114–115, 134, 140, 202
LPA (Libya Political Agreement),
 191–193, 203

LSF (Libyan Shield Force), 151, 156
lustration law, 95, 212, 218

Macron, Emmanuel, 190, 193
Maghreb, 18, 48
Mahmoudi, Umar al-Baghdadi al-, 103
Maiteg, Ahmed, 162
Mali, 6n15, 111, 147, 200
Mansour, Issa Abdul-Majjid, 111
Marzouk, Mohsen, 173
Marzouki, Moncef, 22, 68, 93, 97, 171
Mebazza, Fouad, 21–24, 26, 29–30,
    58–59, 75n48, 89, 210
media censorship. *See* press freedom
Medvedev, Dimitri, 139
MENA (Middle East and North Africa),
    7–8, 207, 219, 223
Merkel, Angela, 130
Middle East, 18, 132. *See also* MENA
    (Middle East and North Africa)
Middle East and North Africa (MENA),
    7–8, 207, 219, 223
mini-constitution. *See* Destour Sagheer
Mismari, Abdelsalam al-, 110n37,
    155–156
Misrata, 113, 122, 133, 162, 164, 167,
    192, 195, 199n105
    militia, 200, 202
Misrata Military Council (MMC), 122,
    213
MMC (Misrata Military Council), 122,
    213
Mohammed Ali Square, 1
Monastir, 19
Montasir, Mohamed, 113
Morocco, 36, 191
Morsi, Mohammed, 71, 202n119
Mouvement de la Tendance Islamique
    (MTI). *See* Enahda
MTI (Mouvement de la Tendance
    Islamique). *See* Enahda
Mubarak, Hosni, 223–224
Mugharbi, Zahi, 110n37, 155–156
Muslim Brotherhood, 71, 73, 114–116,
    141–142, 149, 202n119

Nafusa Mountains, 122, 124
Naguedh, Lotfi, 70
Nasr, Abdelmajid al-, 113
Nasr, Mansour Saif al-, 113

Nasser, Gamal Abdel, 101, 209
National Army, 120
National Commission for Information
    and Communication Reform
    (INRIC), 37–38, 47–48, 76–77,
    79–81, 86, 187, 211
National Conference of Libyan
    Opposition (NCLO), 2, 114–115,
    117
National Constituent Assembly (NCA),
    24–60, 65–67. *See also* Troika;
    Tunisian Provisional
    Administration (TPA)
    of 1956, 68
    Bardo sit-in, 71
    bylaws, 65, 87
    Consensus Committee, 179
    constitution drafting, 3–4, 9, 12, 60,
        65, 70–73
    election of, 24, 31, 41, 44, 53, 56, 65,
        67
    mandate and competencies of (*See*
        September 15th document)
National Council for the Protection of
    the Revolution (CNPR), 25–27,
    48, 87, 89
National Dialogue
    Libyan, 188, 225
    Tunisian, 67, 70, 72–74, 95, 97, 179,
        226
National Economic Development
    Board, 108
National Fact-Finding Commission on
    Corruption and Embezzlement. *See*
    Amor Commission
National Forces Alliance (NFA),
    148–149, 155
National Gathering, 115–116
National Libyan Salvation Front
    (NLSF), 115n60, 117, 148
National Oil Corporation (NOC), 129,
    192–193, 197, 200
National Transition Council (NTC),
    3–4, 12–15, 99–169. *See also*
    General National Congress (GNC)
    "secular" profile, 115–116, 141
    Constitutional Declaration, 3, 114,
        141–142, 154, 156, 161, 165, 218
    Executive Council, 110, 121, 128,
        156

federalism, 155, 192, 205
finances, 118, 129, 135, 158, 167
formation of, 99–100, 102–106
human rights, 140, 143, 159,
    162–169
international assistance, 99, 127,
    130–139, 147, 158–160, 169
judicial reform, 165–168
lack of experience, 126–130, 156,
    161
lack of vision, 15, 99, 108, 134, 140,
    146–147, 149, 161, 170, 188,
    199–200, 203
legislative council, 112–114,
    165–166
roadmap by, 3, 15, 99, 109,
    137–145, 149, 156, 160–161, 165,
    190–193, 203, 213, 221
stabilization committee, 110, 124,
    129
Supreme Judicial Council, 165, 167
weapons monitoring, 121
Nationalistes Démocratiques, 68
NATO (North Atlantic Treaty
    Organization), 120, 123, 125,
    132–134, 138, 201, 215
Nayid, Aref, 110, 124, 149
Nayid, Rafiq, 110
NCA (National Constituent Assembly).
    See National Constituent Assembly
    (NCA)
NCLO (National Conference of Libyan
    Opposition), 2, 114–115, 117
Neo-Destour, 18, 29, 49n111–111
neocolonialism, 132. *See also*
    colonialism
NFA (National Forces Alliance),
    148–149, 155
Nida Tounis, 69–70, 98, 171, 173–174,
    176–177, 181
Niger, 200
Nigeria, 139
NLSF (National Libyan Salvation
    Front), 115n60, 117
no-fly zone, 131, 133n137, 139
NOC (National Oil Corporation), 129,
    192–193, 197, 200
North Atlantic Treaty Organization
    (NATO), 120, 123, 125, 132–134,
    138, 201, 215

Operation Odyssey Dawn, 133
Operation Unified Protector,
    133n137, 134
NTC (National Transition Council).
    See National Transition Council
    (NTC)

Obama, Barack, 68, 132, 139, 160
Obeidi, 125
Obeidi, Suleiman Mahmoud al-,
    120n84, 125
Odyssey Dawn, 133. *See also* NATO
    (North Atlantic Treaty
    Organization)
oil in Libya, 101n4, 102–105, 129,
    134–135, 155, 157–158, 192–194,
    196–197, 200, 209. *See also*
    National Oil Corporation (NOC)
Operation Dignity, 154, 190, 197n100,
    199
Ottoman Empire, 47, 100, 208–209
Ouled Suleiman, 164

Palermo, 193
Paris, 22, 108n34, 109, 122, 131–133,
    172, 193, 202
Parti Démocratique Progressiste (PDP),
    22, 24, 56
Parti Socialiste Démocratique (PSD),
    29–30
PDP (Parti Démocratique Progressiste),
    22, 29, 56
Peace and Security Council (PSC). *See*
    African Union (AU)
Pelt, Adrian, 100
People's Represenatative Assembly
    (ARP), 171, 173, 186–187
people's rule. *See Jamahouriya*
Personal Status Code, 49, 208. *See also*
    gender parity; women's rights
Petroleum Facilities Guard (PFG), 155,
    192, 196
PFG (Petroleum Facilities Guard), 155,
    192, 196
PIL (Political Isolation Law), 152–153,
    167–168, 199
Political Isolation Law (PIL), 152–153,
    167–168, 199
Political Reform Commission. *See* Ben
    Achour Commission

Presidential Guard, 36, 83n81, 172
Press Code of 1975, 80
press freedom, 37, 77–81, 219–220. *See
also* INRIC (National Commission
for Information and
Communication Reform)
Black Book, 93, 97
PSC (Peace and Security Council). *See*
African Union (AU)
PSD (Parti Socialist Démocratique),
29–30

Qadhafi Development Foundation,
110, 116
Qadhafi, Moammar, 163, 166
1969 coup, 110, 197, 209
death of, 114, 128, 160
government of, 2–3, 101–102,
106–108, 133, 137–139, 147, 154,
157, 164, 167–169, 189, 195
overthrow of, 12, 99, 112, 117–118,
120, 130, 134–136, 215
protests against, 2, 115, 208
sanctions against, 130–131, 138
weapons cache, 201
Qadhafi, Saadi, 2, 104n20
Qadhafi, Saif al-Islam, 104, 110, 112,
116, 163
Qatar, 122, 127, 129, 131–132,
134–137, 140, 158–159, 201
Qelb Tounis, 177
Quartet, 72–73

Rada militia, 194
Rajhi, Ferhat, 89
Ras Lanuf, 196, 200
RCD (Constitutional Democratic
Rally), 21–24, 28–30, 32n56, 89,
93–95, 180–181, 184
Renaissance Party. *See* Enahda
Republican Pact, 67–69
Revolutionary Command Council, 101,
209
Rome, 140, 202
roundtable negotiations, 6
Russia, 131, 137–139, 192, 203

S17, 182
Sabha, 113, 194
Saed, Kais, 177

Sahmein, Nuri Abu, 191
Salamé, Ghassan, 193–194
Saleh, Agileh, 191, 193
Sallabi, Ali al-, 115, 117, 156
Sanalla, Mustafa, 200
Sanusi order, 100–101, 110, 113–114,
209
Sanusi, Abdullah al-, 2, 154, 163
Sanusi, Ahmed al-Zubair al-, 113
Sanusi, King Idris al-, 101, 209
Sanusi, Mohammed Rida al-, 114
Sarkozy, Nicholas, 108n34, 109,
130–131, 134n141, 159
Sarsar, Chafik, 187
Saudi Arabia, 1, 111n46, 201
SCAF (Supreme Council of the Armed
Forces), 223–224
September 15th document, 47n107, 58,
65, 86–87, 221
Sergiwa, Sihem, 195
Serraj, Fayez al-, 191–192
Sfax, 72
Shalgham, Abd al-Rahman, 104
Shamam, Mahmoud, 105
Shamia, Abdallah, 116
Shokri, Mohammed, 197
Sidi Bouzid, 25
Sidre, 196, 200
Sirte, 3n6, 110n40, 163, 202
Skhirat. *See* Morocco
Social Democratic Movement, 30
Social Democratic Party (PSD),
29–30
Sousse, 19
attack in, 172, 181
South Africa, 132, 138
Sovereign National Conferences, 10
Soviet Union, 6
SSC (Supreme Security Council),
150–151, 156
starting conditions, 4, 10, 208, 215
Stephens, Christopher, 151, 215
Sudan, 135–137, 224
Supreme Council of the Armed Forces
(SCAF), 223–224
Supreme Magistrates Council, 75n45,
96–97
Supreme National Elections Council,
142. *See also* High National
Elections Commission (HNEC)

Supreme Security Council (SSC), 150–151, 156
Syria, 160

tammarod, 71
Tarhouni, Ali, 105, 126
Tatouine, 70
TDC (Truth and Dignity Commission), 90, 92–93, 96–97, 174–176
Tebu, 111, 157–158, 164, 199–200
Terbil, Fathi, 2, 109–110
Thinni, Abdullah al-, 162, 189n66, 197
Third Wave, 5
thuwwar, 156, 162
Tobruk, 2, 153, 190, 192
Togo, 10
Touareg, 111, 113n49, 164, 189n68, 199–200
TPA (Tunisian Provisional Administration). *See* Tunisian Provisional Administration (TPA)
Trabelsi, Leila, 1, 91n115
transitional justice, 11, 225
    in Libya, 143, 162–169, 205
    in Tunisia, 36–37, 72, 88–98, 171, 175–176, 180, 182–183, 188, 212–214, 218
Tree Square, 129
Tripoli, 102, 114, 116, 128–129, 139, 146
    battle for, 117, 122–123, 136, 156, 159
    fall of, 124, 150
    liberation of, 123, 125, 143, 149
    militia in, 117, 153, 190, 194
Tripoli Central Bank, 197, 200
Tripoli Local Council, 124
Tripoli Military Council, 123, 149
Tripoli Revolutionaries Battalion, 123
Tripoli Taskforce, 123–124, 149
Tripolitania, 100, 189n68
Troika, 4, 60, 65–66, 69–71, 74, 81–82, 86–87, 89, 91–93, 96–97, 170–171, 181, 183, 205, 212, 218–219
Truth and Dignity Commission (TDC), 90, 92–93, 96–97, 174–176
Tunis, 13, 19
    protests in, 25, 71
Tunisia, 17–99

civil society in, 19, 25, 27, 34, 36–37, 40–43, 48–49, 52–55, 60, 66, 70, 84, 93
Constitutional Council, 21, 75n48, 96
Constitutional Court, 32, 177–179
history of, 18–20
Ministry of Defense, 36
Ministry of Foreign Affairs, 50
Ministry of Health, 36
Ministry of Information, 75 (*See also* Tunisian External Communications Agency (ATCE))
Ministry of Interior, 1, 36, 77, 83, 90–91
Ministry of International Cooperation and Foreign Investment, 28
Ministry of Justice, 75, 179
Ministry of Justice and Human Rights, 93
Ministry of Planning, 28
National Archives, 37
National Broadcasting Office, 77, 81
National Frequency Center, 77, 81
national identity, 18, 64, 67–70, 74, 78, 87, 209, 212
National Internet Agency, 77, 81
startup act, 174
Tunisian Association for Constitutional Law, 74
Tunisian Association for Democratic Women (ATFD), 25n27, 36, 43n93
Tunisian Bar Association, 25, 53n127, 72, 74
Tunisian External Communications Agency (ATCE), 75–76, 81
Tunisian journalists' union, 37
Tunisian judges' associations, 37, 53–54, 96–97
Tunisian Magistrates' Association (AMT), 96n135
Tunisian Provisional Administration (TPA), 17–59
    bridging role of, 28, 32–33, 54, 60, 210
    decree laws, 25, 30, 34–35, 39–41, 47, 76, 80–85, 91
    institutions of, 33–39

Tunisian Provisional Administration
(TPA) (cont.)
  judicial reform, 66, 75, 82, 88–89,
    96–97
  legitimacy of, 39–51
  media reform, 77–81 (*See also* INRIC
    (National Commission for
    Information and Communication
    Reform))
Tunisian Supreme Court, 24
Tunisian Union of Industry, Commerce,
  and Handicrafts (UTICA), 72–73
Turkey, 7n19, 134n141, 138n161, 159,
  201

UAE. *See* United Arab Emirates
Ubari, 194
UDHR (Universal Declaration of
  Human Rights), 47
UGTT (General Tunisian Workers'
  Union) l'Union Générale des
  Travailleurs Tunisiens, 1, 19, 22,
  25, 27, 43–45, 48, 53–54, 70–74,
  173, 178, 184, 212
UK. *See* United Kingdom
UN. *See* United Nations
Unified Protector, 133n137, 134. *See
  also* NATO (North Atlantic Treaty
  Organization)
Union Générale des Travailleurs
  Tunisiens (UGTT), 1, 19, 22, 25,
  27, 43–45, 48, 53–54, 70–74, 173,
  178, 184, 212
Union Tunisienne de l'Industrie, du
  Commerce, et de l'Artisanat
  (UTICA), 72–73
United Arab Emirates, 123, 123n97,
  135, 137, 192, 197, 201
United Kingdom, 132, 158
United Nations, 100, 104, 124,
  130–131, 150, 159n40, 159, 165,
  188, 190–191, 194
United Nations Security Council
  (UNSC), 130–131, 138–139,
  143
  Resolution 1970, 131
  Resolution 1973, 131–133, 138
United Nations Support Mission in
  Libya (UNSMIL), 143, 159n39

United States, 6, 50, 130–133, 139,
  151, 159. *See also* American
  consulate in Benghazi; American
  embassy in Tunis
Universal Declaration of Human Rights
  (UDHR), 47
University of Pittsburgh, 108
University of Washington, 105
UNSC (United Nations Security
  Council), 130–131, 138–139, 143
  Resolution 1970, 131
  Resolution 1973, 131–133, 138
UNSMIL (United Nations Support
  Mission in Libya), 143, 159n39
USA. *See* United States
UTICA (Tunisian Union of Industry,
  Commerce, and Handicrafts),
  72–73

Venezuela, 137, 222n29
vertical parity. *See* zipper parity

Warriors Affairs Commission, 150
Washington, DC, 13, 202
West, the, 20, 48, 50–51, 101–102,
  109n35, 131–132, 139
Western Military Council (WMC), 122
WMC (Western Military Council), 122
women's rights, 49, 55, 70n32, 71n36,
  110, 174, 177. *See also* gender
  parity

Yemen, 8, 160
youth, 53, 110, 150, 183
  involvement in protests, 31, 37, 92
  representation in government, 27,
    31n49, 41, 43–46, 87
Yunis, Abdelfatah, 112, 124–127, 134,
  142, 157, 195

Zawiya, 122, 133, 157, 164, 200
Zeidan, Ali, 149, 162, 169, 189n66
Zintan, 122, 153, 163–164, 195
  militia, 163, 192
Zintan Military Council, 111
zipper parity, 43, 83, 186. *See also*
  gender parity
Zuwara, 113
Zway. *See* Zawiya

Lightning Source UK Ltd.
Milton Keynes UK
UKHW020229250223
417635UK00023B/253